The ACCORDION PLAYER

The ACCORDION PLAYER

My Journey from Fear to Love

ICHAK K. ADIZES

books@adizes.com

Website: www.adizesbooks.com

For information, please contact WS Press by email at wspi.353@gmail.com

ISBN: 979-8-9860483-0-7

Library of Congress Control Number: 2022944076

Published by WS Press, Newtown, PA

Printed in the United States

To my parents,
Salamon "Moni" Adizes and
Diamanta "Duka" Kalderon Adizes,
and my dear wife,
Nurit Manne Adizes,
for helping to make me who I am.

"Three passions, simple but overwhelmingly strong, have governed my life: the longing for love, the search for knowledge, and unbearable pity for the suffering of mankind. These passions, like great winds, have blown me hither and thither, in a wayward course, over a great ocean of anguish, reaching to the very verge of despair."

—Bertrand Russell

CONTENTS

PART III
OPENING THE CAGE

INTRODUCTION

As I finish reading this book written by my friend Dr. Ichak Adizes, I am filled with only one feeling: the feeling of love. Dr. Adizes is perhaps one of six Jewish men I have known in my life who endured the pains of the Holocaust and survived. I know him not merely as a Jew or a European or a management guru, but as what my spiritual teacher, Ram Chandra of Shahjahanpur, would call *insaan*—a true and integrated human being.

What makes a human being truly integrated? It is pain and pain alone, for it not only brings all the aspects of a person together but also connects human beings with each other. Pleasure rarely integrates, but rather disintegrates or disconnects. What makes people truly integrated is this aspect of pain they all undergo, using it as a stepping stone toward greater success. Great human beings overcome difficult life situations by using these periods of pain to integrate themselves, and Ichak Adizes is no exception. While most of us obstruct our own growth by sulking under pain, Dr. Adizes is one of that rare breed who did not let his pain go in vain.

His ideas and solutions have always been original. His most famous contribution to corporate success all over the world is the Adizes Factor, which constitutes the formula for success in any organization. His ideas, even about topics that have been shared before, are simpler; he shares them with clarity and transparency. For example, what the concepts of Yoga took several chapters to explain, this genius of a man does in a few simple words.

My favorite part of the book is Adizes's discovery of love in his life. He not only describes the lessons he learned through the years of physical, emotional, and mental pain, but also shares the great lessons of the heart that came to him as part of his spiritual quest. He shares his experience of the Heartfulness practices—how they helped him conquer fear and paved his way to love.

While reading this remarkable autobiography, some chapters stand out. In the chapter "Follow Your Heart," Adizes says, "I make the clients solve their own problems. I only give them the tools." He does not talk of solutions. He shares thoughts and inspiration. Two other chapters also left a mark on my heart: "A Change Has a Price" and "Seek the Light in Your Own Heart." To borrow from Adizes's language, "The more you love, the younger you will feel and the less energy you will waste. And the longer you may live." What a wonderful thought!

It is not fair to compare authors or books. Can you compare oranges with apples? Yet *The Accordion Player—My Journey from Fear to Love* is one of the best books I have read so far. Just like *Man's Search for Meaning,* written by Victor Frankl, who was also a Holocaust survivor, this book leaves a deep impression on the minds of the readers, inspiring them to overcome fear by embracing love. In fact, it is an inspiration to rise above the feeling of love and *become* love.

I recommend that everyone read this book through to the very end, as the conclusion is the most important part. I do not wish to reveal everything and deprive you of the joy of reading it for yourself. As a parting note, all I can say is that we shall forever be indebted to people like Ichak Adizes, who choose to share their lives as a beacon for the rest of humanity.

Daaji
Spiritual guide of Heartfulness Meditation Worldwide

FOREWORD

Let me begin with a confession: I have been a fan of Ichak Adizes since we met at UCLA a half century ago. I was immediately attracted to his capacity to take wide swaths of human activity and find significant patterns within them. At that time, he was perfecting his brilliant work on lifecycles of corporations; while pioneering in the field of arts administration, where he recognized the huge challenges for cultural institutions as they gained power and influence. Here was an amazingly dynamic being almost from another planet, a Balkan-Israeli, now in California, instilling new forms of cosmopolitanism in an increasingly complex Los Angeles. That was a half century ago.

Now, as I've just finished reading his memoir, I love that its title honors the accordion as a kind of metaphor for his life. Here are some qualities of the instrument, well played: passionate, improvisational, authentic, inclusive, open hearted, zealous, cross cultural, democratic, tragic, and celebratory of national, regional, and religious diversity. The accordion uses charm and enthusiasm to cut through the walls people build around themselves and bring them together.

All these characteristics describe the Ichak Adizes I know to a tee.

Reading his words is at times like listening to a powerful performance on this unique instrument—I could almost hear strains of the Holocaust, echoes of Macedonia, and the treasures and pains of an assembled and divided Yugoslavia. There are the melodies of an Israeli childhood and the construction of a nation. And there's music in listening to Adizes, the guru, advising leaders of nations and business executives.

Adizes writes, as good memoirists must, in a way that embraces achievement and failure, and tries to come to grips with the dramas of life with immense honesty and self-reflection. As he searches for the formulae for a new philosophy of entrepreneurship and management, he shows why he became a poet laureate of "founders," those individuals singularly responsible for major cultural and financial breakthroughs. And then he strives to apply that formula to his own life, in finding a mate, in successful parenting, and—most painfully—in allowing himself at last to believe in love.

An elder Adizes explores the qualities of love and meaning as a supplement and perhaps a substitute for his long focus on the corporate and the managerial—think of his efforts to establish and institutionalize the Adizes Methodology for Organizational Transformation. In his humanity, he learns of the limits to transcending the physical and the medical—see his passages on obtaining a kidney transplant.

Adizes, like Whitman, contains multitudes. He is a man of the historical vicissitudes of the twentieth century reinventing himself for the twenty-first. His journey through many shifting circumstances and locations, from the Balkans, to Israel, to Southern California, to Mexico and Central Asia . . . all of this is a thrill, and one that embraces and communicates a remarkable life.

Monroe Price
Professor (retired) Annenberg School for Communication,
University of Pennsylvania
Former Dean, Benjamin N. Cardozo School of Law of Yeshiva
University

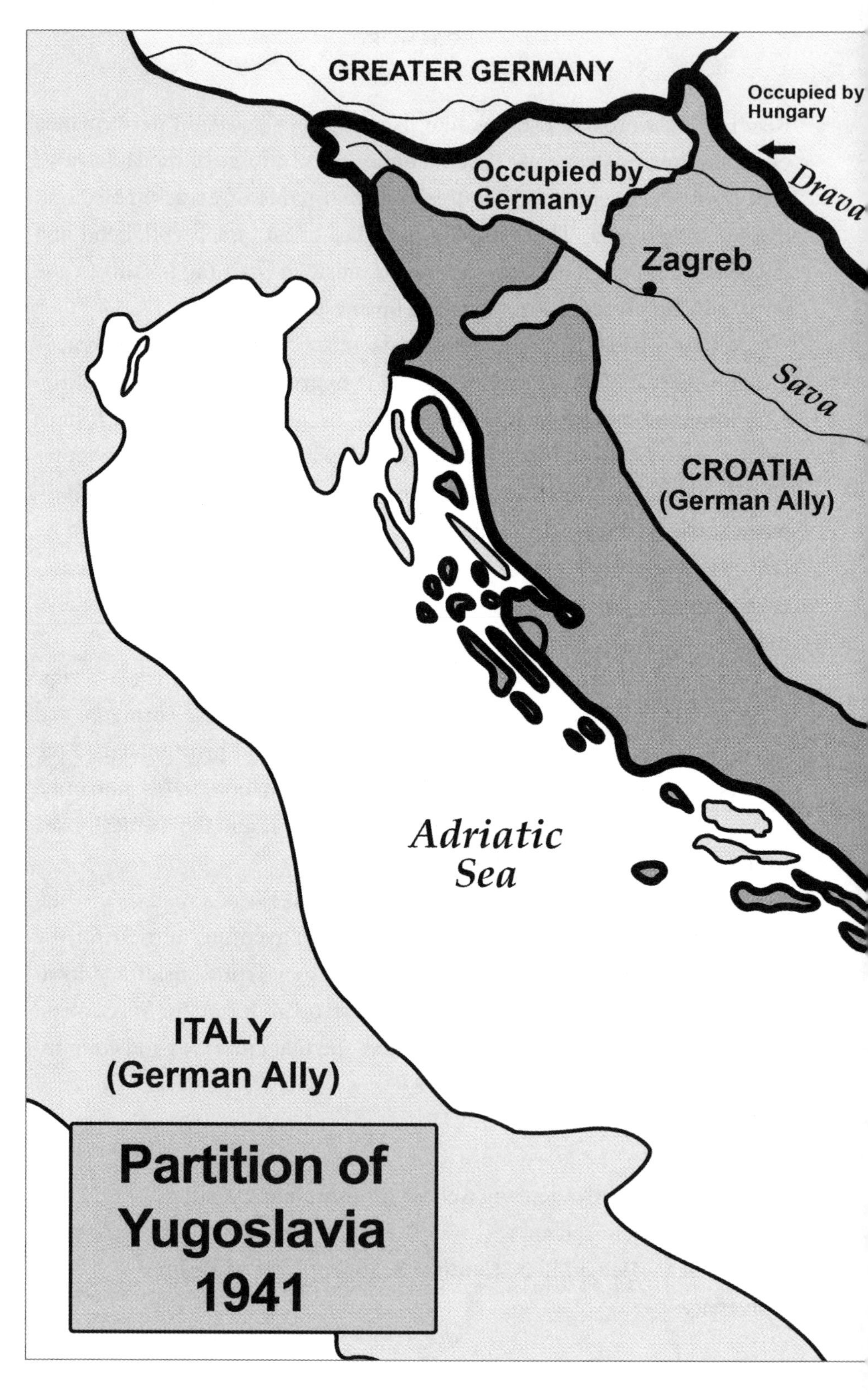
GREATER GERMANY
Occupied by Hungary
Drava
Occupied by Germany
Zagreb
Sava
CROATIA
(German Ally)
Adriatic
Sea
ITALY
(German Ally)
Partition of
Yugoslavia
1941

HUNGARY
(German Ally)
Danube
Tisza
ROMANIA
(German Ally)
Occupied by
Hungary
Belgrade
SERBIA
Occupied by
Germany
Sarajevo
Danube
Nis
Drina
Occupied by
Italy
Albanian Alps
Pristina
BULGARIA
(German Ally)
Shkodër
Bërdicë
Skopje
MACEDONIA
Occupied
by Bulgaria
YUGOSLAVIA
1940 BOUNDARY
Tirana
Lake Ohrid
Bitola
ALBANIA
Occupied by Italy
Occupied by
Germany

PART I

CAGING THE HEART

With my parents, Salamon and Diamanta in the late 1930s, before the war came to my hometown of Skopje, the capital of Macedonia.

PREFACE

I am watching my mother weep.

She sits quietly in the kitchen, sewing a yellow star on every piece of our clothing. The clothes are piled on chairs, on an ironing board, on the kitchen table. She sews steadily and carefully, not uttering a sound. Tears course down her face.

I do not move. I am frightened. A barely audible *"Zašto, Mama?"* escapes from my mouth. Why is she doing this?

She looks at me but seems to look through me. "Because we are Jewish."

I wonder, what does she mean, Jewish? I have no idea.

It is March 1943. I am five years old.

Soon we will be on our way to a concentration camp.

Nearly eighty years have passed since that memory of my mother. On the surface, it looks as though I have overcome the tragedies of my youth. I have risen—not quite from the dead, but something close to it—to a role of prominence as a management theoretician and consultant.

You might say I am a success. But is it true? What is success?

I was once invited to give a lecture. As is customary, my host began by telling the crowd of my accomplishments, how I had started my own institute, advised prime ministers, and helped to turn around hundreds of companies; that I had written twenty-six books, translated into thirty-six languages; that I was awarded twenty-one honorary doctorates and granted honorary citizenships of two countries. That I was named one of the ten communicators of the world, together with the Dalai Lama and the pope.

Sitting next to me on the stage were two men I did not recognize, and I heard one say to the other, "But is he happy?"

No, I was not. My heart was in a cage. My life was a long struggle to find happiness, to overcome fear, and to find love I had lost. I did not give up, and that is what my story is about. By following many of the same principles I used in transforming companies around the world, I found I could transform myself as well and find happiness.

This book is an account of my life—as true an account as one can provide when mining memories that go back decades. The portrait in the mirror is unvarnished, and at times it is not pretty. Throughout the process, I learned more than I could have imagined about myself, that being unhappy is not a terminal disease. It is a choice we make to change or to stay in misery.

I made the choice. I changed. I believe we all can change to love. The future of our civilization may depend on it.

Today, the human race is going through a major transition. We started as chimpanzees; the strongest was the leader. Then we became a nomadic society. The best hunter was the leader. When we settled, we became an agricultural society, and the one with the most land and sheep was the leader. The common denominator? Strength. Muscle. Power.

With industrialization, the brain took the position of importance. Planning. Budgeting. Organizing. Now, we are in the postindustrial, information society and moving to something new; let us call it the digital age. In the new society, robotics will replace the muscles, and artificial intelligence will replace the brain. So, what is our future next?

If civilization continues on the present trajectory, developing more and more brain and muscle, are we going to end up like Nazi Germany? It was highly educated, cultured, with music, art, literature, but no heart. Imagine our future: a society with a vast arsenal of nuclear arms, with high technology and chemical and biological warfare capability, but without a heart?

What will save us, then? The heart.

A restaurant that I like has a big sign on the wall that says, "We will not feed you food that we would not give our children." Well, if you love me as much as you love your children, I am your client for life. I call it managing with a heart. Not just for profit.

When my son asked me why I was writing my story, he asked, "Is it an ego trip?" I do not think so. I think that there are many people who will read this book and identify themselves somewhere. Maybe you are one of them. I hope this book will stimulate you to make changes in your own life. To share love. To feel love.

Ichak K. Adizes
Santa Barbara County, California, and Tel Aviv, Israel

On March 21, 1943, more than two thousand prisoners at the Monopol concentration camp, including my grandparents, aunts, uncles, and cousins, boarded a train to the Treblinka extermination camp.

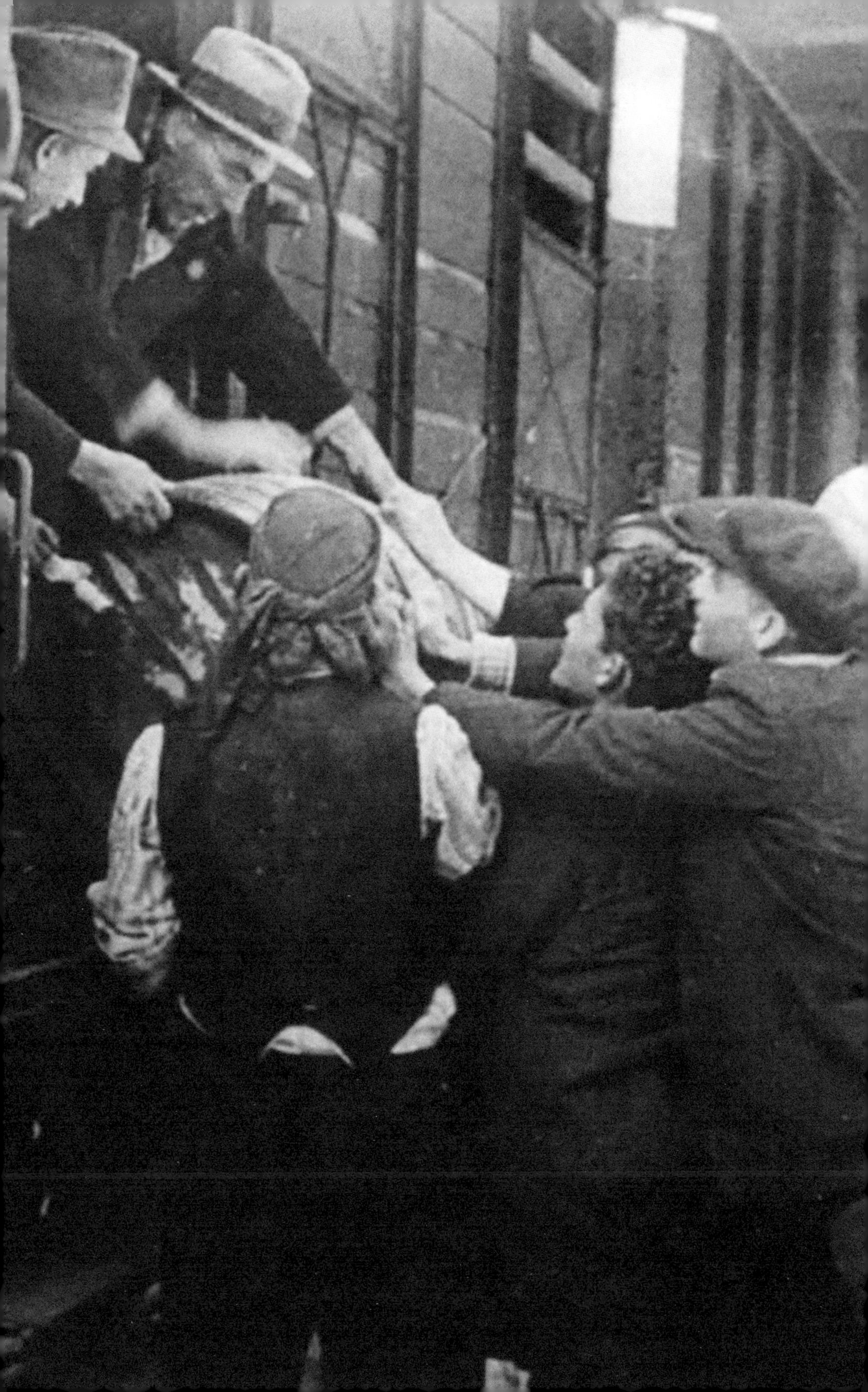

Me, around age four. After five hundred years of Turkish occupation, its influence could be found across the region, from the clothing and food to the backgammon tables in the old bazaar.

A SUDDEN SILENCE

Quietly we gathered, the Jews of Skopje, Macedonia, at the foot of the Jewish Bridge. That wooden bridge where we assembled has been rebuilt with stones. It is not called the Jewish Bridge anymore, as there are hardly any Jews left in Skopje.

Here, by the bridge, families huddled together, not daring to speak or even to look at one another. The signs around town had told us to be here, where we would depart for work camps. No one had any more information, but no one wanted to be the first to raise any questions, to call attention to himself and his family. I sensed the uneasiness in the air and clutched my mother's hand.

She had dressed me that morning in my warmest clothes, as if they could somehow protect me from where we were going. Her fingers had trembled as she tried to secure the top button of my coat, her face twisted to keep from crying.

We stood together in a ragged line in the cold morning air, waiting for an order, a command that would bring us to life. Soon enough, soldiers in uniform shouted at us to advance across the bridge. Their faces showed no emotion as they shoved us ahead with their rifle butts.

We moved forward, an awkward mass, without uttering a word. The bright yellow stars visible on every chest, conspicuous on that somber morning, proclaimed not only our low status but also the fate that awaited us. I still remember the deepening gray of the sky, which seemed lower than I had ever seen it before, and the smell, a fetid, musty odor of sweat drenching everyone, staining the air. I remember shivering and putting my hands under my mother's arms, hoping to warm them somehow.

My family crossed the bridge, dragging a cart, following the soldier at the head of the crowd. He seemed to be the only one who knew where we were going. Except for the voices of the soldiers and the rhythmic slap our shoes made on the Turkish-built cobblestone street, all was quiet. It was a long journey for a little boy. My feet were unsteady on the uneven cobblestones, and I started to cry. I begged my mother to carry me in her arms, but she refused. It made me cry even more. Why would she not take me in her arms? Only after the war would I find out why.

On the side of the road, all along the route, stood Macedonians, our countrymen. Some watched us tread by silently; others jeered and shouted insults, calling us *chifuts,* a derogatory name for Jews. Was that what my mother meant when she had told me we were Jewish? Why were they exhibiting so much hate? I looked to her to explain it all, but she was consumed by her tears.

Finally, we arrived at Monopol, our concentration camp. Its gates were open. We were pushed inside.

Before this, I remember a sudden silence blanketing our household when the Bulgarian fascists put signs over the whole city. Jews must gather to leave for work abroad, they said. Silence and fear overtook our family. When we sat together to eat, we looked away from one another. There was no laughter, no humor—just an overwhelming awareness of emptiness and deep sadness. Something grave and unknown had taken over our lives. What would be our fate? I knew without being told that it was important I remain quiet. No questions could be asked. There would be no crying.

I spent the last days of my childhood—though I did not know it was ending then—sitting in a corner, afraid to speak. I had become a silent observer. Invisible.

While my parents were frightened, they thought we would be back, as did most of our Jewish neighbors. Everyone believed what they wanted to believe, what they needed to believe. They would all take their house keys for the day they would return.

That morning in March the air was cold, and the sky was slate gray. When the time came to leave, my father was all action. He went next door to ask our neighbor whether he would mind storing our mattresses and blankets until we returned. Then, one by one, I watched him throw our meager possessions over the fence into the yard next door.

My grandfather rarely showed emotion. He was the patriarch of the household, the king. No one ever challenged that. No one ever argued with him. But that morning, his shoulders were bowed. Suddenly, before my eyes, he had turned into a powerless old man. He seemed to recede into the background. My grandmother—who was always compliant with her husband, who addressed him using the formal form of "you"—hesitated as she held the knob to the front door. Unable to speak. Unable to move. She waited for directions, for an order from him, but he gave none.

My father took charge. *"Hajde, hajde,"* he urged us. ("Let's go, we can't be late.")

I was born in Skopje, Macedonia, on October 22, 1937. It was a Friday at sundown, just as the shammash, the synagogue servant, began calling the Sabbath service.

The Jews of Macedonia were Sephardim, the descendants of Jews from fifteenth-century Spain. We had been banished by the Inquisition, wandered through Europe, and finally found a resting place in Macedonia.

Left alone to live apart, we had built a traditional community surrounded by rituals, religion, and customs that dated back centuries.

Skopje is a four-thousand-year-old city on the banks of the Vardar River in the heart of the Balkans, famous as the birthplace of Mother Teresa. In the thirties, Skopje's Jewish community numbered about five thousand. Most lived in a *mahle*, a Jewish ghetto, under an ancient wall built during the Ottoman Empire.

The Turks have been gone for nearly a hundred years, but the Turkish influence can still be found everywhere. Turkish rugs, hookahs, and backgammon tables are displayed on the streets, and the vendors invite you to—actually, more like insist that you—visit their stalls. In a photograph of me at about age four, I am wearing a fez and a vest of traditional Turkish design.

At the beginning of the twenty-first century, the Macedonian government spent millions of dollars modernizing the city but kept its old bazaar. In the outdoor market, people move slowly, as there is all the time in the world. It is reminiscent of a bazaar in Istanbul, with cobblestone roads called *kaldrma.* The aroma of grilled meat and Macedonian folk music drift from the coffee shops as *burek* and baklava are served. Men sit at small tables drinking Turkish coffee served in tiny cups along with a glass of cold water and a sweet candy called *rahat lokum* (Turkish delight).

This is how Skopje looked at the time of my birth. Parts of it still look almost the same—except today, the city no longer has its Jews. They are ashes in Treblinka.

My parents' marriage was a traditional one. That is to say, it was arranged by their parents. In some ways, however, their engagement was unconventional. My mother, Diamanta Kalderon, had been promised to another man until her betrothed insisted that the dowry was too small and demanded a larger sum. My grandfather became incensed. He pounded his hand on the kitchen table, yelled, "My daughter is not for sale!" and abruptly canceled the engagement.

A canceled engagement was a serious matter. My mother's chances of making a good match were now greatly diminished. But it became an excellent opportunity for my father, Salamon Adizes, a manual laborer in a flour mill, to seek her hand in marriage.

The Kalderons were not wealthy but would have seemed out of reach for someone like my father. They possessed some education; they valued knowledge and had a feeling for music and literature. They were cosmopolitan and lived in Belgrade, the capital of Yugoslavia, while my father's family was poorer and lived in the less-developed city of Skopje, which was about a day's journey away. From the beginning there was an imbalance. He married up, and she married down.

There was no courtship. Their parents made all the arrangements. It was a relationship based on commitment and loyalty. That was what was expected. That was what was delivered.

They married and moved in with my paternal grandparents, Yitzhak and Venezia Adizes. This was the tradition: after the wedding, a bride joined her husband in his parents' house so that her mother-in-law could teach the new wife how to cook for her new husband and treat him properly.

Like most girls of that era, my mother had been taken out of school after the fourth grade. By that time, she had learned to add, subtract, and read. Nobody saw any reason to keep her in school. She was simply supposed to learn be a good mother and wife. She had a beautiful voice, almost operatic, but she was allowed to sing only for the extended family. According to tradition, singing in public—where men might ogle her—was shunned.

My father had also left school after the fourth grade, but for a different reason. He could not read. He was dyslexic. Since no one knew anything about dyslexia at the time, his teachers simply thought he was dim-witted, and he was dismissed from further schooling. He trained to be a barber but ended up working in the family flour mill in Kumanovo, a little village

outside of Skopje. Since he was the son with the least education, he was often mocked by his father and older brother Leon and assigned the most menial tasks.

We lived in a modest stone house built around a courtyard in the Jewish Quarter of Skopje. I was born in that house. Like most houses in Macedonia in the thirties, it did not have central heat or running water. In winter we slept under blankets that had been warmed over the stove. Water was hand-pumped from a well in the center of the courtyard.

The language we spoke at home and in the *mahle* was Ladino, a medieval version of Spanish with Hebrew and Turkish influences. My grandmother knew no other language. Centuries after the expulsion from Spain, we sang traditional songs in Ladino on Sabbath evenings after sundown. Some of those songs I still sing today, but now I sing alone. No one in my present family speaks Ladino. Of those who knew it, most perished

My father Salamon Adizes, bottom left, with his brother Leon and mother Venezia, at a family wedding, c. 1920. On the right are his father Yitzhak, and sisters Esther and Rashela.

during the Holocaust. In my family, I am the last in a chain that lasted five hundred years who speaks it.

Peace, honor, and respect dominated the atmosphere in our home. I do not recall ever hearing my grandparents argue or even raise their voices. My grandfather, whose name I carry, was the king and my grandmother the queen. When I was a child, I would kiss my grandfather's hand each time we sat down to eat, and he would put his hand on my head to bless me.

Friday evenings marked the start of the Sabbath. We didn't go to temple, and we didn't say any prayers. Coming together was our ritual. Those meals were a matter of great pride for the women in my family. My mother would start cooking on Wednesday for the Friday and Saturday gatherings.

I spent my earliest years at the modest stone house of my birth. It was built around a courtyard in the Jewish Quarter of Skopje. 1938.

Uncle Leon and Aunt Anna and their children would come over, and everyone would sit around the table, with my grandfather seated at the head in the chair of honor. No one would eat until he raised his fork. Then the women served the food. Invariably, during the meal, one of the men would say, *"Bendichas manos,"* which in Ladino, the old Sephardic language, means, "Blessed are the hands that cooked this meal." My mother or grandmother would respond, *"Bendichas bokas."* ("Blessed are the mouths that eat it.")

We ate typical Sephardic food. Every Saturday morning, we had *burekas:* leaves of filo dough filled with cheese or meat or (my favorite) spinach. They were served with a boiled egg, a drop of olive oil, salt, and pepper. Or there was *pastel de espinacas* (spinach pie) served with yogurt and a cup of coffee.

That world ended for me on March 11, 1943.

All the Jews of Skopje were rounded up by Bulgarian fascists on March 11, 1943, and imprisoned at the Monopol concentration camp, a tobacco factory.

MY PAIN

Why had the Bulgarian military rounded us up? Bulgaria had sided with the Nazis after the outbreak of the Second World War. As part of its alliance with the Germans, Bulgaria annexed its next-door neighbor Macedonia in 1942. At first, it looked as though that might be a good thing. Bulgarian Jews had not perished like the rest of European Jewry. Tsar Boris, the king of Bulgaria, had refused to send Bulgarian Jews to extermination camps. Macedonian Jews, however, were another matter. Maybe he had to concede us to the Nazis in exchange for being granted Macedonia. Jews for land. It wouldn't be for the first time in our history.

My parents, grandparents, uncles, aunts, cousins, and I had been collected with all of Macedonia's 7,144 Jews—every Jewish man, woman, and child in the country. Among them were the communities of Shtip and Bitola, whose roots went as far back as Alexander of Macedon, Alexander the Great.

My mother's parents, my *nonu* and *nona,* Mushon and Gentil Kalderon, were not supposed to be with us. They lived in Belgrade but had moved to Skopje at my mother's insistence. Her hope was that Skopje under Bulgarian rule would be less dangerous for Jews than Belgrade under German rule.

My uncles were not supposed to be in Skopje, either. Their aunt, Tia Sol, had immigrated to the United States in 1928, and invited her nephews to join her when the German persecution of Jews began to make headlines. But my grandmother would not let them go. She wanted her children nearby.

My mother's oldest brother, Haim, had studied business in Czechoslovakia but earned his living as a singer. He had even produced a record, which was a major accomplishment at the time, and it looked as though he was about to launch a promising career. Uncle Rako had joined his father in the refurbished clothing business, and Uncle Yosef was in his first year of medical school. I remember watching him play the violin, a private concert just for me. My aunt Hermosa was married and came with her husband, too.

With my beloved maternal grandparents, Mushon and Gentil Kalderon, before they perished at Treblinka. c. 1940.

I was my maternal grandparents' first and only grandson, and they held me close. The Kalderons showered me with unconditional love. *Izakito querido* they called me, never for a moment letting me forget I was loved. When I would visit, it felt like a celebration. They hugged me, played with me, fed me my favorite *burekas* and *fizon* (Sephardic bean soup), and sang me Ladino songs I loved.

Now my only connection to my maternal family is a battered envelope of faded sepia photographs. That and the dim memory of the sound of their voices. Even today, I can close my eyes and hear the lullaby my *nona* used to sing to me at night: *Nani nani, nani kere el ijo. El ijo de la madre. De chiko se aga grande.*[1]

Monopol was, and still is today, a tobacco factory and a warehouse. The Bulgarian fascists had converted it into a concentration camp.[2] The idea was to collect the Jews from across Macedonia into one location and then transport them to labor camps or extermination camps. It was supply-chain management at its most efficient, and the Nazis were certainly efficient. Years later, during his trial in Jerusalem, the world learned that Adolf Eichmann was personally responsible for arranging those transports. His defense? He "just organized the train schedules."

Upon arrival, my parents, my grandparents, and I, obedient to the officers' commands, entered the building where we were to live. Inside, rows upon rows of horizontal wooden shelves were pushed against the walls where tobacco was normally spread out to dry. The slabs carried the smell of decay. They stretched from floor to ceiling and were spaced three feet apart. But there was no tobacco. We were the tobacco.

---

1 Savina Yannatou and Primavera En Salonico, "Nani Nani," YouTube video, 3:31, February 1, 2009, https://www.youtube.com/watch?v=QPSlpQTQQmg.

2 More history, including photographs of Monopol, are on the United States Holocaust Memorial Museum website: https://encyclopedia.ushmm.org/content/en/article/the-holocaust-in-macedonia-deportation-of-monastir-jewry.

Each family was assigned one bunk or wooden slab. My mother, father, and I had one three-foot slab for ourselves. Below us were my maternal grandparents. Next to us were my paternal grandparents. Nearby were my father's sister-in-law, Anna, and her two children, Yitzhak, six, and Yoshko, four. Yitzhak had been blind from birth and could only feel and hear what was happening. Leon, his father and my father's brother, was not there yet.

Leon had hidden in the attic at home to try to save himself. When the Bulgarian soldiers came to the house to validate that everyone had left, he watched through a crack in the attic floor as they captured his wife and two sobbing children. Anna glanced up toward the attic as she and the children were dragged away. Her eyes locked with his, but Leon did not come down.

Leon eventually escaped from Skopje by bribing a Kosovo Albanian with gold to smuggle him into Kosovo, which was under Italian occupation.

Each family at Monopol was assigned a single "bunk," a wooden slab that had been used to dry tobacco. March 1943.

The Kosovar realized that Leon must be carrying more gold to aid him in future escapes and proceeded to rob him, but Leon's hard luck was not at an end. His guide saw one more opportunity for gain, so he turned Leon over to the Bulgarians, who awarded a bounty to anyone turning in a Jew. Leon was beaten mercilessly and brought to the Monopol concentration camp, where he joined his family, all stuffed into their compact cell.

We were crammed into those tiny cells along with the 7,144 other Jews from across Macedonia. One slab, of course, was too narrow to accommodate a large family. Many slept in the damp corridors. After the war, when photographs of Auschwitz were released, I noticed that it looked just like our Monopol "home." It was as if all the camps had been mass-produced.

My overriding memory from this place was that we were all constantly hungry. I cried a lot and begged for food. Our only meal, served once a day, was a white bean soup with a great deal of water and not many beans. The bell would ring, and like hungry animals we would rush from our cells and wait. There was no complaining. It took hours to move up the line, and when we finally reached the server, it took just minutes to drink the soup. My grandmother, my *nona,* spooned me her portion. She was starving, visibly wasting away; nevertheless, she would give me her ration. "Eat, eat, Iziko, I'm too old anyway," she would whisper, quieting my fears, holding me in a loving embrace.

To this day, I can recall the feeling of that hunger in an instant. If I am even slightly hungry, I become anxious and aggressive. When food is placed in front of me, I eat it, even if I am not hungry at all.

It was the hunger that made me forget where I was and the dangers of that place. One day, I noticed what appeared to be goldfish darting around in the water of the little fountain that belonged to the owner of the tobacco factory. Food, I thought. I dashed there to try to catch the fish, but when I reached the fountain, a Bulgarian soldier appeared out of nowhere. He was angry. Without a second thought he lifted his rifle butt and slammed me in the face near my left eye. The force of the blow left me cross-eyed, and by the war's end it was too late to heal the damage. I lost the use of that eye.

In spite of all this, somehow, I do not remember Monopol as depressing.

It was not a place where people fought or raised their voices. Yes, people were scared, but the place was also full of warmth, love, and caring. Like a family reunion. I attribute it to the Sephardic culture. The Jewish people of Macedonia were either Sephardic, like us, or Romaniote—the ancient Jews the Romans exiled and scattered across the Roman Empire after destroying the sacred temple in Jerusalem in the first century of the Common Era.

At Monopol, my father quickly reinvented himself as a medic, thinking there might be a gain for him and for us. One night I watched with wonder as he simply wrapped a white band around his arm and drew a red cross on it with lipstick. Where he found lipstick in a concentration camp, I never learned, but that made him a medic. He had no formal experience with medicine. He had been a hospital orderly, not even a nurse, during his military service in the Yugoslav army, so his total exposure to medicine was that he had observed basic medical procedures. But his quick thinking allowed him to move freely throughout the warehouse, from one building to another.

Ten days after we had arrived, the order came: more than two thousand of the prisoners in the camp were to board a train. This was the first shipment.

From the little window of the converted warehouse, I saw the Bulgarian soldiers loading my grandparents Gentil and Mushon Kalderon, my aunt Hermosa, and my uncles Haim, Rako, and Yosef onto the train. Before I could even cry out to them, my father's sisters, Lea and Hanna, filed by with their husbands and their children. Kathi (I believe she was eight) and Matika with her husband, Aaron, were pushed forward into the train's cattle cars by soldiers with the butts of their guns, disregarding the cries of the children. Altogether, one hundred and three of my relatives, the near entirety of my extended family, were herded onto that train.

I believe my beloved *nona* knew, as she was lifted aboard that cattle car, that it was death that awaited her and her children—the same children she had stopped from fleeing to America.

I can still see her waving at me from the train. Behind her, peering over her shoulder, is my uncle Yosef. My uncle Rako, who used to pull my ears playfully, is beside him, rising on his toes behind my grandfather. And then, suddenly, I see my father. As a medic, he was assigned to help people onto the train. Slowly, without hesitation, without emotion, he slides the heavy door of the cattle cars shut, and the train pulls away. How could my father do that? I wondered then, and I still wonder now.

The moment that door closed on my beloved grandmother, my grandfather, my cousins and uncles, the door to my heart closed, too.

THE JEWS OF SPAIN

During the war and for years after, we had no word from anyone who had boarded that train. We did not know what happened to them or where they had been sent. I always hoped they would show up one day. Instinctively, from time to time, around dusk, I would glance out the window to look for them walking up our street.

Even years later, when I was an adult traveling the world as part of my work as a speaker and consultant, I would compulsively open the telephone directories in new cities I passed through. Perhaps someone named Kalderon or Adizes or Adiges or even Adijes was living there. Perhaps someone was still alive. The uncertainty always gave hope room to grow. Perhaps my lost family would show up somehow.

I understand now how important it is for people to know what happened to their lost loved ones. Without knowing their fate, one always lives in hope, never-ending hope. Maybe someone survived. Maybe just one person.

Sometimes miracles do happen. There is a story—a true story—I heard about a young man from Israel who fell in love with a Jewish girl from Canada. Their families met for the first time at the wedding. Waiting in line to select food from the buffet table, the groom's Israeli grandfather found himself standing directly behind the bride's Canadian grandmother.

As she extended her hand to pick up a plate, he noticed she had a number tattooed on her arm. He had one, too, a sign they each had been in a German extermination or labor camp. Politely, he asked to see her number. It was from Auschwitz. He was startled to see that it preceded his by one digit. It was his own wife, the wife he thought had perished at Auschwitz.

Macedonian Jews carry a macabre distinction: it is the only Jewish community from which no one—not a single soul—transported to the extermination camp survived to tell the story. All who boarded those trains either died on those trains or were gassed with carbon monoxide but did not die from it. They just lost consciousness. Then they were put on piles on top of one another like logs, set on fire, and burned for days until they all died.[3]

About a dozen Jewish Macedonian families were not on that train. They were not even in Monopol. They escaped to the mountains, joined the Partisans, and did not end up as burning logs. Our family survived a different way.

The source of our good fortune dated back to the early part of the twentieth century, when the Spanish consul in the region came across the Jewish ghetto in Prishtina, Kosovo. In 1924, the Spanish government of dictator Primo de Rivera had legislated that all Jews of Sephardic origin could apply for and be granted Spanish citizenship, regardless of their residency or nationality.

Sephardim had been the Jews of Spain for centuries. They were doctors, poets, and advisors to kings. But in 1492, the golden age of Jewish

---

3 In fact, it was even more gruesome: https://muzeumtreblinka.eu/en/informacje/method-of-killing/.

culture in the Iberian Peninsula ended. With the Christian victory over Muslims in Spain, King Ferdinand and Queen Isabella ordered my ancestors to convert to Christianity. Those who refused were expelled during the Inquisition and spread themselves throughout the Mediterranean. Some found their way to the Americas with Columbus.[4]

My ancestors fled to Italy, where the Sephardim adopted the names of towns or rivers as their surnames. My father's family took its surname from the Adige River, which flows through Verona. My paternal grandmother's first name was Venezia, after the city of Venice. In 1635, the Adige family left Verona for Prishtina, which today is the capital of Kosovo. In Prishtina, our name evolved to become Adiđjes and then Adižes. At the beginning of the twentieth century, they moved to Skopje, where I was born. Our people were always looking for a place to survive.

I have traced my mother's family, Kalderon, to Aragon in the northeast of Spain, and even found the Calderon family's coat of arms. (In Yugoslavia, the *C* was changed to a *K*.) My maternal family settled in Manastir, now called Bitola. It is one of the oldest Sephardic communities in the Balkans. According to the inscription on the gates to the cemetery, it opened in 1495, three years after the Jewish expulsion from Spain. When I visited the city cemetery in 1997, I bent down and brushed the dirt off a random gravestone until its carved letters became legible. It read "Haim Moshe Kalderon." Of all the graves in that ancient cemetery, the one I had unearthed belonged to my great grandfather.

So when the Spanish consul discovered the area's Sephardic Jews, it was as though he had uncovered an archeological relic: the Jews of Prishtina all spoke Ladino. He proposed that his government offer these Sephardic Jews Spanish citizenship. It did not matter that they were not living in Spain and had not lived there for more than five hundred years—they were Spanish descendants.

The proposal was approved, but most families refused the offer. The

---

4 See "El Último Sefardí" (in the Ladino language): https://www.youtube.com/watch?v=Gkfa2cPlacQ.

The Kalderons: my mother, Diamanta (Duka), in the front, age five, with my grandmother Gentil Kamhi, behind her Rako and Haim and on her left, her sister Hermosa in Bitola, then Monastir, Macedonia, c. 1922.

Spanish Inquisition was such a painful part of the communal memory that there was an unwritten oath among Sephardic Jews that they would never return to Spain. The Adizes family was among the twelve families of Prishtina who, nevertheless, accepted the offer of Spanish citizenship "just in case." (I can imagine how they felt. I carry five passports.)

How did my family escape? The Bulgarian soldiers guarding Monopol had demanded that everyone with a foreign passport turn it over, supposedly to check that the passports were not forged. My father refused to hand over our Spanish passports.

My mother became hysterical. "We will all be killed if you refuse to turn those passports in," she cried. "Please, for my sake. Please, Moni, for our son's sake, give them our passports. They have the right to inspect our passports." She was openly weeping. "If you refuse, they will kill us all."

My father would not listen. "I don't trust the Bulgarian fascists," he said with irritation. "I'm not handing our passports over. We'll never see them again if we do."

Sure enough, he was right. Those who handed over their foreign passports never saw them again and were transported with everyone else to the fire pits of Treblinka. The members of the Adizes family who did not comply with the orders were spared. We were Spanish citizens. We were Jews, of course, but still citizens of Franco's Spain. To harm us was to violate citizens of a German ally, so after ten long days in the concentration camp our release was approved.

We were standing at the gate when my cousin Mosha, just a year older than me, ran to us and tried to hide under my mother's skirt. "Tia Duka," he cried. "Tia Duka, please take me with you. Please." My father dragged him out from beneath her skirt and ordered him to go back to his mother, my father's sister, Lea. They were put on the next train.

For years my father would try to explain his action. "I was scared," he would say. "Mosha had no passport. The Bulgarian fascists would punish us by taking our passports away for trying to smuggle even a child out of the camp."

We would listen and not say a word.

After escaping Monopol, we fled to Prishtina, where my father was born. There I was befriended by Gianna, the daughter of an Italian officer. I loved her, but I was afraid she might turn me in. c. 1943.

FUGITIVES

When the Bulgarian soldiers released us from the concentration camp, my mother, my father, and his parents had to quickly come up with a plan for what to do next. Yes, we were free, but where should we go? Every destination looked dangerous. To the north, Serbia was occupied by Nazis. So was Greece, in the south. Bulgaria, in the east, was sending any Macedonian Jew they could find to Treblinka.

My grandfather was numb, quiet, but my father was all action. "We need to move," he said. My mother asked, "Where to?"

My father paced while he spoke as if he was already on his way. "Prishtina," he replied. "We have to go where we can." My father, the realist, pushed on. "Prishtina is where I was born. The Adizes family has lived there for three hundred years. We know the city well. Furthermore, the Italians who occupy it are not as dangerous for us as the Bulgarians or Nazis are. There is no other choice."

We took a cart with our meager belongings and moved. Taking pity on us, an Albanian man in Prishtina gave us a place to stay, a storage room in an underground cellar.

The dominant memory of the few months we stayed there is of hunger.

My stomach ached for the nourishment of food, and my mouth for the taste of it. There was never enough to eat. It was the constant in our life. It occupied our thoughts all the time.

One day I found a rope and pried it apart into several small cords. My thought was that I could sell them on the street as shoelaces. I leaned against a store window, an undersized and undernourished six-year-old, and shyly held the thin strands out to people passing by. I said not a word. I was just holding out the strands of what I hoped everyone would see as shoelaces. No one looked at me. No one stopped to speak to me. No one bought them.

I did not speak Albanian and was very lonely in Prishtina, but not for long. A girl in our new neighborhood adopted me. Gianna was tall and dark-haired and seemed beautiful to me. Her smile had a real sweetness to it. She would look at me, take my hand in hers, laugh, and play children's games with me; I felt a great surge of feelings. I could sense her affection as soon as we were in a room together. She was thirteen years old, which made her more than twice my age. She was also twice my size. I suppose I was the baby brother she had always wanted. Gianna provided the love that had disappeared when those train doors closed on my grandmother.

But Gianna was the daughter of an Italian officer. I wanted nothing more than to be with her, but I was frightened. I might say a wrong word or do something careless to indicate that we were Jewish. And if she found out, she would cease loving me and turn us over to her father and the Italian police. And they would kill us all.

Prishtina may have been my father's birthplace, but we recognized that we were not safe there. It was only a matter of time before the occupying Italians, or the Germans, who were not far away in Serbia, discovered us.

My father exercised his newfound authority in the Adizes family. On his own, without even a mention to his father, he searched for and found a guide, a wiry Albanian with a prominent mustache. He knew of an unmonitored route over the mountains into Albania, which was under Italian occupation, too, but less visible to the Nazis than nearby Kosovo. "That's where we should hide," my father concluded.

"But do you trust him?" my mother asked, turning her face away from the man. "Remember what happened to Leon."

The guide sensed our hesitation. "I give you my *bessa,*" he told my father. "I will find a safe way to get you into Albania." At that time, when an Albanian gave his *bessa,* or his word, only death would prevent him from fulfilling his promise. It was stronger than any legal document. It was an oath to which a man was bound.

The route we took felt like an eternity. We stole across mountain paths, some by moonlight, and eventually arrived in Shkoder, Albania's second-largest city. It was a dusty town with dusty roads. Carts hauling soil or produce were pulled by skinny, starving horses.

Shkoder had a sizable Muslim population but only one Jew, an Albanian Jew named Arditi. He was a pharmacist and, more important, another Sephardi. We could communicate in Ladino. Arditi helped us find a tiny apartment, which had one room and a pocket-sized window that let in a small amount of light and very little air. It looked down into a garden that always seemed to beckon me. But I did not dare play there. Someone might ask a question and my reply might lead to our exposure. My father, seated at the one table in the room, drummed the idea into my head: "You must never leave the apartment," he told me. "You understand? Never leave the apartment." He made me repeat it, twice daily, as he looked me in the eye. His eyes narrowed and he stopped breathing for a few seconds. I felt how serious he was about his instruction. I understood the punishment that would befall me if I disobeyed him. So I stayed inside that apartment for weeks at a time.

My father slipped out to work as an errand boy in a store to earn money to feed us. He was thirty-one years old and responsible for the lives of his parents, his wife, and his young child. His job, which mostly involved delivering boxes from one place to another, did not require him to speak much. When night fell, he would rush home to the small apartment with the one small window.

We lived in constant fear. Any small noise made us jump out of our skin. Each time a gate slammed, or we heard loud voices outside, the five of us would huddle together, silent, frozen. Maybe these were the Blackshirts, the Italian equivalent of the Gestapo. Maybe they were searching for Jews like us who were in hiding.

I also feared the dark-robed priests who lived in the church across the street. Why them, I do not know. But they never smiled.

One night, my father's cousins Telo and Salamon Konforti came to our apartment, along with Leon, who was living down the street. They arrived in silence. *"Que haber?"* my father greeted them with the usual Ladino greeting. Telo was short and round, with a booming voice that dominated the room. Salamon was tall and quiet, almost pensive. They were hiding in Shkoder with their families as well, and they were eager to leave.

The Konfortis had come to discuss a plan, a way to cross from Albania into Italy. Telo reported that with enough money, we could hire a boat in the Albanian port of Durrës, sail across the Adriatic Sea, and sneak into Italy. They believed it was safer there than in Albania, an undeveloped Muslim country. But the passage was considered risky. There were stories of boats' captains collecting a fee for the trip, setting sail, and then in open sea ordering the crew to throw the Jewish passengers overboard. "Safety in numbers." Telo argued. "We should all go together." Salamon nodded his head as Telo spoke. He agreed with Telo: this was an opportunity, and we needed to seize it.

My mother had listened silently but could no longer contain herself. "Please, Moni, let us stay here," she begged my father. "I am afraid."

My father often disregarded her. She was always afraid, always believed that we would have no money, that we would be captured, that we would be discovered and put to death. For many years, she was subject to bouts of weeping and, when the crisis seemed overwhelming, fainting.

In our room that evening, I watched and listened intently. I tried to understand what was at stake. I watched and bit my nails, as I continued to do for many years thereafter. My father wanted to join Telo and his brother. The end result meant possibly greater chances of survival, but we were just another family of poor Jews, and the danger seemed enormous. It was one of the few times he could not decide. He turned to his older brother, who had joined the meeting, too.

"I am not going," Leon said. "It is too dangerous. The Albanian who robbed me almost got me killed. How can I sail on a boat with a stranger who is taking us just for the money?"

In the end, both my father and Leon decided against the trip, and Telo and Salamon pressed on alone. Years later, we heard that they made it to Italy and eventually to South America, Telo to Argentina and Salamon to Brazil.

Meanwhile, Uncle Leon decided to strike out with his family to seek shelter elsewhere in Albania. It was all done very quietly. One night, they simply dropped from sight. They left Shkoder without saying a word to anyone. They had to do it that way because if we knew where they were and if we got caught, we would be tortured to disclose their place of hiding. Soon we, too, were forced to settle on a plan to flee.

THE JEWISH WILL TO SURVIVE

History tells us that many Jews from Spain had to cast off their religion in order to survive. During the Inquisition, some Jews converted to Christianity but continued to practice Judaism in secret. They are called Marranos. I have met some of them when traveling as part of my work.

One encounter stands out to me. In the early seventies, when I was lecturing in Monterrey to the chief executives of Mexico's major industries, I did not speak modern Spanish. I lectured in English via simultaneous translation. Midway through my lecture, I realized why I disliked using simultaneous translation: it feels like taking a shower with your raincoat on. I like to sprinkle my talks with humorous anecdotes, but it takes a couple of seconds after I deliver them for the audience to get the Spanish translation. At that point, the joke sounds flat and unfunny, the illustration meaningless. Frustrated, I asked the audience whether they would mind if I lectured in medieval Spanish, in Ladino, the language I used to speak with my grandmother, who did not know any other language. I think they were amused. Go ahead, they said.

By and large, they understood me. At a certain point in my Ladino presentation, it seemed as if they could not hear me well, so I asked them,

"Me sentieron?" From the word *sentir.* The people in the front row looked confused. So I asked in English, "Did you hear me?" One man said, "In modern Spanish, *sentir* is to feel. *Oyir* is to hear."

It dawned on me then that in the fifteenth century the word for "hear," "listen," and "feel" was one and the same: *sentir.* There are remnants of it in modern language. In Italian, *sentir* is "to hear." In Spanish, "hard of hearing" is *mal de sentido.* When you feel sorry for someone and want to show you care, in modern Spanish you say, *lo siento,* which is: "I feel you," "I hear you."

Five hundred years ago, apparently, people were more in touch with each other. When they heard, they listened, and when they listened, they felt. Today we have three different words, which means we can hear and not listen; we can listen but not feel.

This illumination rang a bell for me and, ever since then, when I work in developing countries, where people are less sophisticated or educated, I feel closer to the person I am talking to and it is easier to communicate.

During the break, the underutilized interpreter came to me and said, "Sorry, Professor, I hope this does not sound offensive, but it does not become a person of your stature to speak like a peasant from the mountains."

I wondered what she was talking about but didn't question her.

A month later, when I returned to continue my lectures, she introduced me to the director of the archives of Nuevo León, the Mexican state of which Monterrey is the capital. In his research, he discovered peasants in the neighboring mountains who spoke Ladino. They lived in a village called Doctor Gonzáles. He took me to visit them.

It was December and, by coincidence, the middle of Hanukkah, when Jews celebrate the miracle of the oil found in the Holy Temple in Jerusalem as it was liberated from the Hellenic occupiers. The limited supply of oil was expected to last only one day but burned for eight, which is why Jews worldwide light candles in a menorah for the eight nights of Hanukkah.

Instead of candles, the people of Doctor Gonzáles had a blazing bonfire in front of every house for the same eight nights in December. They had no idea why they followed this custom.

The villagers had another holiday that coincided precisely with the worldwide Jewish observation of Sukkoth, during which practicing Jews live in cabañas. The families in this mountain hamlet built cabañas outside their homes, too, and lived there for the duration of the holiday without knowing why. "It is just our tradition," they told me in Ladino.

They couldn't explain their tradition of not eating pork or of marrying only among themselves, either. I discovered that while the rest of Mexico ate mostly corn tortillas, the Catholics of Doctor Gonzáles ate wheat tortillas—de facto matzah, the unleavened bread served during Passover. When the Marranos at Doctor Gonzáles made their tortillas, they set some aside and kept them in a secure place. The director of the archives didn't understand why. I informed him that it was custom in the Jewish religion to set some *matzah shmura* to the side when making matzah during Passover.

At one moment, the director posed a question that gave me goose bumps. He asked me, the first Sephardic Jew he had ever met, if I knew the meaning of a word the locals used which did not exist in Spanish. The word was *imma,* the only word that survived generations of assimilation. It means "mother" in Hebrew.

My Mexican host, the director of the Nuevo León archives, told me that the ancestors of these villagers were Sephardim who, escaping the Inquisition, had sailed from Spain to Mexico and settled on land granted by the king of Spain to Admiral Luis de Carvajal y de la Cueva. The admiral named it Nuevo León, or "new lion," after the symbol of the tribe of Judea, one of the twelve Jewish tribes emancipated from slavery in Egypt more than three thousand years ago.

The members of the Spanish Inquisition discovered that this admiral was a Marrano, a practicing Jew posing as a Catholic. He and his family were seized and burned at the stake. Some of the one hundred families he had brought from Spain to Monterrey escaped to the mountains, where they settled; today, their descendants live as Catholics but practice rituals and prepare food typical of Sephardic Jews, unaware that their origin was Jewish. Those who remained in Monterrey built it into an economic powerhouse.

One of my clients, a devout Catholic named Elizondo, came from a family with deep roots in Monterrey. Their ancestral home in the nearby city of Saltillo went back generations. He decided to remodel the house when it was his turn to live there and discovered a menorah and a Jewish star hidden behind a beam in the frame of the house.

Once, I attended a conference at the Center for Democratic Institutions in Santa Barbara. The Maltese ambassador to the United Nations was sitting across from me, and the name on his name tag seemed to me to be Sephardic. My neighbor in Israel had the same name, Pardo, as did the former head of the Mossad, the famous Israeli intelligence agency. During the coffee break, I approached the ambassador.

"Are you a member of the tribe?" I asked in passing.

"Shhh," he said, glancing around, clearly uncomfortable, and pulled me to the side of the room. "Yes, I am." He knew which tribe I was referring to without my saying it. "But nobody, even in my family, knows," he continued. "I have the family crest in a safe in Switzerland. We keep our Jewishness a secret, but on his deathbed, the father calls his firstborn and only then tells him that we are Jewish. He then gives him the key to the safe. This has been going on for generations."

Even hundreds of years after the Inquisition, fear is still in our blood.

Many Jews concealed their identity and did not return to Judaism until they were on their deathbeds. Heinrich Heine, the German poet, was one. The painter Amedeo Modigliani was another. Ivan Gabor, a Hungarian psychiatrist and a member of my institute, was, too. He used to argue with me nonstop on any subject. It was painful for him to agree with me. In the Jewish tradition, this is called Talmudism. The Talmud is the book of records of the debates rabbis had when interpreting the Old Testament or establishing rules of conduct. Religious Jews dedicate their life to studying and debating the Talmud.

Since Ivan behaved like a Talmudic scholar, I asked him, as I had asked the Maltese ambassador, if he was a member of the tribe. He denied it.

"But your behavior is so Jewish," I said.

"No, you are confusing Jewish culture with Central European culture. I am Hungarian, and you are Yugoslav. We are similar."

He clearly was denying his origins. We knew a Hungarian doctor who claimed she was his neighbor in Hungary, and she had no doubt he was Jewish. I took him on a trip to Israel, hoping that it would stir some emotional ties, that it would lead him to face his identity. I took him to Jerusalem and told him the story of the Jewish people, hoping to get a response. Nothing. I took him to Masada, the last stronghold of the Jewish people who fought the Romans and committed suicide when they could not protect the fortress any longer. No response. He gave away nothing until he was dying. Only then did he confide in me that as a child he was sent by his parents to live with a Christian family during the Second World War. He swore to wipe away any traces of his Jewish identity. And he did, until he was on his deathbed.

Jews did not only convert to Christianity. Some converted to Islam. During an Adizes Institute convention in Istanbul in the 1990s, we were taken by boat to sail the Bosphorus. Along the shore, I could see beautiful villas, their owners' boats tied to large, sun-drenched docks. I asked the guide who lived there.

"Oh, they are mostly Sabbatais," he said.

Sabbatai Zevi was a seventeenth-century Jewish community leader within the Ottoman Empire who claimed to be the new Messiah. He promised to lead the Jewish people back to Zion, our homeland. Thousands believed him. The Ottoman sultan considered this movement dangerous and threatened Sabbatai Zevi with death if he did not convert to the Muslim religion. A realist, he converted. Thousands of his disciples followed. But to this day they do not intermarry with the local population; they marry mostly among themselves. They are industrious and financially successful. The local Muslim community does not consider them real Muslims. Instead, they call them Sabbatais. There is a rumor that Kemal Ataturk, the founder of the modern state of Turkey, was a Sabbatai.

It is, of course, a truism today that being Jewish has been both painful and dangerous throughout history. To survive, families concealed their identities.

The Catholic peasants of Doctor Gonzáles, the enterprising residents of Monterrey, were clearly Marranos. The Maltese ambassador, Ivan Gabor, and so many others hid or denied their origins to save themselves. We shared a common ancestry; our lives had roots that were intertwined in Spain more than five centuries ago. They converted to save their lives. Five hundred years later, my family did, too, to save ours.

STRAY BULLETS

One day at the store, an Albanian customer stopped my father and asked him a question. When he realized my father did not speak the Albanian language, he became suspicious. He demanded to know why my father was in Albania. My father spoke some Italian because it has the same origins as Ladino. A hasty answer sufficed for the moment, but our presence in the city had been exposed. It had suddenly become very dangerous to remain much longer. We needed to depart from Shkoder, and swiftly, but where would we go? And how?

My father developed a story and took it to the leader of the local Muslim community, the qadi of Shkoder. Luckily, the qadi spoke Italian, so my father was able to patch together a story the man could understand: we were fellow Muslims from Bosnia fleeing a blood feud and needed his help.

In Albania, due to a very ancient tradition, a blood feud would start when someone from one family killed a member of another family. Even if the killing was an accident, honor required revenge. The family now had an obligation to retaliate. A cycle of killing would begin, going back and forth between the two families. It became a matter of obligation defined by a tribal code that was still practiced into the early twenty-first century.[5]

Fortunately, there was also an Albanian tradition that compelled Albanians to offer refuge to anyone whose life was in danger. My father took advantage of the custom. He told the qadi his story, obliging him to offer us some kind of assistance. The qadi thought quietly for several minutes.

"There is a village by the river," he finally offered. "We could hide you there."

When my father came home and told us what had transpired with the qadi, we were scared. Did the qadi believe my father? Could we believe the qadi? Would he turn us in? In the end, we had to accept his offer. We had no choice.

The qadi was a very old man. He had a long white beard and a gaunt, wrinkled face, and he wore a long black dress, like the priests across the street from us, and an imposing white turban. He arrived in front of our house and urged us into his carriage. To split the risks of getting caught, my grandparents were going to join us later. I was seated next to him, facing forward, the direction we were traveling. I made myself as small as possible. I wanted to be invisible. I tried not to shake. I sat as still as I could, staring at my feet. I remember thinking, I must not faint, I must not faint. He seated my parents facing us, and we set off.

To leave the city, it was necessary to cross a bridge on the River Drin guarded by Italian soldiers. Was this a trick of the qadi to hand us over? Even if not, there was still a probability that the soldiers would ask for our identification papers. Our names alone would cause trouble by singling us out as Jews. To even the most uneducated Italian, it was clear that Salamon

5 Dan Bilefsky, "In Albanian Feuds, Isolation Engulfs Families," *New York Times,* July 10, 2008.

and Yitzhak were Jewish names. Would our Spanish passports save us one more time?

The two horses pulled, and the carriage moved ahead. The only sound, which seemed magnified, was that of the wheels rolling over the cobblestones. The qadi was tense, though he tried not to show it. Why? I did not know at the time.

We approached the bridge. The carriage stopped. I tried not to make a noise, not even to breathe. A soldier opened the door and peered in. He saw a child and the familiar face of the long-bearded qadi. He saw only my parents' backs. He closed the door. Apparently, the qadi had enough stature and authority to pass through the checkpoint without interrogation. The carriage began to move once more, and we all started breathing normally again.

We soon reached Bërdicë, the village where we would spend the rest of the war. It was just across the River Drin from Shkoder, but for me, a child of six, it felt like it took hours to get there. The village had no roads. Small houses built of mud and rocks lined a single dusty path. Chickens roamed the yard of nearly every house. There was no electricity or running water. Villagers warmed themselves with the heat from their hearths. Women had to fill jars with water from the river almost half a mile away and carry them back home on their heads.

Our new home was a two-story farmhouse belonging to two brothers, Ali and Rajib Brahimi, and their families. They lived on the second floor, and they offered us their first floor, where they usually kept their animals.

We lived a primitive life there, without much money and ruled by the fear of being discovered. Each evening, we would listen to the rats scurrying over the wooden planks above our heads. Sometimes, one would drop from the ceiling and start running around our room. Once a rat fell into the container that held our drinking water. Even today, I have an inordinate fear of rodents. I am the one who jumps on a chair and screams when I see a mouse. It is my wife who chases the creature out of the house.

My father told the Brahimi family our story of being Bosnian Muslims escaping a blood vendetta. But what would happen if they discovered our true identity? According to Albanian tradition, the brothers were armed at all times, each with a gun and a big knife under his belt. It was wartime. If they believed that we had violated some rule or tradition, if they discovered that we were Jews and not Muslims as we claimed, we feared there would be instant punishment. Maybe death. There was no law to protect us and no one to turn to.

Our fears were not unfounded. We had no idea how to behave like Muslims, how or when to observe their holidays. We did not know how to pray. My father, always able to improvise, told our hosts, "In Bosnia, Muslims pray differently." We were all hoping their provincialism—the fact that they rarely, if ever, spent time outside the village—would work in our favor.

Underscoring everything was the more substantial and immediate reality: we had arrived in Bërdicë without money. How would we eat? Again, my father's ingenuity came into play. Our arrival had coincided with a wedding, and we were invited. There were maybe fifty or sixty people dancing, singing, and firing their pistols into the air. Suddenly, there was a shout. One of the stray bullets had caught someone in the neck. The festivities came to a halt. Random suggestions were pitched from the crowd of wedding guests, but there were no doctors present. In fact, there was not a doctor in the entire village. Everyone crowded around the wounded man.

My father saw his chance. "Let me look at him," he called out. He looked authoritative. They let him through. He set about cleaning the wound with water. There was no other disinfectant. He saw that the bullet had not damaged any arteries and became more assertive. "This man must expose his wound to the sun for two hours each day," he said, "until the wound heals."

It was, of course, not a particularly sophisticated form of treatment, just common sense on the part of someone with cursory hospital experience, but it worked, and my father became the village doctor. While still trying to learn how to pass as a Muslim, he suddenly became sought-after in the community. Villagers would come to see him when they were sick or injured and bring us eggs and chickens as payment. My grandparents arrived to join us a few weeks after the wedding, and my grandmother became his advisor. She knew some grandmotherly remedies for treating colds and even delivering babies.

On one occasion, a woman in the village had difficulty giving birth. She was screaming. My grandmother, with my father's help, made a fire and heated some mud bricks. The woman was told to crouch over those heated bricks. Apparently, the heat opened her birth canal. Still, there was considerable yelling and screaming, which frightened me as I huddled in the far corner of the room.

It was my mother's job to make regular trips back to Shkoder to buy medicine and supplies. She wore a chador, a black garment covering her body and face, as was tradition among married Muslim women. Only her eyes were visible. In this way, she could move around the city without attracting notice. She went to the pharmacy owned by Arditi and purchased alcohol, iodine, gauze, and cotton balls. Sometimes he offered her a small supply of aspirin. It was a bare-bones medical practice.

Without drugs, my father relied on placebos, but he also introduced twentieth-century hygiene to a village whose residents still lived what was mostly a primitive life. When in doubt, he fell back on sun treatment. "Spend more time in the sun," he would tell a patient seeking a cure. The air of confidence, the manner of behaving like a doctor, came naturally to him—more naturally than pretending to be a Muslim. He was also lucky—his record was a good one. His patients eventually recovered. Word soon spread to the neighboring villages. If you were sick, or about to give birth, there was a good doctor you could see in Bërdicë.

One day when my mother arrived at Arditi's pharmacy, it was closed.

Arditi had been arrested. We waited anxiously for some word of him, and then it came from one of his neighbors: the Italian fascists had rounded him up. They executed him without a trial. He was Jewish. That was enough evidence. This frightened my mother even more than usual. We would be next, she was sure. "Don't be so visible," she pleaded with my father. "Don't be so boastful."

But it was no use.

THE RISK HE WOULD TAKE

For the first and only time in his life, in the village of Bërdicë, Albania, my father was proud of who he was. Even his walk changed. No more dragging his feet or slumping his shoulders. He strutted now, with his head held high. He seemed to believe he actually *was* the village doctor.

On many days, the yard in front of the house was jammed with sick patients waiting in their oxcarts for their turn to be treated. They would shuffle into the small, bare house with a look of gratitude on their faces before he had even said a word. With each one, he projected benevolence. "After all," he would say if asked, "I *am* the village doctor."

He was happy and proud. He was not just able to feed the family. He felt he mattered, and he basked in the respect the villagers gave him. But the rest of us lived in abject fear. My parents argued incessantly. My mother would beg my father to lower his profile, insisting over and over that his growing exposure increased our chances of being detected. The Italian Blackshirts might hear about the famous doctor in the remote village up in the mountains with no electricity or running water and decide to check him out. There was no way we could maintain the fiction that we were Muslims if they showed up at our door. The moment they asked for our identification papers, we would be doomed. Another fear was that one of his clients would die and the patient's family, as was the custom, would seek retribution. She had a point.

One morning I followed along as two women from the village walked to fetch water. On the winding path that led to the river, we came across a pair of men on horseback, dressed entirely in black. They each carried a knife tucked into a cloth belt, a rifle, and plenty of ammunition on bandoliers across their chests. Their faces were nearly hidden by their bandanas. They looked like the villains I would later see in Western movies. The men's eyes were fierce, their gestures hostile. They seemed to scowl directly at us. It took every bit of my courage not to flee. Behind them was an old peasant woman riding a donkey, who wept to the rhythm of the beast's every step. Her arm was wrapped in gauze, and dark blood oozed through the gray cotton.

"Grandma," asked one of the women, "why are you crying?"

The old woman told us her story. The two armed men were her sons. One had recently married. For his wedding, she had baked some bread. A large splinter from the wooden pallet she used to slide the dough into the mud-brick oven in the yard had punctured her hand. She had ignored the wound, and it had become infected. Her whole hand had swelled up, and the infection had begun to travel up her arm. At that point, she had gone to see an Italian military surgeon in Shkoder.

"It's too late," he had told her. "Your arm is badly infected. It must be amputated."

The old woman could not imagine living without her right arm. She would not even consider it. She decided to return to her village and die. Her sons were taking her home.

"No, no, don't cry," the women from our village reassured her. "Wait until you hear how fortunate you are that your path led you here!" They were excited. They kept talking over each other. "Right here, in this very village, is a doctor who works miracles!" they announced. "Look! Here is his son!" They pointed at me with a flourish, as if my existence were proof of my father's miracles. They were very insistent that she should see "Dr. Selman," the name my father had taken. "You'll see, he will save your arm!"

I thought I was going to die right there from fear. I was only seven years old, but old enough to feel certain that this was a medical problem much too serious for my father to undertake. I knew he had no medical education. The army surgeon had given his diagnosis. This was a matter for surgery. How could sunshine and good hygiene fix her infected arm?

Terrified, I kept silent. The men nodded in the direction of our village. I had no choice but to lead them to the clinic. In a daze, I retraced my steps along the familiar path to the village, the wailing woman and her terrifying sons trailing behind me. My knees were trembling. If anything was to happen to their mother, these men would be quick to anger. We would probably be beheaded. During the war, up in the mountains, far from civilization, there was no one to protect us.

We entered the examination room. My father assumed his brusque but kind doctor's voice. It rang with confidence. "Please, Grandma, remove the bandages." She followed his directions dutifully. While he examined her arm, she told him about the Italian military surgeon's diagnosis.

My mother saw the condition of the woman's arm and overheard the surgeon's diagnosis. She could hardly fail to notice the old woman's sons. Trying to hold back tears, she pleaded in Ladino, *"Estas loku? Tu no sos doctor! Que estas haziendo? Mos vas a matar a todos!"* ("Are you crazy? You are not a doctor. What are you doing? You will kill us all!") She was in a state of panic.

My grandparents were distraught, too. They tried to reason with him. He should agree with the military surgeon's diagnosis. He should tell the woman that there was nothing he could do for her and send her away. Any other course of action would risk the lives of the tiny remnant of his family that remained.

My father nodded, but he was not listening. He was looking for something in his shaving kit. My grandparents started to weep. My mother fainted. It barely fazed my father. He returned to the examination room to prepare for surgery.

"Get that metal basin on the shelf over there," he directed me. "Hold it steady beneath her hand." I dared not disobey him, ever. There would be beatings if I objected. He took a razor blade and held it to a candle flame for a few minutes. He disinfected the blade in this way with such natural ease that it was easy to believe he really was a doctor. Then, without hesitation, he cut into the tender skin of her inflamed hand. She hissed in reaction to the pain. He made only a shallow cut, skin-deep. Then, using both hands, he squeezed as hard as he could around the incision. Blood and yellow-green pus oozed into the basin that I held, shaking. I thought I was going to pass out. I was frightened but I managed to stay conscious and do precisely what he ordered. By sheer luck, I believe, he had barely missed cutting into a vein, a fact that still sends my heart racing. To this day, I still cannot stand the sight of blood.

When the flow of pus ceased, my father relaxed the pressure, took the woman out to the yard, and told her to expose her hand to the sun—his favorite remedy. When she had regained her composure and looked calm, he ordered her to come back every day for the same treatment with the razor blade and sunshine.

Each day, my father repeated the treatment on a different part of her arm. Each time, I held the metal basin. Each visit, after draining the pus, my father sent her outside to expose her arm to the sun for one hour. I don't know what he would have done if the weather had been cloudy and rainy or if he had hit a vein. At the end of the treatment, she healed. My father saved the old woman's arm. Her sons became our guardians, and we had food.

Many years later, I saw the movie *The Bridge on the River Kwai.* I recognized my father's behavior in that of the movie's British captain, a prisoner of war. In the film, his Japanese captors order him to take a team of fellow prisoners and build a bridge over the River Kwai. The captain becomes so obsessed with finishing the bridge that he forgets he is a prisoner and at war with the Japanese.

Similarly, my father somehow erased from his consciousness the fact that he was a Jew hiding from fascists, who would murder us without thinking twice. He seemed to forget that in reality, he was an illiterate barber with no knowledge of medicine, a fake Muslim and a fake doctor.

But he was drunk with his success, the first of his life. Before the war, all he knew was misery and mockery. He had been less than a man. After the war, even his children—my sister and I—made fun of him, unaware of his dyslexia. Whenever he was behind the wheel, we needed to give him instructions. He was unable to tell left from right. We had to tap him on his shoulder to guide him, pointing out the direction he needed to take. While my mother was a voracious reader, my father had never read a newspaper or a book. We were ashamed of him, as his father and older brother had been before the war. But during the war, he was a hero. What was the most wretched time of our lives was the highlight of his. That brief period in Albania was the time in his life that my father was admired and respected. To the people of the village, he was an important man. He delivered babies, performed "surgery," and treated people who believed him capable of performing medical miracles. People knew of him far beyond the boundaries of Bërdicë. He was a celebrity, a person of consequence. He mattered.

The admiration my father received made him bold. My mother would say, reckless. During Ramadan, one of Islam's holiest observances, Muslims are forbidden to eat from sunrise to sunset for forty days. My father decided he would not fast, even though our lives depended on successfully impersonating Muslims.

I was to be his scout. He dispatched me upstairs, where our hosts, the two brothers and their families, lived. I was to act as if I were playing, but in reality, I was there to listen for any sounds of my father eating that might filter up through the wooden floor. If I heard the sound of dishes being scraped or the metallic clink of cutlery, indicating that food was being consumed downstairs, I was to jump up and down as if in play. That would signal to my parents that their meal could be heard.

My father made sure I understood the gravity of my responsibility. "If you hear us eating but fail to warn us by jumping up and down or even if you warn us too late, and they discover that we are really not Muslims, we may all be beheaded," he cautioned. "Not one slipup," he said.

I went upstairs, scared to my core of the responsibility, the life or death of my family on my seven-year-old shoulders. I pretended to play and listened carefully for any sounds coming from below. I was horribly anxious that I would fail in some way, that through my error we would be discovered and put to death. My fear was made more immediate by the constant presence of our hosts. Ali and Rajib always seemed to loom up suddenly beside me, catching me unaware. I fixated on the guns and big hunting knives the brothers wore tucked into their belts and believed without a doubt what my father told me: we would be beheaded if I erred in performing the task I had been assigned.

For more than a month this was my daily ritual. I did not hear my father eating, but the stress was simply too much for me. It caused me to buckle and then, some days later, to snap. I was outside, in a cornfield near our house. The sun was setting and the shapes around me were indistinct. In the middle of the field, I caught sight of a strange figure. It seemed to be a man. No, not just a man. A German soldier. It's all over, I thought. My heart started beating faster and faster. Sweat covered my body and dripped over my eyes. The Nazis had finally come to arrest us. I could not catch my breath, and everything went black.

Eventually, my mother came out and collected me. For more than a month, I remained delirious, drifting in and out of consciousness. From time to time, I would wake up and eat, then slip away again into an uncertain world of hallucinations. I would cry out at the recurring sight of a huge snake slowly uncoiling from the ceiling above my bed. I screamed nonstop.

No one knew exactly what illness had taken hold. And through this, my father, the miracle doctor, could not help. It was my grandmother who stopped the hallucinations. During a brief period when I was awake, she asked me what the trouble was. "It's the snake," I whispered, pointing my finger toward the ceiling.

"Oh," she said, in a simple but direct way. "I know about that."

"You do?" What a relief. She knew. Then she walked over to the kitchen area and rummaged around for a while. She returned to my bedside with a metal pot and a big wooden spoon she beat against the metal, again and again and again, creating so much noise I was sure it would frighten the snake away. Finally, she threw the spoon aside and said triumphantly, "No more snake."

I believed her.

Only years later was I able to piece together what had actually happened. I was experiencing traumatic stress at age seven. The shape of the cornstalks in the twilight had been playing tricks on my imagination. What I had seen was simply a larger-than-average cornstalk, its "German beard" swaying in the wind.

But I did not just imagine the danger—it was quite real. There was no question that our situation was grave. When Italy surrendered in September 1943, Albania was occupied almost immediately by Germans. A German occupation was, for us, a potential death sentence. It heightened our anxiety. Our fears were magnified because we were largely ignorant of what was happening outside in the larger world. We were isolated. We had only our imaginations, which offered little reassurance.

I stopped hallucinating, but I did not stop fearing for my life. During the remainder of the war, and for years afterward, I would suddenly faint for no apparent reason. I would faint, or even worse, sometimes I would also lose control of my bowels.

Even today, if I feel a little lightheaded or dizzy at the prospect of fainting, it can send me into a tailspin, consumed by the fear that I will never wake up. I have learned how to self-soothe, how to ward off flashbacks from that lost childhood that never seem to disappear. Deep breaths, counting, meditation: I have learned how to keep myself from fainting when I begin to feel anxious or under stress.

Years later, in trying hard to open my heart, I even simulated a death experience to be freed from my fears.

PEACE IS COMING

In the midst of a world war, in the middle of a poor Muslim village, we had no idea who was winning or losing. We were beyond the range of newspapers and radio. We knew nothing. Were we destined to live in disguise in this place for the rest of our lives? Would our village become a battlefield?

My father speculated about what it would look like when the war would come to an end. "When the military trucks on the road stop because they have run out of fuel," he reasoned, "that probably signals that the war is drawing to a close." Why? "Because the supply chain is no longer working."

It made as much sense as anything else. We began to watch for stalled military vehicles on the road on the outskirts of the village. It led to Tirana, the capital of Albania.

Then one day it actually happened. Looking out of our window, I saw a mob of villagers run past our home heading toward the main road. They were red-faced, enraged, shouting words I could not make out as they ran by the house waving pitchforks. I followed them. Around a bend, alongside the road, I saw a motorbike lying on its side and beside it a boy in a German uniform. He was perhaps twelve years old. He was petrified, his eyes looking around wildly for a friendly face, a way to escape. There was none.

At the time I did not understand: how could a boy be a soldier? After the war, I learned that toward the end the Nazis began sending children to the front lines. This boy had probably been a courier whose motorbike had run out of gas. He had been forced to stop, just as my father had predicted.

The villagers, wielding pitchforks and knives, surrounded him. The German boy was shaking. His eyes sought me out, pleading. I returned his gaze, but I was as frightened as he was. After all, they could just as easily decide to kill me, too. Here we were, our fates dictated by war: he, a German boy in uniform, and I, a Jewish child hiding in Muslim clothing. Both fearful for our lives.

I looked on silently, terrified for him. Terrified for myself. The mob took him away. I do not know if they killed him. I never wanted to know. But I have never forgotten his eyes—desperate, scared, searching for a sympathetic face, and then locking with mine. Years later, when I was living in Israel, it was his memory that inspired me to do something few Jews at the time would volunteer to do.

Soon after that incident, there was another sign that the war might be drawing to a close. One day we heard a loud, dense droning in the air. Airplanes were flying over the village, filling the entire sky. My parents ran outside, and I followed, hanging on to the back of my mother's skirt. Large American bombers, with the distinctive American star clearly visible on their wings, were making their way northward. My father tried to be indifferent, as usual, but this time his perpetually iron voice trembled. "They are flying toward Germany," he said.

My mother started to sob. She whispered over and over words that I could not make out. I moved closer to her, to hear her. *"Esto es. Esto es,"* she was whispering through her tears. ("This is it, this is it.") *"Si mos salvamos, Dios Piadoso, vamos a ir a Palestina, estar con nuestros i no mas escondir. No mas sufrir, Dios Piadoso, Dios Piadoso.*" ("If we are saved, dear God, we will go to Palestine. To be with our people. No more hiding. No more suffering, dear God.") That day, for the first time, we were hopeful. It was possible we might survive.

The sight of those bombers with the stars on their wings and the sound of my mother's prayers shaped my very first image of America. I was only eight, but the word itself, *America,* brought with it a special feeling: the country of the free, the country that fights to free the oppressed, the country that cares.

Soon we could see for ourselves that the war really was coming to an end. The Albanian Partisans fighting the Germans were drawing closer and closer to Shkoder. They started bringing their wounded to the village for my father to treat. One Partisan had stepped on a mine and lost both of his legs. He was brought in on a stretcher and stayed with us for several days. He was a grisly sight: no legs, shrapnel scars lacing his body, his bed blood-soaked. I tried to look away, but there was no way of concealing the sight. This time, my father could not do much for his patient. The man died after two feverish days and nights.

One day the Partisans descending from the mountains were crossing through our village on their way to Shkoder. They were weary, their clothes filthy but their facial expressions triumphant. One of them stopped to answer my father's questions, confirming what he already suspected: the Germans had surrendered.

At first, an eerie silence fell over all of us. Then, I remember a lot of crying that soon turned to sobbing. There was a sense of uncontrollable joy but also, to my surprise, one of emptiness and fear. We were suddenly free, presumably, but we had not thought of what would be next. We wanted out. We wanted to go home, but where was home? We wanted a place we could call our own.

Shkoder was not our home. It was a Muslim city, and no Jews lived there. What choice remained for destitute Jews who had lost everything? My mother knew: a Jewish homeland. We did not know if, let alone how, we would ever make it to the land we knew as Palestine, called Israel today. That was the dream—the Promised Land, the land of our ancestors, a place where we could finally be safe. (Clearly, that hope has not been realized. Israel is still far from safe.)

Our first step was to leave the village and return to Shkoder. From there, we would move back to Yugoslavia and then figure out how to immigrate to Israel. We started assembling our few belongings and prepared to say good-bye to the people of Bërdicë. We loaded up a cart led by two bulls. Blankets covered the small hill of our things, and I was placed atop the blankets. The whole village gathered to say good-bye to us. Thinking back now, I know it was a spare, bleak place: bleached hills, small farmhouses crammed with many families, barren farms, and no running water or electricity. People in developed countries would think of it as an area marked by poverty, a place destined for abandonment and destruction, but to us it was home for more than two years.

It was a place where our lives had been saved, not blighted, by friendly people who took us in. Although we were in hiding, we nevertheless became part of that village. We had belonged, and when we were leaving, my mother became emotional and started crying. The villagers were moved by our departure, too. Their voices were soft, and some of the women wept. They would have welcomed us if we had chosen to remain. However, my father was, as usual, all action. He was ready to leave.

Despite the villagers' obvious affection for us, we were still afraid to confess that we were not Muslims and especially that my father was not a real doctor. We just thanked them for their hospitality. As a sign of gratitude to our hosts for having hidden us from the vendetta, my father promised to return someday and dig them a well so that they would no longer have to fetch water from the river. It seemed boastful to make such a pledge, particularly given our circumstances. But it also was part and parcel of my father's sense of grandiosity then. He was still the village doctor helping these poor but kind peasants.

As we crossed the bridge into Shkoder, I remembered the fears I had crossing it for the first time, with the qadi. This second time, we crossed it to freedom, but where would we go? Where would we live? What would we do? We had no food, no money, and no friends. We were still outsiders, though we no longer had to conceal the fact that we were Jews to avoid capture.

My father, ever the survivor, adapted almost effortlessly to our new surroundings. Practically overnight, he found a new identity: he was a liberating soldier. He joined the Communist Partisans to search for Germans in hiding. It was not communism that attracted him. The undertaking was a means of getting us the food and resources we needed. The hunted became the hunter. Once again, the adrenaline, the status, and the power transformed him. He found an opportunity to serve as an active combatant against the small groups of demoralized, defeated fascists who remained in the area. He became a leader, a self-appointed liberator of his people.

One day he found a German soldier hiding in a container typically used to store flour. Approaching cautiously, he opened it and discovered a young man peering up at him, scared to death. The Albanian who owned the container had been hiding him, trying to save the German's life. The Albanian was not a fascist—he would have helped anyone who was in danger asking to be saved. Yesterday, the Jews. Today, the Germans.

My father and the German stared at each other. I do not know what thoughts went through my father's mind. Was he thinking of Monopol and of all our relatives shipped off in those cattle cars? Was it the years of fleeing and hiding, of being uprooted? He did not tell us what he did to the German soldier.

My cousins, Kathy, Mosha, and Zaki, all burned alive in Treblinka. Mosha begged to take him with us and save him, but my father was scared.

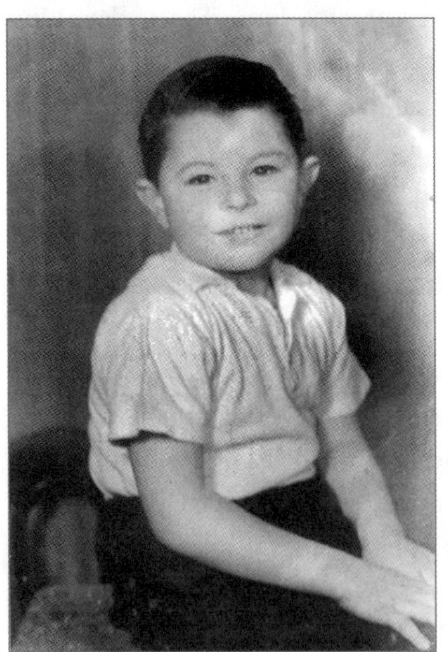

I suspected my father had killed him, and I started crying uncontrollably. True, the Nazis had treated us as though we were less than human. They killed my grandparents, my uncles, and cousins—all my relatives. But I felt sorry for that soldier. I remembered the twelve-year-old courier and the overturned motorbike. Maybe this soldier was just an older kid sent to war, his mother waiting for him to come back.

The Partisans appointed my father to the rank of captain and provided him with a jeep and a driver. He was hunting down German soldiers, but he took it upon himself to also find Jews who were still hiding in the mountains. In a number of trips to and from Shkoder, he brought them to safety.

One day he was driving through the mountains, looking for a back road that led to a remote mountain village. The road was steep and rutted, and it was impossible to drive the jeep any farther. My father jumped out of the car and, leaving his driver behind, climbed the rest of the way on foot. He was determined to find any Jews who might be hiding there. The village was so remote that it was possible they had not heard that the war was over and that it was safe to emerge from hiding.

As he came closer to the edge of the village, he realized he was wearing a military uniform, which from a distance probably resembled the German uniform. It was possible that if he called out to the Jews who were hiding there, they would mistake him for a German soldier and flee. How could he communicate to these terrified people that he was not the enemy?

He stopped where he was at the edge of the village and shouted, *"Shma Israel, Adonay Elohenu, Adonay Ehad!"* He shouted the most sacred Jewish prayer over and over again. My father reasoned that any Jews still hiding in the village would hear the prayer and understand that he was one of them and that it was safe to come out.

Who should emerge but his own brother, Leon. Ana, his wife, appeared as well, their two children following close behind her. My father and Leon had not seen each other since their days in Shkoder, when everyone took his own route to escape. None of us knew whether Leon and his family were dead or alive, though the assumption was that they had perished.

But here they were, alive.

The two brothers approached each other slowly at first, a disbelieving look on each face. Then they both began to run, shouting and crying. They hugged each other as though they would disappear again if they were to let go. Through their tears, the words poured out. They spoke in Ladino. Who survived? Who did not? They wept and clasped one another to make sure, once again, they were both alive.

One of Leon's sons, my cousin, is only two years my senior. His name is the same as mine, though he spells it differently: Yitzhak Adijes. We were both named for our grandfather. My cousin Yitzhak, the same boy who slept only a few feet from me at Monopol, had been blind from birth. During the war, hidden in that village in Albania, his only friend was a hen that he kept as a beloved pet. He would hold it, feed it, and lead it around inside the house, chattering to it as though they were siblings.

The family went hungry quite often, and one day, in desperation, his parents decided to slaughter his pet chicken. They did not tell him, concerned he would cry and make a scene. They also believed that being blind, he would not realize what he ate. That night, the whole family, including Yitzhak, feasted on the chicken. It wasn't until after the meal that Yitzhak was told by his younger brother that he had just eaten his best friend. I do not think he ever overcame the pain. He never ate chicken for the rest of his life.[6]

---

6 Yitzhak became a man of considerable accomplishment. In later years he wrote a book about his life in Albania: Yitzhak Adijes, *Childhood in a Shelter in Albania* (Jerusalem: Yad Vashem Publications, 1994). In 2004, he won the world championship in sailing for the blind.

IN SEARCH OF HOME

Shortly after his reunion with Leon and his family, my father found a convoy of British trucks making its way from Greece to Serbia by way of Albania. The English captain who was leading the convoy needed an interpreter, someone who could speak Albanian. My father volunteered and, in his broken Italian, convinced the convoy's captain to transport the Jewish families who had hidden in Albania—the families he had rescued from the different villages scattered throughout the countryside—to Yugoslavia. They loaded up one family per truck, and a convoy of Jewish refugees found their way to what they hoped would be safety and their abandoned homes.

We became a part of the gathering sea of Jewish refugees who had survived the Nazi onslaught in Europe; a people in motion yet again, whose provisional destination may have been Yugoslavia or Poland or Hungary or any of a half-dozen other countries, but whose true homeland was as yet uncertain.

Each family was given several bags of food and containers of water that had to last until the end of the trip. The water was stored in old gasoline containers, so it smelled and tasted of gasoline, making it virtually

My father Moni Adizes in Skopje after the liberation in 1945. On the right is Lubica Stankovitch, who helped teach me how to read in Serbian.

undrinkable. It was only as we crossed the mountains and saw snow on the ground that we were able to stop briefly, jump out of the trucks, and eagerly scoop up the snow to quench our thirst.

Finally, we crossed the border into Yugoslavia and arrived, ravenously hungry, at Lake Ohrid. There, I ate a fish, a trout, for the first time in my life. It sent me back to Monopol, when I had drifted outside in search of food and, trying to scoop up a goldfish, found myself rewarded with a Bulgarian soldier's rifle butt. This time the fish was caught for me and roasted over a campfire. A knife slipped under the crisp skin to pull out the backbone, and the whole buttery trout was mine. I ate it slowly—very slowly, scared it might disappear too soon.

Our initial destination was Skopje, where we went searching for the possessions left behind the day we were taken to the concentration camp. But everything had disappeared.

My father said that some of our neighbors had looted the house once we were gone, but we could hardly demand to look around inside their homes, and there was no other way of proving what had happened. We were unable to recover anything, and we were facing a new reality: there was no work for my father, and thus no food for us. Once again, we went hungry. My father could no longer pretend he was a doctor, nor were there Partisans he could join in hunting down remnants of the German army. He had returned to Macedonia to find neither home nor food—only his old identity: the poor, dyslexic boy who could not read.

While in Skopje, my grandmother Venezia died. I did love her, but do not remember crying. I would not allow myself to feel with anyone that I loved. I do not remember much of her funeral, either. She was buried in a Jewish cemetery, destroyed years later to make space for a highway.

There was nowhere left to go but Belgrade, the capital of what was then Yugoslavia and now is Serbia. We went there because it was where my mother had been born and raised. Her family home was still there. We assumed and prayed that it would be available for us.

I still remember our address in Belgrade: Kralja Aleksandra Street, No. 120. It was a small, simple two-bedroom house, but it was everything when we had nothing. In the front was my grandfather's shop where he had bought, repaired, and sold used clothes. There was a plaque affixed to the building above the entrance with a family crest and the inscription MK 1894. MK for my grandfather Mushon Kalderon and 1894 for the year the house had been built.

Belgrade had been a battleground. Not a single house stood intact.

My grandfather's shop had been half-ruined during the bombardment of Belgrade in 1941, and again in 1944, and the years that had passed since had been rough on the building.

We could not do much about the lack of heat or terrible cold, but we tried at least to repair the house and the surrounding streets, which were still pockmarked from the bombings. The government set up work brigades, teams of people who lived in the neighborhood and volunteered to clear the rubble. The work brigades were all self-managed. The government barely functioned beyond calling on its citizens to clean up the city as much as they could. Like so many of us beaten down by years of war, I finally had a purpose.

I had just turned nine, and until school started, I was a member of the Pioneers, a youth group. We wore red handkerchiefs around our necks and worked during the light of day, red flags blowing in the wind. My glands were swollen from malnutrition, and with my small, weak hands I truly could not do much. But I wanted badly to be part of something. To get out of my isolation. To try to make friends. My task was to put broken bricks on a pile.

It was up to us to build a new nation. We were the future of Yugoslavia, and we used to sing as we worked: *Druže Tito, ljubičice bela, tebe voli omladina cela.* (Our friend, Tito, you are a white flower. You are loved by all the young people of the nation.)

Many of the songs glorified Josip Broz Tito, the Communist leader of Yugoslavia. His army, the Partisans, had hidden in the mountains and fought the Germans throughout the occupation, and with their backing he ruled the land. Yugoslavia consisted of many nationalities and religions, all of which had been (and still are, to some degree) locked in fierce combat and perpetual enmity. In the new Communist Yugoslavia, however, there was supposed to be only one nation-state united by a dictatorial leader. There was no room for dissent or challenge to Tito's authority, and his order was succinct: no more fighting among different states, religions, or ethnic groups. We were all Yugoslavs, and Tito was our nation's father.

Strange as it might seem, no one knows the real story of the man who had named himself Tito. He claimed that his real name was Josip Broz and that he was born in a little village in Croatia. But in that small village where everyone knows everyone else, no one had ever heard of him or his family. He played classical piano, which he never could have learned in that small village, and did not speak Serbo-Croatian, the local language, well. All people knew was that under Tito they had a chance at peace, so the people chose to believe the legend.

Beyond the personality cult, we would also sing about *bratstvo i jedinstvo* (brotherhood and equality), which I now recognize as a shortened version of the French Revolution slogan. Our version of the song, though, was only about égalité and *fraternité—liberté* was left out.

My father, ever resourceful, renovated the little shop in front of our house and began to sell shoes. Leon, who moved with his family to an apartment a block away, joined as the store manager. My father became his assistant again. No more a respected village doctor. No more the liberator who rescued Jews. Just another tradesman attempting to make a living in a catastrophically distressed postwar economy. He could not even put enough food on our table.

The absence of food took a serious toll on me. I was woefully thin, and beyond the swollen glands, I seemed to be chronically sick. My mother gave me fish oil twice a day, which I hated. It made me want to throw up each time I had to swallow it, but a better remedy was unavailable. When our Pioneer youth group went to visit the mountain next to Belgrade for a bit of supposed R&R, I found a plum tree—the fruit still green, not ripe. I did not care and ate some of the plums. When you are really hungry, you eat whatever looks edible. I got a terrible stomachache and spent the trip back crying from pain.

One afternoon my father burst into the house with a small package under his arm and handed it to my mother. Her eyes opened wide when she saw what was inside. She looked for a moment into my father's eyes and immediately got to work. "Izi, here, take this," she said, handing me a few coins. "Go to the corner store and buy a cup of flour." I obeyed without a moment's hesitation, too excited to question what might be in the package.

By the time I got home, an onion was already cooking over the fire in our one little pot. My mother took the flour and began to mix in other things. My father, grandfather, and I all watched her work, dizzy from the smells and hunger, entranced. "Just a little taste?" I asked my mother. She scraped the pot with a spoon and handed it to me. I sucked on the sweet flavors in my mouth to draw out the moment as long as I could. She rolled out the dough, and I knew she was making a *burek*—a *pastel de carne,* or meat pie—which we hadn't eaten since our Sabbath dinners back in Skopje.

We celebrated as if we had won the lottery. My grandfather reminisced about the *burekas* my grandmother used to make and said something I had not heard since before the war: *"Bendichas manos,"* he said. "Blessed are the hands that cooked this meal." *"Bendichas bokas,"* my mother replied. It was automatic.

As we were eating, I asked my father, where he had gotten the meat. "It is horse meat," he replied shrugging his shoulders. In Albania we did once eat a cat, but I had never eaten a dog or a horse before. I choked, but with effort, kept chewing. I was hungry. Very hungry. When you are really hungry, you will eat anything.

The rest of that winter of 1946, though, we did not feel so blessed. We had little food and no heat, and we lacked adequate clothing to protect ourselves against the constant chill. My grandfather by now was like a ghost in the house, an almost invisible presence, dependent on his son. He was no longer the leader of the clan.

THE ACCORDION PLAYER

My education officially began in Belgrade. I was nine years old, two years older than the other children in class. The war saw to that. As there was no money for the tram, I walked to and from primary school. The journey was a torture. Along the route the neighborhood children would throw stones at me and call me a *chifut,* as our neighbors in Skopje had done when we walked to Monopol. To add to the suffering, I did not have enough warm clothing to protect myself from the cold, and when there were blizzards, my ears, nose, and toes would freeze. Each day, I would come home in tears. My mother would heat water and put my face and hands over the vapor to warm them up. As they defrosted, it would hurt even more.

Frail, cross-eyed, and poorly dressed, shy, and still numb from the four years of war and hiding, I made an irresistible target. At school, I wasn't just a *chifut;* I was also a *shiptar,* a slur for an Albanian. On my very first day, I heard both of these words, not whispered but said bluntly, with scorn. How was I supposed to reply? Was I supposed to fight? I was too small, too frightened, and could barely speak the language.

My anxieties added gasoline to the fire. I had fainting spells at school and on the street, and it was not uncommon for me to lose control of

Europe, c. 1946.

my bowels. I became the class object of laughter, rejection, and physical bullying. There seemed to be nowhere to turn, no one I could appeal to. My father was traveling to buy shoes for the store, and my mother was struggling to find food and keep the dilapidated house functioning. I felt alone and scared.

My misery did not stop me from becoming entranced by a girl from my class—a dark-haired girl, Milica Milosavljevic. All I dared to do was watch her from a distance. I could not imagine even approaching her, much less speaking to her. I was a *chifut.* I was a *shiptar,* too. The children reminded me of this daily.

Cira, a boy from my class, was my major tormentor. One day at school during the break, when our teacher was out of the room, Cira began pushing me and insulting me more than usual. *"Chifut! Shiptar!"* he shouted. He seemed to be goading himself. He cursed me and my mother. His voice grew louder and louder, and his blows came harder and faster. This had happened many times before, but this time someone ended up protecting me.

My second-grade teacher, Mr. Vukadinovic, entered the classroom and interrupted Cira's bullying. He ordered Cira up to his desk. My name was called next, and I followed the instruction to join them in front of the class. The room was quiet for what felt like a full minute before Mr. Vukadinovic spoke.

"Look at them," he said to the class. "Don't they look like brothers?"

A long silence settled over the room.

"Both of these boys have a heart. Both have a mother and father who love them," he continued. At first, I thought this would be one of his usual sermons reminding us of Tito's call for unity. But this time was different.

"Hate is what destroys people," he said. "To live together we need to cherish that we are all one. To respect our differences and trust and take care of each other. We are all human."

The classroom was silent except for the squeaking of the chairs as the kids moved uncomfortably in their seats.

Then he told Cira and me that we were to sit at the same desk for the rest of the year. I don't know which of us was more upset by this command, but we had no choice. It sounds so unlikely, but because of that talk and the time we spent sharing that desk, my chief tormentor became my only friend.

Even though I had a friend in school, my life was still one of constant loneliness. I begged my parents, "Please, I do not want to be alone anymore. I need to have a sister or brother."

The war had just ended. There was hardly any food. How could they even imagine providing for another child? My grandfather explained to me that my mother had been pregnant when the war broke out and had a miscarriage in the concentration camp. She just couldn't go through that experience again. At that moment I understood why she had refused to pick me up and comfort me on our walk to Monopol.

But I would not take no for an answer. I pleaded and cried daily. My argument was always the same—I do not want to be alone in this world. And the day I prayed for finally arrived. But instead of joy, my mother's pregnancy brought conflict. My father started coming home late at night. He was often away on buying trips, and sometimes he would not return even when the workday was over. My mother suspected him of pursuing other women.

One night my aunt and uncle came over, and, together with my grandfather and pregnant mother, confronted my father. I was in the other room, but I could hear the conversation. My mother was crying. Hard. Leon was raising his voice and reprimanding my father. I fell to my knees, hands clasped in front of me just like religious icons I had seen. Please, God, please. Don't let them get divorced. Please, God. It was hard to imagine how life could be worse than it already was. Who would feed us? Our extended family had been murdered!

My father said he would change. He asked them to give him a chance. No one really believed him, but my mother did not want a divorce. Without him we would not survive. The country was in ruins. She had no profession, no way to earn a living, and now she was pregnant. She was trapped but continued taking care of the family. "This is life, son. This is life," she would tell me. "You have to take life as it is and go on." This became my mantra. No matter what difficulties I encountered in life, I would remember my mother and her words and keep going.

In the spring of 1947, my prayers were answered. My baby sister was born. She was given the name of my *nona,* Gentil. In Israel she changed it to the Hebrew translation, Adina. I was more than just excited, but I had not considered the added demands on my mother. I was now even more alone than before.

Outside of going to school, I didn't leave home. I stayed home and read a stack of books that my mother's cousin Mara (changed from Miriam) gave me. That cousin made it through the war because she had married a Christian Serb. Her parents strictly prohibited her dating a gentile, so Mara and Sinisa had eloped and hidden in Kosovo. That is how they survived while her whole family—parents, sisters, brothers—ended as ashes of the Holocaust. (They had two daughters, one of whom eventually became the chief justice of Serbia. The other became a professor of literature.) I read and reread as many books as I could find. They helped me to learn the Serbian language. They were my only life raft, and I clung to them fiercely.

For toys, I turned to what was at hand. I made a game out of my mother's kitchen cutlery. The big spoon was the Indian chief, and the big fork was the leader of the cowboys. The rest of the kitchen forks and spoons were Indians or cowboys, characters I took from my favorite books by Karl May about the old American West.

Having to make my own toys, I believe, developed my imagination and thus my creativity, which were a godsend later, in my professional life. I have found that my clients who are the most daring entrepreneurs had similar experiences. They were isolated in childhood either by being rejected or by being sick, and were forced to think out of the box. I considered it a lesson worth learning, and worth teaching to my children. When they would sit in their chairs, kicking their feet back and forth, complaining there was nothing to do because at that time we had no TV, I told them to get up and *find* something to do.

One afternoon, walking home from school, I encountered a boy about my age playing an accordion on the sidewalk. I watched as complete strangers strolling by tossed him coins. I stood transfixed, remembering my attempts to sell "shoelaces" to strangers when we lived in Prishtina. I was mesmerized by this child musician. There he stood, effortlessly earning attention, money, and even affection.

I was stunned by his confidence, by the way he carried himself with dignity despite his ragged clothes, losing himself in his instrument. The beauty of the simple tunes he played seemed to help others forget their troubles and, in so doing, help him forget his own.

From that moment on, my life was devoted to acquiring an accordion. (In Yugoslavia, as soon as children are old enough to play on their own, they often pick up an accordion, not unlike American kids who might pick up a guitar.) I begged my father even more than I had pleaded for a baby sister. It was nonstop. Usually, he would silence any nagging behavior with the back of his hand. That would end the "conversation." But my father loved to sing, and if I had an accordion, I argued, I could accompany him. The idea appealed to him, and one day, a few weeks later, there it was on the kitchen table—a tiny, gleaming, black-and-white contraption, the smallest version of the instrument, a thirty-two bass.

True, it was a cheap accordion, but to me it felt like a form of salvation, a miracle that could give me the love and friendship I missed. Since we could not afford a music teacher, I set about teaching myself to play. On Friday nights after dinner, my parents, my grandfather, my uncle, and his family, would gather in the living room to sing. I was always included because I could play that tiny thirty-two-bass accordion. That I had no training was beside the point. I learned a song by ear. "Just play," I was commanded. If I failed to play well, it was, "In the bathroom, and don't come out till you've practiced." I cried while I fingered the keys, but I quickly learned to play, at least well enough to satisfy my family.

There were no prayers on the Sabbath, but there was always singing. It was a tradition we maintained for years until my mother suffered a stroke and lost her ability to sing. We would sing Yugoslav or Ladino songs, and I would accompany them. Between songs, they would reminisce about the war and those we once knew.

Life in Belgrade was very stressful for us. We felt the ever-present hand of the OZNA, the Communist secret police of Yugoslavia, known formally as the Department for People's Protection. They had ordered my father to spy on other Jews in the community, especially his own brother. They believed he was a good candidate. Was he not a captain with the Albanian Communist Partisans?

He refused, and they did not like that. OZNA agents made a habit of materializing on our doorstep in the middle of the night, banging on the door and demanding to search our two-bedroom home. "We know you are trading gold," they would shout in my father's face. (Ha! If he had had gold, we would not have been happy to eat horsemeat.)

We had feared the Germans before. Then the Bulgarians. Now we feared the Communists. After the fifth or sixth time they appeared at our door, OZNA arrested my father and "nationalized" the shoe store. He was charged with trading gold and sentenced to a year in prison. He was a capitalist. An enemy of the state.

Graciously, they allowed my family to continue using a portion of our own home after confiscating the property. My mother, sister, and I were confined to one room. The other bedroom was given to Communists from Montenegro who had settled in Belgrade.

My grandfather died that year. I remember coming home from school and my mother taking me aside and telling me to go to the room he was lying in and kiss his hand and say good-bye to him. He was going to die. I did as I was told. But I was numb. I did not cry. I could not feel.

My mother was all alone now and had to find a way to support our little household. She had to take care of a new baby and me, rely on help from friends to get us food, and make time to visit my father in prison.

"Dios piadoso," I heard her praying at night, *"solo salir de aqui a Palestina."* ("Gracious God. Only to leave for Palestine.")

SAILING TO FREEDOM

The year was 1948. The United Nations voted to recognize Israel as a sovereign state for the Jews. After two thousand years of persecution, being gassed, burned, and expelled to wander the world looking for a safe place for themselves, the Jews finally had a homeland.

The Jewish people celebrated with tears but were very worried at the same time. A coalition of Arab states attacked Israel and tried to destroy the country in its infancy. I was eleven when I heard a newspaper vendor crying out, "Arab planes attack Jewish Jerusalem!" I had no idea where Jerusalem was or who the Jews were who lived there. I was just concerned it was likely to upset my mother.

Who were these Jews and what did they have to do with me? I understood we were Sephardi. We ate *burekas,* did we not? And *fizon,* the bean soup, which I later discovered the Spanish called *las Judias* ("the Jewish women"). And my grandparents spoke Ladino with my parents. But *being* a Jew was alien to me. I never had any Jewish education or upbringing.

One day in the courtyard after the war, I had seen my grandfather wrap tefillin (small prayer boxes with ribbons) on his head and hands, a ritual traditional Jewish men observe each day when they pray. I had never

Yugoslav Jews on the deck of the SS *Kefalos*,
sailing from Bakar, Croatia, to Haifa, Israel for two weeks.
We almost sank. December 1948.

seen him do that before, and I panicked. Was he going out of his mind, tying himself up like that?

During the war, we pretended to be Muslim and didn't dare to show that we were Jewish. In Belgrade at school, we were told that religion and God were creations of the capitalists to rule the masses, the opiate to soothe people into being exploited by the greedy rich. Religion, in particular the Jewish religion, was totally foreign to me.

Belgrade was the first place I remember us celebrating Passover. We had no Haggadah, no prayer book to read from. My grandfather led the seder dinner, nevertheless, recounting the story of the Jews' liberation from slavery in Egypt. He recited some of the prayers and sang some songs in Ladino. My parents and Leon and Anna mumbled along where they could, but it was pretty obvious they knew only a little more than I did about what we were doing. At one point, my grandfather nodded to my mother, a sign. She handed me a piece of matzah that had been set aside earlier, wrapped in a big napkin. My initial instinct was to open the napkin and keep eating, but she gestured for me to hold the little package over my shoulder. Then she pointed me toward the door, and the whole family shouted out, "Bye-bye! Next year in Jerusalem!"

Where was Jerusalem? Why the ritual? I had no idea. So I opened a history book to look for any information about Jews. I found only a few words, a single sentence, about the story of Masada, in which the Jewish people fought against the Roman occupation. I read that sentence a hundred times and swelled with pride: Jews did know how to fight and defend themselves, after all. For years, that was all I knew about my heritage or my religion.

It was not easy to leave a Communist country. One of Tito's deputies, Moshe Piade, was Jewish by birth. As a dedicated Communist, he rejected all religions, but when the Jews of Yugoslavia wanted to immigrate to Israel, they went to him for help, and the Communist regime agreed to let us go on the condition that we relinquish all of our possessions to the state. Everything we owned was the price of our freedom.

We were destitute, persecuted, and frightened for our lives. My father was in prison. I was blind in one eye. We were crowded into one small room, hungry and cold. Without a second thought, my mother signed away her parents' home and everything we had. We would leave for Israel with just the clothes we were wearing, a small suitcase, my accordion, a bottle of oil, and several pounds of flour. Just in case there was no food in Israel. A special train was designated to transport the emigrating Jews to the boat that would then take them to Israel. Whoever missed that boat would likely wait years to find another way into the country.

My mother was eager to get to Israel as soon as possible, but I was not. I was one of Tito's Pioneers. We were taught at school that we were all Tito's children and that our loyalty was to him first and foremost. If we heard anyone saying anything against Tito at home, we were to report it to the police immediately. We were brainwashed. Every child had become a spy in his or her own home, and parents were afraid to speak in front of their own children. In my case, I had nothing to report. My father was in prison, and my mother was too busy making ends meet to talk politics.

I did not want to leave Yugoslavia. How could I leave Tito? As my mother gathered our things and my baby sister to leave for the train, I hid behind a shed at the entrance to the house. My mother was frantic. What should she do? Should she try to find me and risk missing the train and thus the ship? Or should she meet the departing train and leave me in Yugoslavia? Fortunately, at the last minute, torn between Tito and my mother, I responded to her frantic calls and came out of hiding.

During the ride to the train, I sobbed. Despite the hardship and the teasing, I did not want to leave Belgrade. I wore the red scarf of the Pioneers. I was Tito's son. I could not abandon him. The cab driver tried to soothe me. "You will come back," he said. "This is not the end."

"I don't believe you," I sobbed in between my tears. Little did I know of the glorious return I would have many years later when Serbia's prime minister would ask me to help keep Yugoslavia from falling apart.

The train ride to the port of Bakar was just the start of a tense and dangerous journey. The train would stop from time to time, and policemen would swarm from one car to the next, ordering us to open our suitcase. They rifled through the small bundles people carried and searched the clothes we wore, looking for gold. We were Jews, after all—we must be rich. They would curse us when they found nothing. *Poor* Jews? How could that be?

We arrived at Bakar around midnight. My father had been released from jail and brought to the port, where he stood waiting for us. He looked gaunt. I had not seen him for almost a year, and he had not seen my baby sister since her birth. Still, he had no time for emotion. He was all business. With scarcely a word to anyone, he took charge and immediately secured a bunk for us on the bottom floor, convinced that the deeper we were in the belly of the ship, the less we would feel the motion of the sea.

Two ships had been chartered to transport Yugoslav Jews to Israel. One was a passenger ship and the other a freighter that had been used to smuggle arms to the Israelis at the start of the War of Independence. We were on the freighter, the SS *Kefalos*—or, as we called it, the Krepalos. *Krepati* in Serbian slang means "to die miserably," and on that freighter, we were doing just about that.

There were more than three thousand souls crammed onto that ship, including Uncle Leon and his family. The Israeli authorities who organized the transport constructed three stories, each outfitted with multilevel bunks, in the bowels of the freighter where cargo was stored. We were the cargo.

Whether or not we would even reach Israel was debatable. A year earlier, the British, who at the time controlled Palestine, had stopped a similar transport of Jewish Holocaust survivors from France in their attempts to limit the number of immigrants entering the country. The SS *Exodus* had made international headlines when British soldiers boarded the ship as it neared Palestine and the passengers resisted, resulting in several deaths and injuries. Many ships were directed by the British to Cyprus, where their passengers were interned as refugees and kept from coming to Israel.

Even though British rule had just come to an end, the stories of their actions still haunted us. To avoid being seen by British planes that we feared would still be trying to prevent ships carrying Jewish refugees from entering Israel, we were allowed on deck only at night. During the day we had to stay in those bunks.[7]

The British weren't our only fear: the sea was rough and stormy, and the old, creaky ship nearly sank during the passage from the Adriatic to the Aegean Sea. The captain sent SOS signals, and two other ships followed close behind us in case we started to go down.

Since the sea was rough, people often threw up, in spite of the fact that there was little food. Their vomit would sometimes seep through the cracks of the bunks all the way down to the lowest floor, where my father had selected a spot for us.

---

7 A photograph of an onboard wedding on our ship, the SS *Kefalos,* can be found on the United States Holocaust Memorial Museum website. My father is in the lower-right corner: https://collections.ushmm.org/search/catalog/pa1087245.

From time to time, he would order me to play my small accordion. People would crowd around us and start singing. All I knew were the Communist songs I had learned as a Pioneer. People sang. Music is music. It kept the spirits up.

I didn't know it then, but that freighter carried us past the coastline of Albania, coming within thirty miles of Shkoder and the little Muslim village where we'd hidden out during the war. Beyond these were Prishtina, and even farther, the Macedonia of my earliest memories. We crossed the Mediterranean, passing Greece. After almost ten days on the high seas, the coastline of Israel was within reach. At last, we were allowed up to the deck in daylight. Slowly we climbed the three flights of stairs toward the bright blue sky. The wind was strong, but it felt like autumn, not winter, and the salty air filled my lungs and softened the stench of the bodies all around me.

My father lifted me up for a few seconds to see what those who were closest to the rails could see. It was the coast of Israel, off in the distance. Here it was, within sight: the Promised Land. Suddenly, people began to cry. Every passenger onboard wept. These poor, hungry people—people who knew what it meant to fear for their lives, who had lost fathers and mothers, sisters and brothers in the furnaces of the death camps and by some miracle survived—looked at the coastline and saw their salvation on the shore that lay ahead.

The ship docked at the port of Haifa. A policeman whose cap bore the six-pointed Jewish star stepped onto the boat. A policeman was wearing a Jewish star—not a policeman who was sent to find me and threaten my life, but one who was trained to defend me. Without a minute's hesitation, I dropped to my knees and kissed the ground. From that moment on, I ceased fainting and soiling my pants. I finally understood what my mother had been praying for all those years.

MY LOST FAMILY

When we reached Haifa, on December 26, 1948, I was eleven years old. As soon as we exited the ship, we were put on military trucks and driven to a military camp abandoned by the British, who had since left the country. My father and I sat on our suitcase so it wouldn't get mixed up with everyone else's tattered belongings, and I held my accordion to my chest like a pillow. As the truck made its way, I watched the roads and fields, looking for a sign, for something that would announce in some profound way that I was a resident of the Jewish state. But these were just ordinary roads and fields and an ordinary night sky. It had not yet dawned on me that it is the people who lend meaning to a landscape.

The Be'er Ya'akov camp was fortified and surrounded by wire, like any other army camp would be, but to me it looked like a concentration camp. Once again, I sank into my fears. Although I was allowed to wander freely from the barracks, I was scared to do so. There was a temptation. On the other side of the barbed wire was an orange orchard. Each day, I looked at those oranges with longing. I wanted to run out of the camp and touch them, pick some. They looked like gold to me. I had tasted an orange only once before, in Belgrade; I cut it into tiny portions and ate it

I had lost nearly all my relatives in the war, but when we arrived in Israel in 1948, Tia Estrea (my mother's aunt) and her extended family welcomed us as one of their own.

one slice at a time over three days. But I also remembered my attempt to leave the concentration camp in Monopol. It had cost me an eye. I was not about to tempt fate again, even in friendly Israel. I stayed put, but we did not remain at the camp long.

There is a Jewish custom dictating that if a Jew dies without ever seeing the Holy Land, a lump of its soil should be placed on his eyes at his funeral; if he did not live to see the Holy Land, he should see it as he departs this world. The most religious Jews preferred to live on and be buried in Israeli ground rather than be satisfied with just a lump of soil. When my great grandfather Haim Kalderon grew old, he immigrated to Jerusalem in order to die there. He is buried on the Mount of Olives, the oldest working cemetery in the world. He took his three unmarried daughters with him to Jerusalem and left his three sons in Belgrade, one of whom was my grandfather, Mushon Kalderon. Now Haim Kalderon's granddaughter, Diamanta Kalderon Adizes, had arrived in Israel, not to die but to live.

My mother knew that she had three aunts in Israel and that one had married a Cohen, but that was a very common surname in Israel, like Smith in the United States. She also knew from her father that this same aunt lived in Haifa and had a son who worked at the post office. My mother reasoned that the son's name was Haim because, as the firstborn, he would customarily have been named after his grandfather. That was all she knew.

Before departing for Israel, she had written a letter and addressed it to "Estrea Cohen, mother of Haim Cohen, who works at the Haifa post office." She wrote the letter in that five-hundred-year-old language, Ladino, because it was the only language in which she could communicate with the aunt. She wrote that we'd survived the war and asked if anyone she might know was alive in Israel. And would you believe it? The letter found its destination. At that time, many people were looking for their families, relatives, and friends. The radio used to broadcast on and on for hours, "So-and-so is looking for a son from such-and-such town. He last saw him in Auschwitz. If anyone knows him or knows what happened to him, please call so-and-so." That's how my mother's letter found its way to her aunt.

How Tia Estrea knew that we had arrived in Israel and where we were is unknown to me, but one day she appeared at the gate of the camp and requested permission to enter. She began asking people if they knew anyone by the name of Kalderon. Eventually, someone stopped her and pointed toward our barrack. She stood at the door and shouted in Ladino, *"Ay Kalderones aquí?"* ("Any Kalderons here?")

My mother stood up and started weeping. Her aunt, whom she had never met, was alive. She was far from the furnaces of Europe. She was in the Jewish state.

The hugging and crying seemed like it would never stop. Estrea asked if her brothers were alive. None were. We did not know it for sure, but deep inside we suspected the worst. How about any of their children? None. She could not stop weeping. My mother joined in. They hugged each other, supported each other. I was quiet. I could not cry. It seemed beyond me. I wanted to join them, to feel something, but inside I felt dead.

Tia Estrea loaded our few possessions on top of her car and sped us to Haifa. The aftermath of the war was everywhere, burned cars and tires along the road. I held my mother's hand and wondered if war had followed us or if war itself was everywhere. But I understood that this time was different. We were in Israel, starting a new life among our own people. We did not have a house or furniture, but this land would become our home.

I had lost nearly all my relatives in the war. In Israel, however, I found I had a large extended family. My mother's three aunts had many children, some of whom were married and had children of their own. Some had perished or had been hurt. Estrea's son had lost his leg from a mine while liberating Beer Sheva during the War of Independence. Years later, her son-in-law was killed during the Yom Kippur War. There is no family in Israel, I truly believe, that does not have at least one family member who was killed or maimed in a war.

Estrea's family reminded me of my Kalderon grandparents: love was the language they spoke, always looking for a way to please with a hug, with being present and attentive.

She took us to her apartment, where she, her husband, and their three daughters, one serving in the army, lived. It was tiny. Two small bedrooms. How was she going to fit four more souls? "With love, there is plenty of room," Estrea said.

The state did not have enough foreign exchange to buy food, while the country needed lots of it for the hundreds of thousands of Jewish refugees coming from Europe and expelled from Muslim countries. They all needed to be fed, and there was not enough, so rationing was imposed by the state. There was never enough for everyone, but we shared it with all.

When Hanukkah arrived, my new Israeli family gathered. They lit candles, prayed, and sang Hanukkah songs. I just watched. It was all very foreign to me, and being in Israel did not help. In Israel, I was taught Zionism, the history of the Jewish people and how we had the right to return to the land of our ancestors. But not Judaism, the religion. True, I had a bar mitzvah and learned a *parashah,* a section of the Torah that pertained to my birthday, but I forgot what I learned within days of the ceremony. I wasn't seriously introduced to Jewish observances that would help me feel that I was part of the worldwide Jewish community. I was not taught any prayers or rituals. In Israel, we, like many secular Jews, sang national songs and celebrated most of the Jewish holidays with a day off to go to the beach or go hiking. Not to pray in a synagogue. Even today, to my sorrow, I feel like a foreigner when I go there.

After a few months of staying at her small apartment, Tia Estrea found us a place to live in a Palestinian neighborhood that had been abandoned by an Arab family during the war.

It was quiet the day we arrived, like a ghost town, not a soul on the street. Small stone apartment houses lined the block. Here and there, people watched us from their windows. Their body posture and facial expressions were not welcoming.

I went to school several blocks away and enrolled in the third grade. An eleven-year-old in the third grade; it was not an auspicious beginning, nor a comfortable one, but I had lost years of my life to war.

Even though the school was in an Arab neighborhood, there was not one Arab student in my class. We were all Jewish immigrants. Some of the children were from Bulgaria and spoke a language I could understand. It was close to Serbian and Macedonian, so I socialized with them. This is why I can understand Bulgarian today.

We lived in that apartment in Haifa for almost a year in only a single room. The other rooms were occupied by other families. I was forced to share a bed with my parents. My father was not discreet about sex with my mother. I would close my eyes and plug my ears and try to think of something far away, but nothing helped.

FOREIGN AGAIN

My father found work as a longshoreman at the Haifa port. One day he was brought home on a stretcher. He had broken both legs in a work-related accident. Suddenly, my mother had to care for my baby sister and my immobilized father. As a result, I had to leave school temporarily and go to work selling newspapers on the street to earn some money for the household.

Unfortunately, it was not enough to feed the family. On the outskirts of Haifa was a *beit olim* (camp for newcomers to Israel), and it gave away food to those in need. I would walk there every day to collect leftover bread from the tables and bring it home. My mother would then mix those crumbs of bread with hot water and add a little cheese, and that was our meal for the day. I went hungry once again. Starvation marks you. It is something your body never forgets. This was the third time in my eleven years that I went hungry. The first was in the concentration camp in Skopje, the second was in Belgrade after the war, and the third time was in Israel. There would be another time, in America of all places.

We had no refrigerator, only an icebox. Every day, a cart would pass through the streets with ice for sale. A man with a wagon and a bell,

My father found work as a driver once we moved to a suburb of Haifa. Our Tia Sol in America paid for his delivery truck, along with our new housing. c. 1950.

shouting *"alter zachen,"* which means "old things" in Yiddish, would visit the neighborhood to buy old clothes or things, which he would repair and resell—just as my grandfather Kalderon had done from his shop on Kralja Aleksandra Street.

We did not have much clothing to wear, much less to sell. Tia Sol, the same aunt who had invited my uncles to America before the war, came to our rescue. She would periodically send a package of clothing to us, never-claimed items that people in America had forgotten at the dry cleaner. The garments looked old and used, but we celebrated when the packages arrived.

I remember when the first streetlights were installed. I watched in amazement from the terrace of my house as the lights changed red . . . yellow . . . green. "The lights are synchronized to create a flow from one to the other," my father told me. I was truly impressed. I gazed at those lights almost every evening before bed until one night. A kid on a bicycle—not yet used to the new system—crossed the intersection on a red light. A car ran him over, killing him.

This was how we spent our first year in Israel. Then we moved to a one-bedroom duplex in Tzur Shalom, on the outskirts of Kiryat Motzkin, a suburb of Haifa, where everyone was either a Yugoslav or a Bulgarian immigrant. Tia Sol paid for our new housing and for a pickup truck. She used money her brother, my grandfather, sent her before the war to protect the family just in case anything happened. I am wondering whether I should do the same, with anti-Semitism on the rise now.

My father began working as a driver, hauling people and packages everywhere in the newborn nation of Israel. Sometimes I would go with him to help carry the packages he delivered. We would stop for a round of dark rye bread, cut it in half, then slice each half and pour oil and salt on the slices. That was lunch, and sometimes it was our only meal for the day.

I enrolled myself in an elementary school in Kiryat Motzkin. I knew I had to do it on my own. My father was busy making a living. My mother did not know the language and had to take care of my baby sister.

We had no money for the bus, so once again I walked to school. It was four kilometers from our house, but it felt like a hundred to me. I found my way to the principal's office, waited until he came out, and said to him in broken Hebrew, *"Ani Yitzhak Adiges, rotze bet sefer."* ("I am Ichak Adizes, and I want to go to school.")

How did I get to be Ichak and not Yizhak or Yitzhak like my grandfather or my blind cousin, or like Yitzhak Rabin, the assassinated prime minister of Israel, or Itzhak Perlman, the famous violinist? When we arrived in Israel, we had to register our names. So I wrote it in the Serbian spelling. In Serbian you write how you pronounce. There are no added letters or missing letters. Write as you pronounce, so I wrote I C H A K, which in Serbian reads "Yitzhak." Also, my family name was a problem. Its origin is the Adige River in Italy, pronounced A-DIDJE, but in the

Serbian language there is no DJ sound, so it was made Adižes—the little mark over the *z* is pronounced close to the way the second *g* in the word *garage* is said. But in English there is no letter Ž. So my name is not at all what people call me. I should be called Yitzhak Adiges. But people all over the world, including Serbia and Israel, call me *Ichak Adizes*.

I do not fight it. I know who I am. Call me what you like. *Chifut. Shiptar. Sabon,* which means "soap" in Hebrew. (That is what some sabras, Israeli-born kids, called me. I was the raw material. The Nazis had made soap from the body fat of the Jewish people they gassed and burned.)

On my first day of school, I was placed in the fourth grade. I was twelve years old and in the fourth grade, pathetic. I must have looked like some kind of a freak to my classmates: small, terribly thin, cross-eyed, wearing a strange winter hat that protected me from the snow in Yugoslavia but I was wearing it in the heat of Israel, struggling to speak Hebrew. The other children ganged up on me and pummeled me regularly.

In the Hebrew language, there are two H sounds, one soft and one guttural. The Hebrew word for "the teacher" is *ha mora* with a soft H. But, because there is no soft H in Serbian, I would pronounce the word with a guttural H. Unfortunately, *kha mora,* with a guttural H, means "female ass" in Hebrew. There would be an uproar when I addressed the teacher. The children would laugh. All the way through the end of primary school, the children called me *kha mora.* They were cruel, as only children can be cruel. And although I was Jewish, I wasn't accepted as an Israeli. The real Israelis were the sabras. We were the diaspora Jews who did not fight. The weak ones. We were the downtrodden, the passive European refugees who came to Israel because we had been kicked out. We hadn't come to redeem the land and build a new country as they had.

I suffered a lot and just wanted the earth to swallow me. There was no teacher like Mr. Vukadinovic to save me. Despite bearing witness to my

With my classmates at Kiryat Motzkin in Hafia. I am in the center row, fourth from left. I may be smiling in the picture, but my years at that school were some of the worst of my life.

humiliation, nonstop bullying, and beatings, not one of the teachers chose to get involved.

My years at that school were some of the worst years of my life. I felt betrayed. To me, it felt worse than the anti-Semitism in Belgrade. These were Jewish kids; they were supposed to be my friends, my allies. At the time, I was the only "foreigner" in the class and thought I was the only outcast. In fact, most any newcomer was shunned. Acceptance comes slowly for the last to arrive in Israel.

When we arrived, Israel's elites were the Ashkenazi Jews, those born in Poland or Lithuania or Russia. They were the Zionists who immigrated to Israel before the war, drained the swamps, and established the kibbutzim, the communal settlements. We, the latecomers, were the Sephardic Jews, called *franks,* a derogatory reference. Then came the emigration from Morocco and Iraq and Yemen, and the Mizrahi Jews became the butt of jokes. Ethiopian Jews—Black Jews—were next. They were the descendants of Queen Sheva, who conceived a child with King Solomon, the son of King David, more than two thousand years ago. They feel discriminated against. Today, the latest emigration is from Russia, and now it is they who are the rejected ones.

Apparently, this was not just my experience. Once when I was in New York City, I got into in a cab and noticed that the driver had a typical Russian Jewish name.

"Where are you from?" I asked.

"Moscow."

"How did you get to New York?"

"Via Israel."

"Why didn't you stay?" I asked.

"Because the Israeli kids made my life miserable," he said. I nodded quietly to myself. I understood only too well.

One of my classmates, Ehud Artzi, took the lead as my main Israeli tormentor. He wrote a script for one of the school plays suggesting that I wore a winter hat because I had lice. The kids laughed and laughed. On my way home, walking that long road by myself, I fantasized about suicide. Or I could try to run away, but where could I live? There seemed to be nowhere to turn. There was no one I could talk to, no one with whom I could share my feelings, no sympathy from anyone. My mother was busy with the baby and apparently did not comprehend what I was going through. My father was occupied day and night driving the truck. I had people all around me but felt utterly alone. The most basic need we humans have is to be part of a tribe, a family, a cult even. Prolonged isolation is a death sentence. That is why solitary confinement in a prison is the most severe punishment. A prison is a punishment by isolation, too.

This doesn't apply just to humans, I learned. When my children were young, we had a Doberman Pinscher. At some point we left for a month. Ignorant me, I asked a friend to just come to the house every day to feed the dog. It stopped eating and died.

In America we are more and more isolated, with fewer and fewer interactions happening "in real life." Even home alone in their rooms, children are bullied on the Internet. No wonder the suicide rate has gone up at an alarming rate, even more so during the isolation of Covid.

In the decades I've spent trying to heal from the pain of my childhood, I learned that the psychologist Abraham Maslow was wrong. The most basic need is not safety and survival but being part of a larger system that accepts you. In other words, integration. And what higher form of integration is there than love? Thus, the most basic need is to love and be loved.

In my career I looked for it from my clients, my audiences. When I became aware of what I was doing and why, I realized I needed to find love not on a stage but here, inside. In order to truly start to love my family, I needed to learn to love myself first.

When my father washed his truck, my job was to dry it to perfection. He inspected my work carefully, bawling me out for any white spots I might have missed.

WHITE SPOTS

My father was always busy driving that little truck. Not only was he no source of emotional support, he was a major source of stress and pain, too. For example, he used to wash his pickup truck not in the shade but in the sun. My job was to dry the truck. The problem was that washing a car in the sun leaves white spots that are difficult to detect. I always missed some because it all depended on the angle from which you looked. My father would always find some spots that I missed, and those elusive spots made him very angry. I dreaded hearing my father's voice calling me to dry that truck. I knew he would shame me and call me a parasite. His anger would only escalate from there until he would slap me across the face.

Looking for white spots when drying the pickup truck became a pathological preoccupation. Unsurprisingly, this obsession later manifested in my work habits. When I consult for a company, or write a book or an article, I am fanatical about perfection. I go over my work obsessively, again and again, to make sure that I do not miss anything, not one single spot.

As I grew older, this obsession with perfection created issues in my marriages. There is a Hungarian expression that says, "Before getting married, open both eyes. After getting married, close one eye." I, however, closed my eyes when courting because I was terrified of love. Did not all those I loved perish? After my first and second weddings, I opened both eyes searching for the "white spots"—for anything I could find that was wrong—compulsively looking for problems. Obviously, neither my partners, my children, nor my associates relished that particular habit, and it took a toll on all of my relationships.

My mother could not do much to protect me from my father's abuse. There was no way to reason with him. His way was the only way—no excuses, no arguments. When it got to be too much for her, she would often faint. I would rush to bring her valerian and beg her not to die. I was terrified that her fainting would kill her, that she would leave me, just as my grandparents had. I did everything I could to prevent her from fainting.

Looking back, I can see that my fear of upsetting her had its comic side, though I was not aware of it then. One day I had a fight with a neighborhood kid. He took some rocks and started throwing them at our house. My mother worried he would break a window. If he did, we wouldn't have the money to repair it. I became alarmed. If she got upset, she might faint, and I equated fainting with a heart attack, which scared me to death. I rushed to her, stood in front of her, and begged her to beat me. Maybe that would stop her anger and she would not faint. "It is my fault he was throwing stones," I said. "Please beat me, but please do not faint. Please do not die." I was hysterical.

For years, even after I became a professor, my extended family called me *Izzy-bij-me-mama,* which means "Izzy-beat-me-mama" in Serbian.

When I graduated from the eighth grade, my father moved our family to Tel Aviv, which was then a suburb of Jaffa, a port city that functioned as the gateway to Israel in biblical times. The prophet Jonah set sail from Jaffa before landing in the belly of the whale. It was in Jaffa that Peter, one of the twelve apostles of Jesus, had a vision to preach the Gospel to non-Jews. The cedar timbers used to build King Solomon's Temple in Jerusalem came through Jaffa's port.

My uncle Leon was living in this ancient city, also in a deserted Arab house. Leon and my father decided to start a wholesale business to distribute oil and flour. The operation even included my blind cousin, Yitzhak, who worked in the store. Uncle Leon would be the brains of the enterprise, and my father would be in charge of loading and reloading barrels of oil and sacks of flour. He was, again, the muscle man, but this time at least he was a partner in the venture. And we had enough to eat.

The move to Tel Aviv seemed to be a harbinger of good things for me. It provided the change I needed—namely, leaving behind the elementary school that had made my life miserable. In Tel Aviv, I was free to start a new life, and I needed to succeed. I feared that if I lagged behind, I would be forced to carry packages for a living—a muscle man, a day laborer, like my father, struggling to earn sufficient income to support the family.

My focus became earning the acceptance and approval of what looked to me like Israel's upper class: the sabras. I spoke Hebrew fluently now and wanted to merge with them and become part of their Israel. But how?

A new school seemed like a way in, and I managed to enroll myself at Gimnasia Herzliya, which was the oldest Jewish high school in Israel. The children of the economic and political elite went there. I observed my sabra classmates carefully and began to imitate them. They wore khaki pants and blue shirts, so that's what I did. When I started to get some hair on my face, I let my mustache grow so I would look like a sabra, too.

One of my friends was Dov, a boy who came from one of the richest families in Tel Aviv. I would go over to his house and listen to classical music. I never before knew anything about classical music, and he would explain what we were listening to. In my desperate efforts to improve myself, I asked him to teach me how to eat properly at the dinner table, with good manners.

After freshman year at Gimnasia Herzliya, I transferred to Municipal School Aleph. I wanted to go to a school where academic performance was the priority, but I overreached. It was far from easy to attend a top school and master English, math, and a host of other subjects while working every afternoon to help the family. I had found a job collecting dirty laundry from laundry stores, helping the driver of the truck, and taking it to a commercial laundering facility. Riding along the streets of Tel Aviv in the back of the delivery truck, every now and then I would glimpse some sabra boys my age walking with girlfriends, laughing, and eating ice cream while I sat on a pile of dirty linen, dreaming of a better future.

Although I wanted to succeed, grades were not particularly important to me at that time. What was important to me was belonging. I was a lost soul looking to be accepted. I initiated many after-school activities and was elected chairman of the student council.

In 1955, when heavy rains caused floods all over Israel, I organized the students in my school to collect blankets and books and then distribute them to families in the tent camps for newcomers called *ma'abarot.* While there, I would play my accordion to entertain them. It was my first volunteer activity, and I needed more.

Not long after, I joined Bnei Akiva, the religious youth movement, though I did not know much about religion. This was followed by Hashomer Hatzair, a youth movement aligned with the far-left socialist political party, but I'd had enough of Marxism in Yugoslavia. Next I tried Mahanot Ha Olim, which gathered every Friday evening to debate politics and dance the hora. That was not enough for me, either. Then, almost by accident, I found Youth to Youth.

People are born twice. Once, physically. The second time, when they realize why they were born. Many of us have not discovered the reason, but once you discover it, it fills you up. If you follow your inner light, your purpose, when you are breathing your last breath and somebody asks you, whether you feel any remorse or sorrow that you wasted your life, you should be able to say, "No, I lived my life to the fullest. I lived the life I was destined to live."

I found my purpose when I joined Youth to Youth. In fact, I was one of the organization's earliest members. The mission was for privileged young teenagers to help underprivileged ones. In reality, I belonged to the latter group, but I was European so I was considered one of the privileged.

Youth to Youth first attracted me because of the influence of a book I had read as a child: *Timur and His Gang,* by the popular Soviet writer Arkady Gaidar.[8] In that novel, a gang of kids decides to eradicate crime from their little village, doing good deeds rather than the usual mischief a gang would be up to. They were renegades of sorts, but ones who did good in the world, and that awoke a desire in me to do something similar.

We would donate time to help other kids who were deprived because they were poor, disabled (polio was still a scourge), or came from a family with a criminal record. We lent assistance to anyone who needed it. We would play with children in the neglected poor parts of the city or transport kids with polio to enjoy Purim carnival celebrations. We taught deprived kids how to read and write if they had difficulties, and more.

Many years later, when I was advising Grupo Elektra (part of Grupo Salinas of Mexico City, and a major multinational corporation), I found myself returning to memories of my time at Youth to Youth. I suggested that the company embark on a campaign to help children in need in the communities where their stores were based. Why not ask the municipality for permission to construct basketball courts and playgrounds on abandoned lots in poor neighborhoods?

The company had retail stores, and employees at those stores would donate time to coach the neighborhood kids. The company's suppliers would contribute whatever was needed for the playground, such as basketball hoops, and get recognition for it. A win-win proposition. The municipality agreed to the proposal, and it worked. Kids came to play, and under the tutelage of the company's employees, they organized to clean the graffiti off the walls of their homes. Eventually, one million kids took to the streets to clean their neighborhoods.

The Youth to Youth philosophy still exists today and is now part of the

---

8 Arkady Gaidar, *Timur and His Gang* (New York: Charles Scribner's Sons, 1943).

education system in Israel. Every high school student must devote time to community work.

There was another major influence that led me to join Youth to Youth. When I was eleven, I read *The Pedagogical Poem* (known to English-language readers as *Road to Life*[9]), a book by the Russian author and educator Anton Makarenko. In his book, he describes running an institution for teenage delinquents, how he made them respectable members of society, and how he helped to heal them by building their self-respect and trust. And I decided that I was going to do the same. I was going to help people, and I was going to write about it like Makarenko did. (Many years later, I am one of the very few recipients of the Makarenko Medal, for my service to humanity.)

When I joined Youth to Youth, one of the opportunities was to work in a prison for teenage girls. I volunteered immediately. I had to take an hour-long bus ride to a police station, where a vehicle waited to take me (and my accordion) to the prison. It was a long, inconvenient commute, but I cherished the role. I felt I had something to offer. I was valued, maybe even loved.

The prisoners were almost all my age. Most of them had been arrested for prostitution. Some had been coerced into sex work by men they fell in love with, who then used them as sources of income. They appeared so vulnerable and innocent to me. I could not imagine them renting their bodies on the street. One girl was a young mother who could see her baby only on the prison's visiting day. I remember watching her cry as she held that baby tightly to her chest.

I did not attempt to reform those girls or teach them more socially acceptable skills. I taught them something I thought they would enjoy: Israeli folk dancing and songs. I cannot say how many of them returned to

---

9 Anton Makarenko, *Road to Life* (London: Stanley Nott, 1936).

sex work when they were released, but for years after that, when I would walk the streets of Tel Aviv, sometimes accompanied by a girlfriend, I would often hear a shriek of delight come from some dark corner. It would be one of the girls from the prison, who had recognized me, and she would run to hug me. Inevitably, I had to do a lot of explaining to my date.

I learned a great deal from my volunteer work in the prison. First, how painfully exploited those young girls were. I watched them sing. I watched them dance. I watched them cry. And I saw into their kind souls.

I also learned that punishment only works as a means of control for a short time. The more you punish, the more frequently and intensely you have to punish to get the same result. These girls had been abused so many times in their lives that they had become unresponsive to punishment. One guard tried hitting a girl. She kicked him back, a hard blow delivered between his legs. She was put in an isolation cell for a few days, but she didn't care. She'd had enough abuse.

What worked was love.

It took an hour and half to get to the prison, and the same amount of time to get back. I was literally risking my life every time I went because terrorists were attacking buses regularly. Why was I making the effort? Yes, I was contributing to society, but in doing so I was also building my self-esteem.

When the students of the pioneering psychotherapist Karl Menninger asked him what course of treatment he would recommend for a depressed patient, they expected some pharmaceutical prescription. His answer was that he would recommend that the patient go across the railroad tracks and find somebody who was in more pain than he was and help him.

My father may have had that same drive when he reinvented himself as country doctor when we lived in Bërdicë. That it was more than survival for him. In helping those poor, uneducated people, he helped build his own low self-image, too. Unconsciously I followed the same script in my life.

My senior year of high school I grew a mustache to try to look like a “real” Israeli, a sabra.

WALKING ON HOT COALS

In 1956, a couple of months into my senior year of high school, Israel's war with Egypt broke out. Suddenly, there were soldiers—our soldiers—marching, tanks on the streets heading for the border, and air raid sirens screaming. But we didn't feel the same fear we felt during the Second World War. The sense of resignation, desperation, and hopelessness had vanished. This time, we knew that we would defend ourselves, not go like cattle to the slaughter.

We cheered with pride for the soldiers headed for the front lines. Nothing but military songs played on the radio. We could fight. The Holocaust wouldn't happen to us again. Never again.

My father was mobilized, and I found my own way to contribute by organizing a campaign to collect books for injured soldiers recovering in local hospitals. The war ended a short time later, but the hostilities did not. Palestinian terrorists were still attacking buses, indiscriminately killing civilians, often children. One day, I heard on the radio that they had attacked a bus on the road to Eilat, a town in the south of Israel on the Red Sea. My friend Yossi and I decided to go there to demonstrate that we Israelis were not afraid of terrorists.

At that time there was no organized transportation to Eilat. You had to hitchhike. So we did. We stood with our thumbs out for hours to get a ride to Be'er Sheva, the capital of the Negev desert. Be'er Sheva means "Seven Wells," as it is named for the spot where Abraham, the father of Judaism and the Arabs, had his tent and built a well.

From Be'er Sheva, the best way to get to Eilat was to go to a restaurant where the truck drivers ate before crossing the desert. The trip was going to take most of the night, and we found a pair of drivers who needed someone to keep them company so they wouldn't fall asleep.

At the time, the road through the desert was dangerous even for cars but much more so for a big semitrailer, especially on the steep descent into Makhtesh Ramon, the largest crater of its kind in the world. The road was narrow and winding. We were still driving as the sun rose. In every direction we saw clay hills across the canyon that looked like they were painted colorful reds, yellows, and browns. At the top of a black cliff, an antelope stood, facing us as we passed by.

In the desert, there is a silence you can experience like nowhere else in the world. In a forest, you hear the wind rustle the trees; by the water, the sound of waves lapping or crashing. But in the desert, the sense of quiet is overwhelming. It's no surprise, then, that so many of the prophets found God in the desert. In silence. In peace. Not chasing a bus or rushing to catch a plane.

Eilat sits on a bay on a slice of land wedged between the Kingdom of Jordan and the Sinai Peninsula. At the time, Eilat was just a few tents and a navy patrol boat in a makeshift port. Across the bay was Aqaba, a typical Jordanian village dotted with little white houses where the enemy lived.

Eilat had no population to speak of, no hotels, no place to sleep except on the beach itself, which cooled off to a chill in the desert night. Luckily, we found some Israeli camaraderie, and the sailors on the frigate in the bay invited us aboard to sleep. The next morning, we waded into the Red Sea to snorkel and see the coral reefs and exotic fish beneath the surface of the water—one of the best sights in the world. We felt good about ourselves. We made the trip. We did not allow the fear of the terrorists to stop us from traveling the country.

This resolve to have hope no matter what has conditioned Jews the world over to walk not merely on hot coals but through the very fire itself. "Next year in Jerusalem," we have said with optimism and hope, generation after generation, even in the face of unspeakable horrors

Lately, however, I have begun to wonder whether the flip side of this attitude—this ability to live with stigma, rejection, and victimhood—is a good thing for the Jews. We did not move out of Nazi Germany in time. Today in Israel, it is impossible to take a bus without fear of an attack from Palestinian terrorists. I suspect other nations would have dealt with the situation more proactively. The motto in Israel is *yihye tov, al tidag* (everything will be okay, don't worry).

Many other nations would not tolerate living for so long in a state not of war but not of peace, either. But we, the Jewish people, we go on.

Like most young people in Israel, I entered the army shortly after completing high school. Not only is military service compulsory for all men and women (some ultra-Orthodox Israelis are exempt), but most people my age actually looked forward to serving and fulfilling their patriotic duty. That is perhaps less true today. The politics around the occupied territories keeps some left-leaning Israelis reluctant to serve. But in the late fifties, when I was drafted, military service was a rite of passage keenly anticipated by nearly all youngsters. It was seen as a large step forward in one's life. If you wanted a career in politics or in the army, that was where you started and made a name for yourself. It was where you formed lasting friendships, made contacts for your future career, and underwent

When I was drafted into military service in the late 1950s, I served in a unit for paramilitary training. Jews didn't have to be slaughtered like we had in the Holocaust. We could fight.

the transition from adolescence to adulthood. I saw serving in the army as an opportunity to become a "real" Israeli. I was going to volunteer for an elite fighting unit.

The day I left for the army, my father wasn't around. He was at work. My mother feared for my safety and started to cry. I was concerned for her but ready to go. My sister was only ten and she had no clue. Why the commotion?

"Let's go, Adina," my mother said to my sister as I put on my jacket to leave. "We're taking your brother to his bus." When it arrived, I hugged them and jumped on board. The bus was full of young faces—Europeans, North Africans, and Middle Eastern. It was easy to identify the sabras. They all seemed so confident, so arrogant. They were loud, while we "foreigners" sat quietly, waiting to see what our future might be.

Boot camp training was physically demanding, but I refused to fail or wash out. When basic training ended, our assignments were announced. My heart sank. Because of the injury to my left eye, I was deemed unfit to serve in a fighting unit. Instead, I was assigned a position as an instructor of paramilitary education. I was to be a soldier, but a soldier who educated teenagers in basic military principles.

Hearing that I was not fit to serve in a fighting unit was a blow to my self-esteem. Though it hurt, I tried to put the best face on my position. I am still a soldier, I told myself. I am a soldier with an important responsibility. I am the one responsible for preparing high school students for the army. In other words—and I laughed out loud when it occurred to me—I am a youth leader once again. It was an extension of the life I had carved out for myself when I was a high school student, and it was a field I excelled in.

In 1958, my friend Rafi Walden and I (on the right) volunteered to lead a delegation of German high school kids visiting Israel as part of a program to establish trust with the Jewish nation.

SERVING THE GERMANS

In 1958, the German government, intent on making amends with world Jewry and particularly with the new Jewish state, sent a delegation of high school students to visit Israel. It was the beginning of an effort to establish links with the Jewish nation after the Holocaust.

That very first group of Germans came on their official visit to Israel early in my military service. They were all from Cologne. The city investigated their pasts thoroughly to ensure none of the students came from families with Nazi ties. Nonetheless, the Israeli army thought it best to ask for a volunteer to guide them rather than ordering someone to do it. No one responded. I stepped forward.

I still remembered that young German courier on the motorbike in the village in Albania. We had never spoken, but when we locked eyes, we had made a connection. Should children pay the price for the atrocities adults commit? The answer was self-evident to me. I would be the one to teach the German students Israeli folk songs and dances.

We communicated in English, which I hardly spoke. But we understood each other well enough. When you like someone, words are not necessary. A nod of the head is enough to convey what you want to say.

⸺

Being with these German teenagers, I remembered the debates in the Knesset and protests in the streets over whether to take reparations from Germany for what the Jewish people had lost during the Holocaust. Israel needed these funds to build the country, but in 1952, Menachem Begin, the head of the opposition party, was against taking them. He claimed we could not free the Germans of their guilt by just taking money. Our gassed ancestors were not for sale.

I was influenced by his rhetoric and refused to take any reparations for the eye I had lost in the concentration camp. And now I was escorting a group of German teenagers to Yad Vashem, the Holocaust museum in Jerusalem. It was one hall after another with pictures of the horrors, of the ovens, of children and women and old men who were gassed to their deaths. One display showed thousands of eyeglasses, then the hair of the people who were destined to die. The hair was to be used to fill pillows and cushions. The Nazis were harvesting the bodies of the people they were going to kill as one harvests as much as possible from a cow.

I watched the students stare at the displays, at first not understanding, then gasping as they understood what they were seeing. Not one of them could hold back from sobbing. They felt guilty, those fourteen- and fifteen-year-old kids. Guilty for their country and for their parents and grandparents who had not committed these crimes against humanity but who had looked the other way.

And as I looked at the pictures, I wondered—and wonder still today—how a human being could lose his heart and treat other people as if they were just bone and muscle, as if they were animals to be consumed. I cannot imagine myself killing a little chick. Or drowning a kitten. How could the Nazis burn little Jewish kids like my five- and six-year-old cousins?

Whenever I find a Holocaust museum, I always go and look at pictures intently, hoping to find a photo of my cousins, my grandparents, my uncles. I look for any sign of my own family, of those who perished. I never give up hope that I might discover something more about them.

As part of their visit, I also took the German students to Eilat, which was still a sleepy little town. (Today it resembles Miami, with high-rise hotels and shopping malls.) We spent a day nearby at King Solomon's mines. The connection to Jewish history, to the Bible, is wherever you go in Israel.

It was summertime, when it is very hot in Eilat, so we slept outside on the terrace of the student hostel. One night, a middle-aged woman gently shook me awake.

"Are you the leader of these Germans?" she asked.

Uh-oh, I thought. Now there's going to be trouble. "I am," I said. "How can I help you?"

"I'm Dutch," the woman replied. "I was in the Dutch resistance, where I met a Jewish Israeli. He fought the Germans as part of the Jewish Brigade." She paused, and I nodded to show I understood. The Jewish Brigade was a contingent of the British Army during the Second World War, composed of Jews from the British mandated territory of Palestine.

"That soldier and I fell in love and got married," she continued. "I moved to Israel, where we had a daughter. I'm here in Eilat with her on holiday now."

"And?" I asked. I couldn't understand why she was waking me from a sound sleep to tell me this.

"In Holland, after the war, we punished women who dated Germans during the war. We would shave their heads bare. I shaved the head of one woman who had fallen in love with a German courier."

I sat up now, fully lucid.

"I woke you up because I wanted you to know that today my daughter met their daughter. She's in your group."

Oh, I thought. Now trouble is coming.

"I want to ask that girl for her mother's forgiveness," she continued. "We were both in love."

Love. *What is love?* I kept asking myself in the hours after she left—the kind of love this woman was talking about. The thought of it kept me up the rest of the night.

FOLLOW YOUR HEART

When I finished my two-year military service, I sought the person I trusted to counsel me on what to study, what to do next. Not many people voluntarily go to prison for career advice, but I took the long bus ride out to the prison where I had taught folk dancing and asked to meet with the warden, whom I respected greatly. He always appeared to love his job. And the girls admired him. He never complained about his work or his pay. I asked him what I should do with my life. "Study something you truly enjoy," he said. The words caught me by surprise. What could school offer that truly interested me? I hadn't been much of a student in high school, but I was a voracious reader and in love with huge chunks of the intellectual universe, specifically the social sciences.

"Find a profession that you are truly passionate about," he continued, "and you will never have to work." To work is to do something we hate but need to do to earn a living. Doing a job one is passionate about is not work; it is a vocation.

Many years later I consulted at Northrop Aviation, the manufacturer of fighter jets. My intervention helped them to change from producing only two-engine jets to single-engine ones, which helped to increase their market appeal. As a reward, they invited me to the Fontainebleau Air Show in France to fly me on their F5.

It was an incredible experience. One hour flying at the speed of Mach 1.9 and 5 Gs. When we landed, the test pilot looked at me and said, "Would you believe it? They pay me to do this."

I followed this warden's guideline. I never worked a day in my life, and I got paid well for doing it.

Psychology, sociology, political science, history—I wanted to study it all, but what university would want me? I had an atrocious high school record,

I paid my way through university in Jerusalem by playing the accordion. What I lacked in technique, I made up for with my ability to get the audience to join in and sing.

all Cs, except for a D in English. The social work program would not accept me. Neither would the department of psychology or any of the other social sciences. To go into natural sciences or law did not interest me, but even if it had, there was no chance of being accepted. The demands of these fields were even more stringent.

I found out that the department of economics at Hebrew University of Jerusalem had a policy of accepting virtually everyone who applied. But there was a catch: after the first year, only the top third of the class would be allowed to advance in the program. I enrolled without even knowing what it was I was going to study. For me, economics was the only game in town. And now, for the first time in my life, I would have to focus on school. No more volunteer work. Study, or realize you are a failure. I accepted the challenge. I eagerly packed my bags and moved to Jerusalem.

I didn't have friends when I first came to Jerusalem. I still felt like a stranger until one day, in my freshman introduction to economics class, another student was answering a question and I realized he sounded just like me. Our accents were identical. I felt an immediate kinship with him. I caught him right after class and introduced myself.

He said he was from Italy.

"But you have such a Slavic accent!" I was truly surprised.

"My parents are from Zagreb, Yugoslavia. During the war, they escaped to Italy, where I was born."

His name was Marko. I had finally found a friend I felt at home with. We became inseparable. We studied together, cooked together, and ate together.

Years later, when Marko died of cancer at forty-two, I found that I could not stop grieving. The impact of his death surprised me—I did not know I could feel so deeply. It felt as though the closest member of my family had died. Even now, so many decades later, I still miss him. When I talk about him, people are always surprised to learn that he was my friend and not my brother. In Serbia they say that a good friend is more than a brother.

My second friend was Shimon. He was born in Israel. Before the country was established, during the British Mandate for Palestine, his father served with the British police. One morning, as Shimon's mother stood on the terrace of their apartment—waving good-bye to her husband, their young son in her arms—two men on motorcycles drew their guns and shot her husband just outside his home. They were members of the Stern Gang, a Jewish terrorist group waging war against the British, trying to force them to leave Palestine. When the time came for Shimon to join the Israeli military service, he was given a job as a clerk in civil defense. It was a totally insignificant role, one that had no military secrecy or significance attached to it. Apparently, the Israeli army worried he might hold a grudge.

Shimon and I shared a room in a little house with two bedrooms near the university. The other one was for two girls, who giggled endlessly, to the point that we could not study and concentrate. So, as revenge, when they studied I would take out my accordion and play. This was a war of who could better distract whom. Or, maybe more truthfully, it was my clumsy way of trying to get the girls' attention. All my life I was awkward in courtship.

Except for Marko and Shimon, I had no other friends at the university. I tried joining the student folk dancing troupe. Students who would go on to become famous artists in Israel were members of this dancing troupe, but no one ever remembers my being there. I became the vice president of the student union and later the president of AIESEC of Israel, an international association of economics students that arranged student exchanges all over the world during the summer months. Still, I found no success in my attempts to feel that I belonged. In an effort to fit in, I tried to date only girls born in Israel, girls with strong Israeli roots. But none of the relationships lasted. I was scared to love and, even more, to be loved.

Since my father couldn't support my education, I earned my living by playing the accordion at weddings, parties, bars, and anywhere else the opportunity presented itself. Performing was more than a way of earning money; I enjoyed bringing people together to sing and dance. I felt everyone's eyes on me—they were connecting with me. On the streets, in

Friday nights at home meant leading my parents and the rest of our family in song, as I had done since learning to play the accordion as a boy in Belgrade.

school, nearly everywhere else but the stage, I felt like an outsider. When I played for an audience, there was a closeness bordering on intimacy.

I played at a famous student bar, Bacchus, and later at Suramello, which artists frequented. (I once watched Ehud Manor make a pass at his future wife as I performed.) In both places there were other accordion players much, much better than me. They could actually read music and studied in a music academy. Their chords were amazing. My playing was really inferior. So how could I compete? How could I keep my position and earn my living?

My strategy was to inspire the audience to sing. I would start a song that I knew was very popular and play it with all my heart, with feeling. When you communicate feelings honestly with music, it is contagious. The audience would join in, and how well I played was not critical anymore. The other accordionists performed. I led the audience to perform.

Looking today at the profession of organizational therapy that I created—which I consider to be distinct from consulting—I realize that I am repeating the same strategy: I make the clients solve their own problems. I only give them the tools.

I completed my degree in economics and political science in 1963. The Central Bank of Israel invited the top economics graduates to work for the bank as researchers. I was one of them. For about six months, I sat locked in a room at the bank. I looked at figures and looked at more figures and compiled statistics and concluded that I'd rather die than live that way.

It was considered a great honor for a student of economics to be invited to work at the Central Bank, and I had the honor of being responsible for the chapter of the bank's annual report on transportation. The guard at the entrance to the bank would address me as *Adoni* (sir, in Hebrew). No one had done that before. And I had my own office. Great honors, but I couldn't imagine working for years with numbers and tables. It would be a life that would suffocate me. It wasn't what the prison warden had encouraged me to pursue. It wasn't where my heart was.

How many people get hooked on a job not because they like what they are doing but because others appreciate them for doing it and they badly need the appreciation? I was one of them, but I wanted to escape.

In July 1963, an unexpected opportunity knocked at my door. The student union asked if I wanted to lead a delegation of students to America over the summer. I accepted, convinced that in America I could learn more about management than anywhere else. Besides, I wanted to escape from my life as a recluse in the Central Bank, to be free from that airless room filled with numbers and statistics. I was going to America. My trip was paid. Maybe, maybe, I could find a way to stay to study there. No way was I going to pass on this opportunity.

PART II

CAGED HEART

Gathering key decision makers in one place, sitting in a semicircle, Clóvis Carvalho, serving president Fernando Henrique Cardoso, uses the Adizes Methodology to help solve Brazil's inflation crisis.

AMERICA

There is an old Sephardic expression that is almost a prayer: *Dios piadoso, solo no esperar de las creaturas*, which means, "God help me to never expect anything from my children." In the Sephardic tradition, to expect your children to live out their lives for you is to curse yourself. Can you imagine the pain you will feel when they do not live up to your expectations? The best strategy is to raise them and let them go on with their own lives, free.

When I was a child, my parents expected me to contribute to the household by drying my father's truck, watching my baby sister, and working to supplement our family income. I was part of the family, and so I was bound to it. But once I finished high school and became an adult, I was free to choose where and how I lived. When I started thinking about studying abroad, my mother did not try to stop me. Her motto was, "If you are happy, I am happy." In all of my years of living overseas, she never asked me to return to Israel. As a matter of fact, once I became an adult, she never asked me for anything. I try to follow this tradition with my own children.

I wanted to study abroad to get my master's degree and then my doctoral degree. I wanted to teach and write. In order to be accepted, I needed a letter of recommendation.

I asked for an appointment with the head of the department of economics, Professor Don Patinkin. In 1963, he was the most widely known and respected economist in Israel. I was seeking a recommendation, true, but I mostly wanted his encouragement, his blessing.

"How old are you?" he asked.

"I'm twenty-six," I answered.

"Too old," he said. "By the time you finish your studies and get your PhD, you will be too old to get any return on your investment in your studies."

He turned back to the papers on his desk. The conversation was over.

Too old? At twenty-six? The rejection left me feeling low, but also infuriated. I would not listen to him. I was not over the hill. I would prove him wrong. Years later, I came across an expression that could have been one of my mantras at the time: Love as if you will die tomorrow, learn as if you will live forever. I could not do much about love at the time, but I believed in my gut and soul I could do something about learning. I decided I would continue my studies and pay whatever price was needed.

In Israel, when the famous and highly decorated military generals retired from military service and were getting ready for the open market or the political arena, they went to Harvard or Columbia to get an MBA. Those universities were beyond my scope. But precisely for that reason, attending those universities became my aspiration. The destination appeared so much higher than I could realistically expect, and the journey there so daunting, but I would try anything to get there.

A friend of mine who was originally from the United States objected to my going. "Whoever goes to America, the country of unlimited opportunities, does not come back," he said. "Go to London. You will come back."

I laughed. "I am an Israeli. I will come back, no matter where I study."

We plan, yes, but God decides.

I left for America as the leader of a delegation of Israeli students with the Experiment in International Living, an organization that arranged exchange programs for high school and university students from all over the world. The host family would take the students in and treat them as though they were their own children rather than tourists or guests. The goal was to make it possible for young people to experience life in different cultures. For the duration of the trip, I was going to live like an American.

Since it was a student exchange program, we were expected to return to Israel. I even had to sign a document to that effect. But in my mind, I was determined to use this opportunity to study management in the United States, specifically business administration. It was not the business world that excited me. It was how to manage it.

Viewing this exchange as a path to study abroad seemed like a worthy plan. But how could I stay in America when I had just fifty dollars to my name. My father had no money to support me. He had cancer and was not working. I had no scholarship or fellowship, either. How would I be able to stay without a working visa, and which university would accept me? Tia Sol was no longer alive. Neither were her son or her daughter. Who would welcome and help me?

Still, I took my chances. I departed with my accordion and a suitcase packed with the shirt my mother had embroidered for me to wear when I performed.

The delegation boarded the plane to Istanbul, where we would join other students from the region for a charter flight to the United States. The flight from Istanbul was a rambunctious one—an entire plane full of students headed out on a big adventure. An occasion like this called for me to pull out my accordion. Music is, of course, the international language. Soon, everyone was singing their native songs, laughing, and joking. The music seemed to create a bond among all of us—strangers when we boarded but not when we landed. We sang for hours.

Prompting those around me to sing together was the only access point I had to experience a sense of closeness with others. The Montenegrin expression that always came to my mind in those moments was *Ko peva zlo ne misli* (He who sings thinks no evil).

In the early hours of the morning, I watched through my window as the plane landed in Hartford, Connecticut. I saw so many small, stand-alone houses with their own yards, houses that in Israel or Yugoslavia we would call villas. There are so many villas in America, I thought in amazement. In reality, they were merely middle-class homes—modest, quintessential American homes. So this is America.

For me, a Holocaust survivor, America was more than just another country on the map. I remembered the American planes flying over Albania when we were in hiding and my mother whispering, tears running down her cheeks, "America. America." I remembered American jumbo airplanes bringing ammunition to Israel during the Sinai War. America, the staunch ally of Israel, the defender of the free world.

The country was an idea loaded with emotion. Not just freedom. It meant tolerance and acceptance, whoever you were. My image of the country came also from the Hollywood movies I'd seen starring Doris Day, films overflowing with abundance. I pictured America as a country of beautiful women and sleek cars. In Yugoslavia, it was said that in America there was money in the streets.

Our first stop was Putney, Vermont, home of the Experiment in International Living. There, I had my first American meal—a steak with applesauce. What a strange combination, I thought. Sweet and salty flavors in the same dish? In America they mixed everything—ethnic groups, religions, races, and even their flavors. And meat was served so casually, as though it were an everyday food.

After getting settled, the next day I caught a night bus to New York to take the entrance exam for the master's program in business administration at Columbia University. I knew it was a long shot, but I decided to apply anyway. As we barreled down the dark highway, I began to dream of my future. If I got accepted, New York seemed perfect for me. There, I could find bar mitzvahs where I could play my accordion.

At some point along the way, the bus stopped and idled, and idled. At first, I thought the driver was simply taking a long break, but time was passing. I eventually asked someone why we had been waiting so long. He said that we were waiting at the police station while the police investigated a car accident.

I was not even aware that there had been an accident. In Israel, if there had been an accident the police were investigating, there would be a commotion among the passengers. Everyone would have an explanation and a story to tell. There would be arguments and maybe even some shouting as people became emotional. But on that bus in America, there was silence.

Americans live and let live. Together, but not on top of each other. Holding on, but not suffocating. These first impressions flooded my mind. The bus passengers let the police do their work and assumed that they knew what they were doing; there was no need to argue or convince or intervene. This was different from anything I had known.

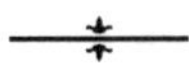

I arrived at the Port Authority bus station in New York City early in the morning. I had never seen a bus station so large. It was like a city in and of itself.

I walked down the block to Times Square, where I stood blinded by the bulbs wildly burning electricity in the morning light. This is America?

I wondered. If I left the lights on at home, my father would punish me severely. "Do not waste electricity," he would say. "The clock is running. It is money." In Times Square, there was so much wasted energy.

As I crossed the square, I noticed a homeless man lying on the sidewalk. At that time, in Israel, I had never seen homeless people. I had seen people begging on the street in Yugoslavia, but just lying there on the sidewalk? Never. And people simply walked around this tattered man as if he were a bundle someone forgot on the street.

I had been warned: America is a country of endless opportunities but also a country where one man is a wolf to another man. If you fall, you are left to lie there. Do not expect pity, I was told. Do not expect help. You are on your own.

There was not much time to stand and gawk. I had to find the right subway to take to Yeshiva University. I, of course, had never been in a subway station and must have looked confused. Fortunately, a kind man saw my bewilderment and offered to show me which subway to take and where to get off. Wait, I said to myself, in America people *do* help.

When I arrived, I was overcome by a sense of anxiety. A great deal was riding on the exam and my desire to attend Columbia University. I sat down and started the test. I answered two or three questions. Then I opened my eyes to another applicant shaking me awake. I had made it through a handful of questions before falling asleep—I had not had a full night's sleep since leaving Israel. The exam was over, and apparently so was going to be my dream of attending Columbia.

There was nothing to do now but rejoin the Israeli delegation in Vermont. The next day, we boarded a bus for the daylong drive to Westerville, Ohio. We were going to live in college dormitories there for two weeks to experience student life in America.

Westerville is very close to Columbus, and during the time we were there, I found my way to Ohio State University. If Columbia would reject me for poor performance on the entrance test, I thought, maybe this university will accept me.

The accordion had propelled me through school in Israel, so why not in Ohio? Next to the campus was a small bar with an open mic where people performed. One by one, students with guitars would come up on stage, adjust the microphone, and play a song by Peter, Paul and Mary, Bob Dylan, or Joan Baez. I had brought my accordion so I could join in, and from that night on, everyone at the bar sang along to the songs I played. I hoped that someone would discover me and offer me a job playing in restaurants so I could make ends meet the way I had in Jerusalem. I found a local Jewish community center and offered to play Israeli music there. I reasoned that they must have bar mitzvahs here, too.

If I could make a living here, I had one problem solved. But Ohio State did not even consider me because I did not apply. My hope, unrealistic as it might have been, was still to be accepted by Columbia. Columbia was the target. The best. How? I did not know. But I had faith.

One day, some students and I were riding in our host's car with the radio tuned to the news. The newscaster reported that Skopje, my birthplace, had suffered a terrible earthquake. Thousands had died. The city was flattened. Then, without even a moment of silence, an ad for toothpaste came on the air.

I was speechless. How could these two messages exist in the same breath? When I lived in Israel and Yugoslavia, neither country had radio channels with commercial ads. Israel didn't have television, either. Israel's prime minister and founding father, Ben-Gurion, was totally against it, saying it would have a decadent impact on Israel's culture.

So, yes, advertising during news programs was totally new for me. I was on the verge of tears. My birthplace had been destroyed, thousands died, and instead of playing mournful music, the radio station had tried to sell me toothpaste. Was this America, too?

LIVE AND LET LIVE

Robert Cortinovis was unlike anyone I had encountered in Yugoslavia, Albania, or Israel. The entire month I lived with him and his family in St. Louis, I tried to put my finger on what was so different about him. He certainly wasn't stronger than the men I had met before, or necessarily smarter. It was, I thought, in part the way he carried himself. He was a stocky man of average height, but he walked lightly. He moved as though he felt comfortable in his skin, as though he did not expect to be stopped by an authority or confronted by someone he barely knew. He wasn't on guard against some criticism or put-down. He was relaxed. As were his wife, Irene, and their children, Steve and Dan.

The Israelis I knew, in comparison, were very intense. Israelis are seldom right but are never in doubt, and they challenge each other all the time. No matter what is said, an Israeli—and, actually, Jewish people in general—have to find a hole in any argument. Never taking anything for granted, the result of two thousand years of Talmudic debate.

There was something familiar about the Cortinovis family and the way they lived. Their home resembled every depiction of suburban America

I'd seen on TV or in *The Saturday Evening Post*. It was the happy life of happy people with happy problems.

There was never a shortage of food—never. I, who had starved in every country I had lived in, couldn't believe it. There were so many different types of bread in the supermarket! How to choose what to buy? The abundance made my head spin. It all seemed so wasteful.

Early in my time in St. Louis, Irene sent me to the store to pick something up. They were out of stock, so the saleswoman apologized and carefully gave me directions to a competing store that had what I was looking for. I walked out in disbelief that in St. Louis—and, I assumed, across America—there was enough for everyone. Where I came from, you learned to negotiate the price vendors asked in the marketplace. You haggled. If you agreed to the price the seller asked, the seller would feel stupid; he should have asked for more. And he would never—ever—send you to a competitor.

It seemed that the United States ran on trust. I encountered this phenomenon the first time I used the public phone system. My dime disappeared, and my call was not connected. I was upset. An American standing behind me said that if I called the operator and told him what had happened, the phone company would connect me for free.

"What?" I replied. "The phone company will trust me and let me make the call for free?" That would not have happened in Israel or Serbia. There, the culture was one of distrust because everyone was always trying to take advantage of one another.

From the boys' athletic games to casual conversations between Robert and Irene, Americans seemed obsessed with the idea of fairness. In the Middle East and the Balkans, fair play was for suckers. Your job was to protect yourself. Cheating was culturally acceptable, and if you were stupid enough to let others take advantage of you, that was your own fault—people would mock you for being a loser. But not in St. Louis. There, if you cheated or took advantage of someone, you were rebuked or ostracized.

It was not just a polite façade, I discovered. Americans *at that time* trusted other people, even people they did not know. I could see it everywhere—in what and how I was served in stores and restaurants, in the way American taxi drivers charged their customers, and in the rules I watched the children play by on the local baseball field.

In America people knew how to live together—live and let live.

I had that experience when I went to a street fair that summer, where a hundred or so vendors were selling merchandise and fast food. There was Mexican food; there was Jewish food; there was Italian food. I saw no American food. American food was all these different foods put together.

Walk down one of many streets on New York, and you will see a Pakistani restaurant next to an Indian restaurant and a Jewish restaurant next to a Lebanese restaurant. No animosity. In their countries of origin, they might be killing each other, but in America they live as peaceful neighbors.

While I loved America, I missed the casual intimacy of my home countries. Family life was different here. Robert would come home from work, have a martini, read the daily newspaper, watch the news on TV, have dinner, and then go to sleep. Each day, the same ritual repeated itself.

"Where is the rest of your family?" I asked Irene one day. "Your cousins and aunts and everyone in your extended family? I never hear about them." In Israel and Yugoslavia, extended family was always present. Here, I did not see anyone.

Many years later, a friend of mine, who had a successful career in Los Angeles and a beautiful mansion next to the beach, took his wife and children and moved back to Serbia. I asked him why. "In Belgrade more people visit my home in one day than in a whole year in America," he told me.

I identified with what he said because sometimes I wonder what price I am paying for the career I have made in America that I could never have made in Israel. It is lonely in America. Maybe not for those born here because they are used to it. But for somebody who comes from a "warm" culture, like those of Greece, Mexico, or Israel, the difference in intimacy and friendship feels significant.

America is a vast country. Children leave for college far from home, get married, and move somewhere else. How often do we see our grown children? I don't mean by video chat; I mean to hold them and kiss them. When I am in Israel and my friends invite me for a Friday night meal, I am jealous. The whole family—children, grandchildren—around the table, every week. Here, you wait for your children to maybe call you. I was surprised, for instance, that in America people do not know their neighbors very well. Everybody keeps to themselves and does not intrude on what their neighbors are doing. This has advantages because you feel free from uninvited involvement. However, there are great advantages when you can go across the street to ask your neighbor for some ingredient you need for a meal.

When my children were growing up, it bothered me enormously that I could not allow them to play on the street in front of the house. Somebody might steal them or hurt them. In Israel, even where terrorism is the norm, children nevertheless play in the street, free to go from one house to another. Once I got home from school and ate, I was immediately on the street to play. We used to play soccer with a ball made of old socks. There was no money to buy a soccer ball. In America—at least in the big cities—you have to arrange a date in advance and drive the children to visit their friends.

But this sense of community is declining in Israel and Serbia, too. It started with the introduction of television, and the sense of alienation has increased even more with the Internet and social media. People spend more time communicating through their devices than they do in person. Walking down the street in the American suburbs feels like walking through a ghost town. Walking down the street of a Mexican village you see children playing, mothers sitting on their terraces knitting.

I love Mexico. One time I flew into Mexico City, and the line at customs for foreigners was at least an hour long. The line for Mexican nationals was empty, very fast. I ducked under the rope and presented my American passport at the immigration booth. "But you are not Mexican," the agent said, looking at me with surprise. I put my hand on my chest and said, "But I am a Mexican at heart." She let me pass.

No sooner had I met Irene and Robert than they quizzed me about my faith. "Do you believe in God?" I hesitated before answering.

There was a crucifix above my bed, a small statue of Jesus crucified on the cross, with blood dripping from his hands and feet. Now, sitting in their dining room with them, another crucified Christ stared at me from the wall. These were Irene's decorative touches, but they reminded me of the time when some kid in Serbia had called me a murderer of Christ.

My father had insisted that if God were there, he would not have allowed the Holocaust to happen. As a child pioneer, my teachers were communists who taught me that religion was the opiate of the masses.

But when I told them, "No," I did not believe in God,[1] they did not ask me to leave and live with a different family. They were surprised, but they accepted my answer and let it go.

That said, when Sunday rolled around, Irene informed me that we were all leaving for church. Together. I paused and remembered a Sephardic expression my father would use when telling me to ignore something: "It is like when you walk by the church: look the other way." For us Jews, a church was not a place to go. What would I do now?

Well, if I could be a Muslim for two years during the war, surely I could be a Catholic in America for a month. I reminded myself that Jesus was a Jew, a member of my tribe.

---

1 It was only years later that I would discover my personal God. I told my story to the alumni of a Jesuit seminary: https://www.youtube.com/watch?v=Z33dt8VWZxQ&t=215s.

During the Roman Catholic Mass, members of the congregation are supposed to kneel at certain points. It's not easy for a Jew to kneel, especially before the crucified Christ. Nevertheless, when Irene and Robert knelt, I knelt, too. According to the rules of the trip, I was their son, so I decided to behave like an obedient son.

They opened their prayer books. I followed suit and opened mine. I read the words of Jesus Christ (in Aramaic, a sister language of Hebrew): *Eli, Eli, lama sabachthani?* (My God, my God, why hast Thou forsaken me?) As I understood it, the passage described the intense physical and emotional suffering the Jews had supposedly caused Jesus. At that moment, I recognized one of the sources of anti-Semitism. If Christians settled into their pews every week and read that the Son of God, their Messiah, was brought to the point of intense suffering by the Jewish people, then it was hardly surprising that some of them emerged from the church hating Jews.

But that is not the only reason, I think. We Jews traditionally live in segregated communities, within walking distance of our synagogues. We eat kosher and will not break bread with our gentile neighbors. Who likes people who think they are better than you and refuse to eat with you? The prayer *Ata behartanu* says that we are the chosen people. It sounds so elitist, but if you continue reading the prayer you realize it is not. The continuation of the prayer says *she kidshanu be mitzvotav,* which means that sanctified us with obligations, so it is not elitist at all. We are chosen to fulfill obligations, to be the conscience of the world, to fight for justice, and to seek the truth.

During the ride home from church, I was quiet and thoughtful. I pondered the importance of understanding what makes people accept or reject other people whose beliefs differ from their own. It wasn't exactly a religious experience, but it was no less profound.

If God is one, the same God of all religions, why the fighting? Why the persecution of one another? We fight about *how* we practice our religions rather than recognizing that we share a common God. Jewish people put on a hat when going to pray. Christians take the hat off, and Muslims take their shoes off. Some see Saturday as the day of prayer and rest.

Others, Sunday and yet others, Friday. Maybe we should start a new religion: Thursday is still available. The fighting is over the form rather than the function, the true purpose of connecting with the divine.

This realization made me very open to pray at any house of prayer. More than once, when I've been traveling alone for business, I have found myself joining Christmas prayers in a church. God is one, and I will connect with the absolute wherever I am.

UNEXPECTED HELP

Attending church, or temple, I was to learn, was how American families socialized. Our delegation was invited to speak about Israel in an Episcopalian church. That's how I met Eliza.

We talked about Israel, sang Israeli songs, and mingled with the congregation. I played the accordion. As I performed, I noticed her in the crowd. She was young and slim, with short hair and the most beautiful large, honey-colored eyes. She had a smile that said it all for me: purity, love, and empathy. I played the accordion better than ever. I tried to make eye contact and succeeded. After my set, I took down her phone number, and we decided to meet again.

I learned that she played tennis. She told me about ice skating on the frozen lake at Wellesley College, where she was a student. What did I, a kid from Macedonia and Albania, know about tennis? About skating? About Wellesley? To me she represented the America that I saw on TV, in films, and in magazine ads. Eliza and I engaged in the usual courtship rituals of many high school and college students, but this kind of romantic intimacy was all breathtakingly new to me. One evening, as we were fooling around in the backseat of her father's car in a school parking lot, a guard suddenly appeared with his flashlight shining right on us. We were barely dressed.

"What are you two doing?" he demanded.

In my most formal voice, I replied, "I am here with the Experiment in International Living."

"You call this an experiment?" he shouted. "Get out of here before I call your parents." Eliza laughed the whole way home.

At the end of the summer, Eliza left for college. When we parted, we made a pact: every evening at midnight, we would both look for the North Star. We would connect with each other by looking at the same star for at least five minutes. It was romantic, but it was not honest. For me, the affair was more of a rite of passage than something like love.

The Experiment in International Living had one final trip scheduled for us: a visit to Washington, D.C., the nation's capital. By coincidence, we arrived just in time to join the March on Washington led by the Reverend Martin Luther King Jr. We were foreigners, strangers to the United States, but it was at that moment that I saw the true glory of America.

If I had a stereotype of an average American fixed in my mind from my time in Ohio and Missouri, that day swept it aside. At the march, I was introduced to the real diversity that is America. Black and white, well-dressed and disheveled, people of different religions and classes marching together for a common mission. There were no fires set, no calls for revolution. No, it was a friendly, loving, singing march. I linked arms with strangers and joined in singing "We Shall Overcome," although, to tell the truth, I had no idea what it was that we had to overcome.

Being Israelis, naturally we pushed ourselves to the front of the crowd. I stood just below the podium when Dr. King gave his famous "I Have a Dream" speech. I stood there and listened to his voice booming out at us in cadences so rich and sonorous they sounded like poetry.

Standing in that crowd, I had no knowledge of the civil rights movement in America and no more than a dim understanding of Dr. King's influence. I certainly had no idea that I was experiencing one of the most significant moments in the country's history. But I was in awe of the sheer number of people who stretched across the National Mall before the Lincoln Memorial and beyond, so far that there was nothing else to see. It was a vast sea of faces and bodies, come together as one.

Before I left for Washington, Irene and Robert Cortinovis were curious to learn what their "summer son" had in mind for his future. They asked me if I had considered staying in America. Robert thought I might fit in and gain a great deal from the experience. I found the courage and revealed that one of the reasons I was excited by the prospect of traveling to the United States was to study management, but obtaining a student visa seemed like a complete impossibility. How could I stay when I had so little money to my name? In order to stay, I needed proof that I had enough money to support myself. And I needed to be accepted to my dream school: Columbia University.

But the Cortinovises, like many Americans I got to know, tended to see challenges as problems to be solved. They wanted to help me. Their first step was to secure a way for me to qualify for a student visa. They gave me a letter guaranteeing that they would take financial responsibility for me. The condition was, however, that I would never actually ask for that help. I was speechless. No one had ever placed so much trust in me. I thanked them, took the letter, and never asked for any help, even when I starved later that year.

Days later, Columbia accepted me into the MBA program despite my miserable entry test score. As luck would have it, there were a lot of Israeli army generals enrolling at the time. Columbia was looking to recruit students who possessed a "leadership profile." The admissions office mercifully ignored my test score and chose to focus on my accomplishments as a student leader in Israel. They gave me the benefit of the doubt that my failure on the exam was because of my deficiency in the English language, and they put me in an English-as-a-foreign-language class for a semester.

The chance they took on me would go on to influence my theories on leadership. A leader is not what he or she knows but what he or she is. It is better to hire someone who *is* and teach him or her to *know* than hire someone who knows and teach the person to be.

As far as tuition went, the university gave me a student loan. That solved one problem. But the offer was conditional on my proving I had the resources to support myself while in school. How was this possible? I was a foreigner and did not have a work permit. Robert and Irene's letter, although sufficient for the immigration office, apparently was not enough to satisfy Columbia. They wanted to see money in the bank.

I stood at the corner of Broadway and Seventy-Second Street with my accordion in one hand and my little suitcase of summer clothes in the other, watching the airport bus depart with the Israeli delegation waving good-bye and cheering me on. I waved back and smiled broadly as I began to sweat. What was I thinking? I had no money, no clothes, no way to earn a living, since I had no work permit and—most important of all—no return ticket. That was it: study in America or bust.

I spotted a restaurant across the street called Tel Aviv. It felt like a sign to me. I went inside and asked the first man I saw, "Do you need an accordion player to play in the evenings?"

He was a short man with an Israeli accent and a prominent bald spot on the top of his head. He looked at me suspiciously, but my knowledge of Hebrew and my appearance gave me away. His eyes showed that he recognized in me a fellow Israeli, fresh off the boat.

He said in a gruff but kind voice, *"Yalla, nagen mashehu."* ("Go on, play something.")

He listened for a few minutes before saying, "You can play here, but we can't pay you anything. All I can offer you is whatever you get in tips."

I wondered if perhaps I was not that good. But if that was true, why would he let me play? There was no time to ponder his motives. I accepted his offer. (Later, I discovered he was the composer of one of the most famous songs of the Israeli independence war: “Bab El Vad.”)

On my first day alone in New York, I played until two in the morning. I made less than five dollars in tips, most of which was in quarters. As they were closing the restaurant, I had a problem. I didn’t have anywhere to sleep. I just stood there, lost.

The waiter, a short, wiry Israeli about my age, was cleaning tables and moving chairs. He noticed that I wasn’t going anywhere and asked me if I needed help. I hesitated a moment, then I admitted with some embarrassment, “Yes, I have no place to stay.”

“What do you mean, you have no place to stay?” He didn’t seem able to comprehend my situation. I was in a restaurant at two in the morning with a small suitcase, an accordion, and no place to sleep. He looked at me curiously for a moment. Then he made up his mind. “You can sleep in my car if you’d like,” he said with a shrug.

So I spent my first night in New York in the backseat of a waiter’s car parked outside his apartment in New Jersey. That was how my life in New York began.

The next day I wandered the streets of the city, my neck craning to take in the height of the buildings. My head spun as I tried to absorb the vast crowds—the way they dressed, the way they walked as though the earth belonged to them. The tremendous wealth in the store windows dazzled me. It was another world, almost beyond my comprehension. I was hungry, but all I could afford was a single twenty-five-cent hot dog for a meal that day. I was so careful to stretch the few dollars I had.

When evening came, I went back to the restaurant and played again until two in the morning. As the restaurant was closing, the waiter asked me, “Where are you going to go tonight?” I said I didn’t know, hoping he would offer the backseat of his car again.

"Okay," he said. "Come and stay with me."

In his little apartment, we took the curtains down from the window and placed them neatly on the floor to serve as a mattress and a blanket for me. The floor was my bed for the night.

The third day, I knew without being told that I had better begin looking for a room, preferably near Columbia University. I found two older Jewish ladies, both refugees from Russia—part of that old world I knew so well—who rented me a room for fifty dollars a month. I asked if I could pay them at the end of the month, calculating that I could earn the fifty dollars in tips by then. They agreed, saying that they understood my situation: they had been refugees once, too.

In a peculiar way, without saying a word, they adopted me. Every morning one of the babushkas would make me tea with lots of sugar to help me through the day. I did not have to speak of the war, of Monopol, of my years in Yugoslavia. But I knew that they had been there, where hardship lives, and that brought me some small measure of comfort.

Now I had to address the problem of proving to Columbia that I had the money to support myself while studying. My mother had reminded me before I left for America that Tia Sol's son-in-law had a brother, Morris Russo. He had passed away, but his wife, Esther, was alive. She had even visited us in Israel. I found her number in a Long Island phone book at the library and called her from the pay phone down the block from the restaurant. To my relief, she was actually happy to hear from me and immediately grasped my situation. "I can loan you the money for twenty-four hours," she offered. "You deposit it in your account and ask for a statement from the bank proving that you have money." I did just as she said.

This was another surprising experience. I wondered, are these Americans naïve, or what? This trick would not have worked in Israel, where you are often a subject of suspicion and assumed guilty, or in Serbia, where you are automatically rejected for being different.

What an innocent country America is, I thought, so guileless and eager to help. In the United States, people seemed to look for ways to help me. In the countries I came from, everyone was on guard—survival was the driving force in decision making. I shook my head in wonder. I felt welcome, trusted, and hopeful. But it was more than American culture. Now I recognize it was the Jewish culture, too, where we help each other in time of need. Where family includes more than the extended family. All Jews are one big family.

That said, I did not find life in New York easy. I spoke very little English. I went to school by day and played the accordion for tips every night to pay the rent and afford food. I put aside fifty cents a day for green pea soup and a hot dog at the Chock Full o'Nuts lunch counter.

I was not in a concentration camp or in Albania or Yugoslavia or Israel. I was in America, where I could see the abundance of food in the supermarkets and the glitter of unimaginable wealth on Fifth Avenue. Nevertheless, it was in America, of all places, that I was on the verge of starving.

My first year in graduate school at Columbia University, I nearly starved, I had so little money. A scholarship from the Young President's Organization in 1964 kept me afloat.

HUNGRY IN AMERICA

I began my first semester at Columbia in the autumn of 1963. One day in late November, I came out of class and everywhere I turned, people were crying in the streets.

What happened?" I finally asked a man walking by.

"President Kennedy was murdered," he answered. I ran home and asked the two landladies if I could watch their TV. I was glued to the screen as it replayed the president's assassination. It was difficult to grasp. A little less than three months earlier, I had been part of a peaceful demonstration that I could not imagine happening anywhere but America. Yet someone had just shot the president of the United States.

What was going on in this country? How could they allow the president of the United States to ride in an open car? The car was driving so slowly! It seemed like a criminal lack of security. I remembered the convoy of cars Tito would travel in during any celebration. His security team would post sharpshooters on every rooftop along the route. His bulletproof car zoomed by with several other cars of the same color and make, so it was difficult to discern which car was his.

Winter arrived quickly, and with it came snow. I froze. I hadn't experienced a real winter since my childhood in Belgrade. I asked another student if he would swap a sweater for the shirt that my mother had embroidered for me. He did, but it did not help much. I was still freezing. There was a shop nearby that had a fire and put all their merchandise on sale. A warm pair of gloves was marked down to a dollar. I did not have the dollar. I stole the gloves.

There was one ray of sunshine that winter. Eliza had returned to Wellesley and every other week or so, she would grab a bus from Boston to visit me in New York. I did not have the money to host her well. We would take the subway from my apartment near Columbia to Times Square for dinner. Tad's Steaks had a window to the street from the kitchen, and we would huddle together watching the chef grill steaks that sold for $1.29 each. Then we would walk one block north, buy two hot dogs for twenty-five cents each, and eat them very slowly. That was our night out on the town.

Was I in love? Eliza, with her beautiful brown eyes, was so supportive and generous. She typed my papers. Ironed my shirts. She would accompany me and give her full attention while I played at the restaurant on Seventy-Second Street. She never asked for anything in return—and I never offered to give her anything, either. My heart was closed, sealed shut, so it didn't matter how much caring she offered; it never got through.

After a few months, Eliza stopped coming to see me in New York. She had enrolled at Harvard Medical School and was very busy. I didn't have the money to visit her, so by a silent but mutual agreement the romance came to an end.

By the time I handed in my final term paper for the first semester, I was so ill from malnourishment that I had to be hospitalized for a few days. It was

December 1963. I knew I could not continue playing accordion for tips all night, be at school all day, and constantly hungry. My situation looked hopeless. I didn't have the money to buy a return ticket to Israel.

When the hospital released me, I heard that the International Student Center on campus was having a holiday party. Free snacks, I whispered to myself and hurried there. I met an Israeli film student, Dan Wolman, who immediately understood my problem.

"You know," he said, "there's a dorm for international students here, where students from all over the world live. Why don't you contact them? Maybe they'll give you a room and food and help you out."

I formulated a plan. Most of the five hundred or so international students living in the dorm probably couldn't afford to fly home for the holidays. They needed entertainment. So on Christmas Eve, I went to the International House, sat down in the lobby, took out my accordion, and without anyone asking me to, began to play like the little kid I saw on the street in Belgrade. I knew folk songs from all over the world because in Israel people come from many different countries and continue to sing their national songs. Soon, students emerged from their rooms and gathered around me. Everyone sang along to the best-known songs from their countries all night. I played tirelessly—my staying in America depended on it.

The next Monday, I went to the program director of the International House, Dr. Gordon Davis. He was tall, friendly, and easy to talk to. "I was the one who played the accordion all night on Christmas Eve," I told him, "and I need help." I did not beg or plead. I just said, "I've got no means of support, and I don't know how I'm going to finish my studies."

He didn't ask for a letter from my bank or any other document that would confirm my story. It had been only days since I was released from the hospital, and my appearance was apparently proof enough that I needed help. Dr. Davis said, "Come back tomorrow."

When I arrived the following day, he told me, "You'll be given a room. It will be paid for by a grant from the Young Presidents Organization. A man named Stanley Rumbough donated two thousand dollars for a needy student. Plus, if you work in the coffee shop in the mornings, your meals will be free."

The YPO was composed of chief executive officers under the age of forty-nine and had branches all over the world. To this day, its members meet every month in their respective cities to learn about good management and leadership.

This help was far more than I had expected. It seemed like an act of profound generosity. Who was I? Someone who had walked in off the street on Christmas Eve and played folk songs. I was a stranger. Only in America, I thought. No letters, no proof, no bureaucracy—just a helping hand.

"How can I repay this?" I asked.

"In the future, help support those in need," Dr. Davis said.

I have tried to pay it forward, as Dr. Davis suggested. I have given lectures to top executives in New York and donated the fee I charged to the International House. For twenty-six years, I have lectured at YPO universities and provided consulting services to the organization, always gratis.

Nearly half a century later, I was awarded the Ellis Island Medal of Honor. The medal is given to immigrants or descendants of immigrants in America who have made a significant difference in the nation. I received the honor alongside one hundred others that day. Among past recipients are American presidents, top business leaders like Lee Iacocca, and entertainers like Frank Sinatra. It was an impressive event, with flags, marches of the armed forces, and, of course, speeches.

Because my family name starts with an *A,* I sat at the top of the receiving line and was among the first to receive the medal. Time passed as other recipients were called to the podium and honored. When the speaker called out the name Stanley Rumbough, I practically jumped out of my skin. The man who had enabled me to finish my studies and advance to where I was came to the podium. He and I received the medal on the same day.

With Stanley Rumbough, whose grant enabled me to finish my studies in 1963. He got an Ellis Island award the same year as me. It is given to those who made a significant difference in the nation.

The International House was the place of residence for many Palestinians. I searched for some point of contact with them, in large measure because of my experiences in Albania and Yugoslavia. I had learned as a child that the people I thought were enemies were often actually friends. The Palestinians, however, did not want to socialize with me. I was an Israeli, an enemy.

I tried a different tactic to get close: music. When I played some traditional Arab folk songs on my accordion in the student lounge, the Palestinian students couldn't resist me any longer. Slowly, we started hanging out together—at a distance, but still together—in the same room, at the same dining table.

One night I asked one of the Palestinians who came from a refugee camp in Jericho where he had lived in Israel. He said he was a refugee from Haifa.

"Where was your house?" I asked him, starting to feel some discomfort.

"Abbas Effendi Street," he told me.

"What number?" I asked, now alarmed.

"Number 32A."

I froze. That was the building my family had moved to when we first arrived in Israel in 1948. Its Arab owners, fleeing the war, had abandoned it. The Palestinian, a child my age at the time, and his family had become homeless and displaced. They lived in a Palestinian refugee camp in Jordan while my family and I, refugees from the Holocaust, moved into their house, seeking refuge ourselves.

I was silent for a very long time. He cleared his throat and waited for me to say something. I could not. I was emotional to the point of numbness. Without a word, I walked over and put my arms around him. We held each other quietly in the dining room of the International House, a Palestinian and an Israeli, each five thousand miles from home.

Later, during the Six-Day War in 1967, my newfound Palestinian friend was worried and frightened. He had not heard from his family in Jordan and did not know what had happened to them. His family lived in a refugee camp in Jericho about an hour's drive from my parents' home in Israel.

Michael Engel, a fellow graduate student with me at Columbia and an intelligence officer in the Israeli army, offered to help me locate them. A friend of his in Israeli intelligence found them and sent us a message: all is well.

Today in the Middle East we have two nations fighting for the same tiny piece of land. Neither has an alternative that could work without the cooperation of the other side. The claim that the displaced Palestinians, a population of almost six million, can settle in other Arab countries is bogus. The other Arab countries don't want them. They can hardly feed their own people. The Palestinians have nowhere else to go. The Israelis do not have another piece of land either.

That is the reality, and the conclusion is that we need to learn to live together. But how can the Palestinians trust the Israelis when their land is increasingly being taken to settle Messianic Jews there? How can the Israelis trust Palestinians—or anyone, for that matter—with the Jewish history of persecution and the experience of thousands of missiles directed at Israeli schools and homes from Gaza? Both cultures do not even respect the different denominations or ways of practicing their own religions, let alone one another's. Without mutual trust and respect, one country is not the solution. It will be continuous warfare.

If the country is split, there's another problem: fear that the Palestinians will use missiles to bombard Israel. They already do so from the Gaza Strip, and they are already shelling from the north, too. Splitting the country will enable them to do it from the Western Jordan region. Israel will be surrounded and have no space to maneuver.

When I was intending to return to Israel in the 1970s, I built a house on the beach close to Netanya. It was only nine miles to the prewar border (the one the Palestinians insist Israel retreat to), not enough to even finish a cigarette along the drive there. What other country in the world would permit potential hostile missiles to be positioned nine miles away?

So what is the answer to avoid hundreds of years of increasing escalating hostilities? A paradigm shift both cultures have to initiate. The solution must be Switzerland and not Bosnia. The difference is a culture of mutual trust and respect.

One evening at Tel Aviv Restaurant, someone accidentally knocked my accordion off the chair where I'd placed it after my last set. It hit the floor and broke into two pieces. I was devastated. The accordion was my livelihood and, in a way that I knew but could not quite articulate, my link to the world. It was my means of belonging. What was I going to do? I had no money to repair it. The person who had knocked it over had disappeared, and the restaurant owner was indifferent. My world seemed to be wiped out in an instant.

I headed home on the subway with the broken accordion in a box, weeping. This, I knew, was the end of the road. I got off the train at 116th Street, the stop for Columbia University, and bumped into my statistics professor, Dr. Samuel Richmond.

"What's wrong?" he asked kindly. He saw my tear-streaked face and genuinely wanted to know.

I told him the story. Professor Richmond was Jewish, and his parents had been refugees from Russia. People used to say that he was among the first Jews to be hired as professors at Columbia. He listened to my story without saying a word. Then—and I will never forget that moment—he took out his wallet and counted out enough money to fix the accordion.

I started to thank him, but he raised his hand to quiet me. It was such an intimate gesture. He cared.

BECOMING JEWISH

In Israel, the Jewish people take being Jewish for granted. It is, after all, a Jewish nation, but only some Israelis are religious. Zionism separated Jewish national identity from religion. The holidays my family observed were considered national holidays. We were secular, but, of course, we identified ourselves as Jewish. Why else did they try to kill us during the Second World War? Why else were we singled out in postwar Yugoslavia? Why else had our ancestors been driven from Spain more than five hundred years ago? Yes, I was an Israeli Jew, but I knew practically nothing about Judaism. That changed in America.

It began about six months after I arrived in New York. One night, as I was playing my accordion in the restaurant, I noticed a couple staring at me from their table. Had I met them in Israel? In St. Louis? During the break, the man called me over to his table. He introduced himself as Moishe Dworkin and explained that he was the director of a Jewish youth summer camp serving Minneapolis and St. Paul, Minnesota, the Twin Cities. Would I like to work for him over the summer as the camp's music director?

Me? Music director? I did not read music—I played by ear. And now, out of the blue, I had received an offer to be a *music director!* But the fact was that I knew nothing about prayers, especially if they needed to be sung. I also had no idea where Minneapolis was. But I knew one thing for sure: I needed the money. It was a thousand dollars for the whole summer, an enormous sum when you have close to nothing. I accepted before he could change his mind.

As soon as classes ended for the summer break, I boarded a bus for the long ride to Minneapolis. When I arrived, I was met by several counselors, among them Abraham Foxman, who went on to become the national director of the Anti-Defamation League. We drove three hours to Herzl Camp, located on Devil's Lake in Wisconsin. I discovered that Bob Zimmerman, later known as Bob Dylan, was a camper there several years earlier.

Herzl was a conservative Jewish camp. Each Friday evening, everyone would put on a white shirt, wash their hands, and solemnly sit around the tables. They would bless the bread and wine. Before the meal, I would lead everyone in singing Jewish and Israeli songs that I had learned from listening to the songs of Rabbi *Carlebach*, particularly the one that greeted the Sabbath. Saturday mornings, we would pray.

I had been Jewish all my life, but Herzl Camp was the place where I learned to love being Jewish. From that summer on, I always wanted to welcome Friday night by lighting candles, singing Sabbath songs, kissing my family, and blessing the bread and wine. While I knew nothing about Jewish traditions and religion, to the people at this American summer camp, *I* was the real Jew. I was Israeli, a Jew from the homeland.

At Herzl Camp, I felt Jewish and wanted to learn the rituals. I wanted to learn how to conduct Shabbat dinner and Passover seder, to find my way around the prayer book. I loved the Jewish culture, but there were certain parts that bothered me, such as the prayers, *Ata Bechartanu* (you, God, have chosen us), *she lo asanu ke kol ha goyeem* (and you did not make us like the gentiles, like the rest of the world). This claim of superiority does not endear us to the world. Why would it? When I became a professor, I could identify the Jewish students in the classroom. They were the first to raise their hands. They argued. They challenged. It made the class lively and interesting, but the rest of the class resented it.

What surprised me at Herzl Camp, though, was not just how ignorant I initially was in the ways of Jewish life, but how much we Israelis had snubbed the Jews of the diaspora. The Jewish community of the Twin Cities that had founded Herzl Camp had sent food, clothes, and money to Israel. They had built up a strong national political presence in America. They raised funds every year through the United Jewish Fund. They fought anti-Semitism with great zeal. But to me, an Israeli, they were the diaspora Jews, the weak ones.

When I returned to New York, I was invited to play at a Jewish retirement home. At the end of my set, an Israeli visitor spoke about how Israel needed help from America's Jews. A very old lady, a resident of the home, rose to speak. She could hardly stand on her feet. She held ten dollars in her trembling hand and with a shaky voice said, "This is for my people of Israel."

It almost brought tears to my eyes.

One can be Jewish and not religious at all. This is true worldwide, but in Israel there is an increasing antagonism between the secular Israelis and the orthodox Jews. But what are the long-run potential repercussions?

When I visited Israel in 1971, I went to see a play at the Tzavta Theatre in Tel Aviv. It was a play with only two characters. One was Theodor Herzl, the founder of Zionism, who is considered the father of the Israeli nation. The other was Sabbatai Zevi, who is considered a false messiah and inspired thousands of Jews to join him in converting to Islam.

At a certain point, Zevi says to Herzl, "Maybe you are a false messiah, too."

What would happen if, God forbid, Israel collapsed? Nations do disappear over the years. What would happen to the millions of secular Jews who found their identity in Zionist nationalism and turned their back on religion? Would Zionism without a country be strong enough to maintain the Jewish identity? Would Judaism lose millions of members of its tribe? I fear that secular Jews in Israel are becoming a different breed of Jews, separate from the world's Jewry. Or, as one of the religious generals of Israel called them, "gentiles who speak Hebrew."

I USED TO LIVE HERE

When I was awarded my MBA in June 1965, the graduation ceremony was disrupted by students protesting the war in Vietnam. During my time in Yugoslavia, no one dared to oppose anything the government did or did not do. I do not recall any protests in Israel, either. Not at that time. We were all too busy trying to make ends meet. How were they able to protest in America? Why would anyone protest in America? The protests puzzled me, but what puzzled me even more was the fact that no one even confronted the protestors.

I had come to America for a doctoral degree, but that summer Columbia, my own alma mater, rejected me because I had received a C in one of my courses. I would have to head downtown to New York University's business school, where Peter Drucker was teaching at the time. Drucker was already very famous, the star of the business school circuit. That's who I had to surpass, I said to myself. (Thirty years later, George M. Gendron, at the time the editor of *Inc.* magazine, wrote in a testimonial for one of my books, "Just about everything I know about managing and leading an organization I learned from two men: Peter Drucker and Ichak

Adizes." Have I made it yet? Not quite. To date, he has been awarded three more honorary doctorates than I have.)

Drucker or no Drucker, I knew right away that NYU was not for me. I reached out to Bill Newman, my professor of management at Columbia, and the next thing I knew, I was admitted to Columbia's PhD program. Another helping hand, another second chance. This was America, a country rich and open enough to offer second chances if you had enough passion and drive to persevere.

With a two-hour cafeteria shift at the International House that earned me free meals and the money I received from a fellowship, it was enough to keep me afloat. Still, I wanted more. I found a job as a night guard at the purchasing office of the Israeli Ministry of Defense in New York. The pay was good, and there were no imminent threats at the time, so it was easy. Every other weekend, from Friday evening until Monday morning, I would lock up the building, with me inside. Food was delivered to my door. Three nights during the week, I would arrive at the office at 5:30 p.m., secure the doors, and study for as long as I could stay awake. On my weekends off, I would play my accordion for the Young Judea youth movement in Brooklyn. During the week, I would play for Israeli folk dancing classes or at the Israeli restaurant. It was work or study, and nothing else.

Who knew when the money would stop? I had settled into my lifelong pattern of putting work first, pleasure last. It took me half a century to discover that the habit, among other things, was a way of avoiding the difficult and perilous challenges of cultivating intimacy. I did not see it at the time. I was behaving like a typical survivor and continued to do so for most of my life—this need to keep proving myself no matter how well off I become.

I hadn't yet decided on a subject for my thesis when Vlastimir Matejic, the director of the Institute for Executive Training and Development of the Yugoslav Federation, arrived on campus to investigate what Columbia University was teaching in the field of management.

I speak Serbian and was asked to show him around campus. He told me that in 1948, Tito had split from the Soviet orbit and Yugoslavia had developed a new system of management called industrial democracy, or self-management, which was neither the Soviet Union central planning system nor the Western market-driven capitalist system. It was a totally new third system. At Columbia, very little was known about the subject, and in a matter of days it was decided: I would go to Yugoslavia to research and write my doctoral dissertation on how this third system worked, and he would help pave my way.

I flew to Munich and bought a secondhand Volkswagen Beetle with my life savings. Crossing from Austria into Yugoslavia, I turned on the radio. The sound of the Serbian language and songs from my childhood unleashed a flood of feelings. I remembered how much I loved Yugoslav music. My family used to sing those Serbian, Macedonian, and Dalmatian songs almost every Friday night after dinner, and we would dance the

Every time I'm in that part of the world, I'm reminded of how much I love Yugoslavian music. Belgrade, 2007.

kolo, a circle dance. Whenever I am asked where I am from, I always say Yugoslavia, of which Macedonia was only a part.

I arrived in Belgrade and went to my mother's cousin Mara. She, her husband, and their two daughters lived in a tiny apartment. In Israel or the States, the size of the space would be unacceptable, even in a student dormitory, but for them, it was home, and they found a corner for me to sleep in.

The first thing I did was visit my grandfather's home, where we had lived after the war. The same black iron gate that I remembered as huge now seemed very small. I slowly opened it and wandered into the courtyard. Here is where my grandfather sat putting on the tefillin. Here is where my mother used to hang the laundry to dry. Nothing had changed. At the end of the terrace, some people were sweeping the ground. They directed their eyes my way, a warning without words.

"Sorry," I said, almost in a whisper. "I used to live here."

My grandfather's shop, which my father had turned into a shoe store, had been turned into a women's clothing boutique. Above the entrance, the Kalderon family coat of arms remained. I did not want to leave, but it was not my house anymore. Time to go. But every time I travel to Belgrade, I find myself making a special journey—a pilgrimage of sorts—to that dilapidated old house with the store in front.

Next, I retraced the steps I had taken as a child to Cira's home—he was the bully who later became my close friend. The past guided me. Suddenly, I was in front of a familiar house. Would he still live there? Would I find him? We hadn't spoken in twenty years. My heart was beating fast. I climbed the stairs to the second floor. It should be the first door on the left. I hoped that whoever lived there now would know who or where Cira was.

I knocked, and a tall bald man opened the door. He looked at me, puzzled for an instant, and then—"Isak!" he shouted with delight.

We hugged for a long time. He invited me in, and we drank shlivovitz, the Serbian plum brandy. We talked and talked and interrupted each other with laughter. I learned that the boy who had bullied me for being Jewish was now a judge and had married a Jewish girl from Bosnia.

Little did I know that I would lose my childhood friend during the NATO bombing of Serbia. Cira had a heart attack and died.

Yugoslavia was still very much a Communist country in 1966, and suspicious of anyone coming from the United States, so it was not simple to conduct research. Reading the newspaper, I learned that the government had imprisoned the director of a marketing research firm who reported how well different retail stores were doing. The Communist government considered it espionage. Even more troubling was that an American doctoral student had been deported. His research was considered inappropriate, and he was labeled a CIA operative. I wondered what would become of me.

It was with some trepidation that I got in touch with Vlastimir Matejic, but his warm welcome allowed me to put my fears aside. As promised, he introduced me to two companies: the Belgrade Cotton Plant and the Belgrade Wool Plant. I studied them, trying to identify the similarities and differences between their management styles. I was permitted to attend all meetings, read minutes of those I could not attend, and interviewed the workers.

It was a field study par excellence. From morning until midnight, I went to the workers' council meetings, interviewing whoever would talk to me. I had not lost the language; even the slang and working-class colloquialisms were familiar to me. I knew the songs they sang and identified with the culture. The men and women I met and interviewed felt comfortable with me and were proud to tell me how their system worked.

In the Yugoslav self-management system, the companies were managed by the workers, for the workers. The workers chose their corporate leaders, set their own wages, and even determined which products would be sold. It was a true workplace democracy. They applied the New England town hall–style democracy to all organizations in the country. A local school's council, for example, would be composed of elected parent, teacher, and student representatives. The principal would be elected by the council and obligated to follow its decisions. Every city block had its own council of residents responsible for the block's cleanliness and for the care of the poor people who lived on that block. It was self-management, literally.

Workers were provided buses and brought in from villages to work in the textile plants. They were peasants. They had no business education whatsoever, but the law required that they make business decisions, approve business plans submitted to them by management, and decide their income.

To my surprise, these peasants made excellent decisions. Here I was, an MBA degree holder and a doctoral candidate, and they were performing as well as—or even better than—I would have if the authority had been placed in my hands. Why? They had common sense. They participated in decision making with fervor. Their livelihood depended on the decisions they made. They were empowered to make decisions, and they took full responsibility for the outcomes. It all seemed so simple, though, of course, it was not.

The problem was that there were no decision-making protocols. They would argue late into the night, constantly interrupting one another. It was exhausting. Some, it should be said, hated the system. They did not want to participate and would rather have someone else decide for them and then complain about the decisions made.

Self-management diverged in one other major way from what I had previously studied: property ownership. In the Soviet Union, all productive assets—land, machines, buildings—were owned by the state. They were nationalized. In America, where capitalism prevails, assets are privately owned. But in Yugoslavia, assets were neither state-owned nor privately owned. They were "socially owned." The best way to explain this idea is by analogy. Who owns air? Who owns the open seas? No one, right? We all have to take care of them because we all own them.

It was during my doctoral research that I developed the concept that would become a cornerstone for the organizational therapy I would go on to develop. I called it CAPI,[2] for "coalesced authority, power, and influence." It predicts whether a decision made on change would be implemented. When three entities—the collegium (the executive management committee), the workers' council, and the Communist Party cell—all agreed on a decision, no one could stop it from being implemented. It would be carried out. This was not a coincidence. There was a principle at work here; if those who were authorized to decide (the workers' council) worked in consensus with those who had the expertise to suggest the decision (the executive committee) and with those who had the power to keep the decision from being implemented (the Communist Party), implementation was assured.

---

2 Ichak Adizes, *Mastering Change: Introduction to Organizational Therapy* (Santa Barbara, CA: Adizes Institute Publications, 2016).

Returning home for a visit where love is. Could I feel it?
My mother and my sister in Israel, 1967.

HYPNOTIZED

While doing my PhD fieldwork in Yugoslavia, I decided on the spur of the moment to visit my parents and friends in Israel. It was not far from Yugoslavia, and I had not been back since leaving for America with the Experiment in International Living nearly three years before. My mother and sister greeted me at the airport with bunches of flowers in their hands, the celebration I had longed for and needed. When we got home, my father was strangely subdued. He had been struggling with cancer, and that had weakened him. Other than my father's health it was like nothing had changed, like I had never left.

While in Israel, I received a letter from Eliza, who had contacted Columbia University, which had given her my whereabouts in Yugoslavia. My cousins forwarded her note to me in Israel. My heart skipped a beat when I read that she and her friend from Harvard would be driving from Greece to Italy via Yugoslavia. Did I want to join them?

"Yes!" I replied immediately and changed my plans to drive with them from Athens rather than fly straight to Belgrade.

But when I arrived at their bed-and-breakfast to meet up for the journey, it wasn't Eliza who stopped me in my tracks, but the beautiful young woman next to her at the breakfast table. She was blonde, green-eyed, and intense looking. Her name was Beth. She was Jewish and a soon-to-be graduate of Harvard Medical School.

I believe that at that instant I would have done anything—renounced my religion, my parents, my country, left school to become a mail carrier—if she had asked. It was a coup de foudre. I do not know if I fell in love at that moment, but I do know I lost my head. I felt as though somehow time and space had colluded to hypnotize me. As I started to speak—to say hello, to say something, anything that didn't sound stupid—I realized that I was having difficulty swallowing. I felt that someone had grabbed me by the throat and was holding tight.

From then on, I only had eyes for Beth. I drove the car and arranged it so that she sat next to me as we cruised along the small roads through the mountains of Montenegro, talking nonstop. At times, the sound of Eliza crying in the backseat would drift forward. I assumed she was crying because she still had feelings for me, but, heartlessly, I did nothing about it. I was not proud of my behavior, but I seemed unable to alter it.

We stopped in Dubrovnik, the medieval city on the coast of Croatia surrounded by massive walls four hundred fifty years in the making. Beth and I wandered the narrow streets. We reached a plaza alive with music from restaurants that were once ancient villas. A Dalmatian song was playing: "Where Palms Flap Their Branches."[3]

For the first time ever, I felt as if I was awash with energy I did not recognize. Was my heart finally opening to love and be loved? My whole body united with something bigger than myself; it was like joining a force of energy and disappearing into it. It was a feeling I had never had before. I admit that even now, fifty years later, when I hear this song, I remember that feeling. When she accepted my advances, I felt like a peasant who had been rewarded with a kiss from a princess.

---

3 Dubrovacki Trubaduri, "Dok Palme Njisu Grane," https://www.youtube.com/watch?v=HcNC5RW34IA.

When I finished my fieldwork in Belgrade, I drove my Beetle across Europe to Holland and put it on a ship for the United States. I rented a flat in Boston a few blocks from Beth's. I was in love or possibly just lovesick. Either way, I knew that I wanted to live as close to her as possible.

Truth to be told, I was not myself with Beth. When she took me to Scarsdale, New York, to meet her family, I purchased a pipe for the occasion although I did not smoke. Her parents were sophisticated people, and I wanted to impress them. I watched her mother's eyelids flutter with contempt as I tried to pack the pipe and tobacco spilled on the floor. Beth's grandmother was there, too, and after the first course I asked her for a spoon, as I would have done if it was my home, since she was the matriarch of the family. The car ride home was hell: "You asked *my grandmother* to bring you a fucking spoon?" Beth screamed. Later, her mother told her, "Watch who you marry; you don't want to be embarrassed for the rest of your life."

This wasn't our only problem. She was at medical school and interning nonstop at the hospital. I was miserable, timid. I did not know what to say or how or when to say it. I was tense, stressed, and scared of losing her.

Then I did. One day, she told me it was over. I was devastated. She was firm. She had no feelings for me. And we had a witness, Eliza, who stared at me through the whole episode with those big brown eyes of hers. I stood frozen in the doorway. She looked so sad. I thought she was feeling sorry for me or perhaps thinking that I should have stayed with her.

I felt guilty and ashamed of how I treated Eliza. I always wished I had behaved differently and not humiliated her. She was such a wonderful woman and a true friend. How could I have repaid her with such indifference? I decided that if I could, someday, I would like to find her and apologize.

Forty-five years later, I did. A friend who inquired with the Harvard Medical School had told me that she practiced medicine in New York, and I was in New York at the time, visiting. It was Yom Kippur, the day of atonement, the day of asking forgiveness. I searched for Eliza's phone number and found it. She still used her maiden name as her middle name.

It took me two hours to gather the courage to call her. I must apologize, I thought. I have felt guilty for far too long. Years of therapy had taught me to explore my feelings and express them without fear.

So I called. She was not in. I was relieved and left a message. "This is Yitz Adiges," I said, pronouncing my name the way I had when we were together. "It is Yom Kippur, and I am calling to ask your forgiveness."

An hour later, she returned my call. Of course, she remembered me, but she did not remember anything I had done that called for forgiveness.

"Don't you remember? I ignored you on the trip we took through Yugoslavia forty-five years ago. I behaved so poorly, and you were depressed because I paid attention only to Beth."

"I remember I was depressed, but not because of you. I missed Scott, the love of my life, who I left behind to make the trip."

"But I was a real asshole when I was dating Beth. Remember when she broke up with me? You looked so sad."

"Yes, I was sad. At that time, Scott had just broken up with me, and I felt really lost and depressed."

On my end, silence. How much of what we feel, I wondered, is a response not to reality, but to the version of reality we have constructed in our heads?

IS THAT ALL THERE IS?

Before I departed for Yugoslavia to start my field research, I had interviewed for positions at several universities. Word came back to me, rejection letter after rejection letter. No one would take me. I looked outside of academia and applied to McKinsey & Company and the Boston Consulting Group. I tried every organization that was interviewing on the Columbia campus. Still nothing. A certain panic began to set in at the thought of being penniless again.

Should I return to Israel to live at home while I completed my dissertation? Many friends had done just that, and none of them ever wrote their dissertations; none completed their degrees. I was determined that would not happen to me.

It was at that moment of desperation and doubt that I received a telegram from the University of California, Los Angeles. UCLA was offering me a position as an acting assistant professor at the Graduate School of Business Administration (today called the Anderson School of Management). I began jumping with excitement. I read and reread the telegram. Yes, it was real. I would be able to teach while I wrote my dissertation.

In the late sixties, UCLA's business school was ranked among the top ten in the nation. Working there was a dream I did not even dare to visualize. But why had they offered me the position? I had not even applied.

It turned out that I had been recommended by the chair of my doctoral committee at Columbia, Bill Newman, who had also mentored Barry Richman, the department head of the Graduate School of Management at UCLA. That's the way the academic world recruits: by word of mouth, within circles of trust. When Barry and I later became friends, he showed me the letter that convinced him to hire me. Professor Newman had written that he had one student who was either going to make it big or fail utterly. On the one hand, he emphasized, I was very creative, which was a precondition for success. But, he said, I aimed too wide and didn't focus well, which could mean failure academically. However, it was entirely possible that I could be the next Max Weber. With that, UCLA took the risk.

When I discovered that he had compared me to Max Weber, the founder of the field of sociology, my head swam. There was no higher praise that I could imagine. Then profound anxiety settled in. I was just beginning my career, but I was expected to live up to the potential that the people I admired had forecast for me. "There is no bigger burden than unfulfilled potential," one of my clients later told me. I still feel this burden today.

When the affair with Beth ended, there was nothing left for me in Boston, so I packed my possessions in the trunk of my Beetle and headed across the country for Los Angeles. My thoughts swung high and low, from my broken heart to my hopes for a fresh start teaching at UCLA.

I arrived in Los Angeles at night, exhausted, and promptly fell asleep in a motel. When I awoke, all I could see outside my window was palm trees and sunshine. After frozen Belgrade, I thought I had landed in heaven.

When I surrendered my Yugoslav license plates, the man handling the registration at the Auto Club asked me if they could hang it in their office. Those Communist license plates with the big red star were the first they had seen that had crossed the United States from ocean to ocean.

I was twenty-nine years old and, after what seemed to be a lifetime of struggle, I felt that I had arrived. I went to a department store and bought a pair of dress pants and the first jacket I had ever owned. I was going to attend faculty meetings and stand in front of a class; I was soon to be an acting assistant professor, and I wanted to look presentable. I also found a place to live, a studio apartment. I did not even have to play my accordion to pay the rent.

When I arrived at UCLA, the secretary of the department was friendly, helpful, and—dare I say it?—respectful.

"Oh," she said, almost as an afterthought, "Here's your green card." In the blink of an eye, I was granted the ability to work in the United States legally. While I was studying at Columbia, I always felt that I might be just one step ahead of the immigration authorities, who would discover I was playing the accordion in a restaurant for tips and throw me out of the country. It was an irrational fear, but at the time I was always looking over my shoulder—perhaps, a remnant of the years I had spent living in a Communist country.

The future I had dreamed of was within reach, but when my thirtieth birthday came around, there was no one to celebrate with. I was earning a decent salary, but I knew no one. Not my family, my friends, or anyone who knew where I came from. Not the Yugoslav workers who not only had been part of my field research but were my comrades around the clock. All at once, my sole companions were my typewriter, my notes, and the library.

I drove to Santa Monica beach, looked out at the ocean, and felt sorry for myself. When I had no money, when I faced constant hunger and deprivation, I did not have the time or energy to pity myself. I had to concentrate all of my faculties on surviving. Now, free from survival worries, I suddenly had time to focus on how I felt, and I felt miserable.

Maybe if I returned to Israel, I would feel better. I decided that when I finished my dissertation, I would leave UCLA and return to Israel. What I had to learn, and did not learn at the time, is that wherever you go, there you are. I could not run away from myself. I had a problem. Yes, I was lonely, but I also felt that I was not loved, that I did not deserve to be loved, that I had not yet earned the right to be loved.

I was spending all of my energy in my brain, and when there was nothing to do and my brain was free from work, that was when I would notice my misery. My heart would ache. Apparently, I was not alone. Research has found high levels of depression among Holocaust survivors, even though they should have celebrated that they survived. The findings reveal that most of them felt survivor's guilt or were overcome by longing for their loved ones. Was this my case? I do not know. But I did know that I was not a happy traveler on the road of life.

I threw myself into my dissertation, mailing each chapter to Professor Newman at Columbia as soon as I had finished writing and endlessly rewriting it. After about twenty chapters, I received a letter: "That's enough! What we've got here is enough for a PhD thesis!"

If Professor Newman hadn't stopped me, I would probably still be writing that thesis today. He had been there for me all along. I remember one critical time when I almost blew my budding career, and he saved me. I was preparing for the oral exam I had to pass before I could begin writing my doctoral thesis. The more I studied for that exam, the more I realized how much more there was to know. I was afraid that I would be unable to answer some simple question and would humiliate myself.

A couple of days before the scheduled date, I asked Professor Newman to postpone the exam because I wasn't prepared. I was even thinking about quitting the doctoral program just to avoid taking it.

He looked at me for a minute, then asked me if I had a girlfriend. I didn't reply. How could I think about girlfriends when I couldn't even deal with this exam? He told me to go to the first hotel I could find and have a good time, and he would see me on Monday for the exam. He just about threw me out of his office.

I walked home along Riverside Park in tears, headed for my little cubicle of a room at the International House, where I tossed and turned all weekend. That's it, I said to myself. Everyone will know the truth. I am a fake. I know nothing. I had played all of my cards and fooled everyone, and the moment of truth had arrived.

When I turned up for the exam, all my anxiety magically disappeared. I found myself answering the questions put forward by the examining committee with a level of knowledge and certainty I had not imagined I possessed. I got the highest grade possible and was advanced to candidacy.

What I learned from that experience was that the best students are those who know how much they do not know. Once a journalist asked me in an interview, "Now that you have achieved so much in your career, what is your wish for the coming year?" I explained that I wanted to be able to say that a concept I currently thought and preached was actually wrong. He looked puzzled by my answer. "In other words," I explained to him, "I want to advance and learn something new about the subject I already know well. I am never content with what I think I know."

I read somewhere the following: Wise people who think they are ignorant are truly wise; ignorant people who consider themselves wise are truly ignorant.

One experience made this point vividly for me. The day I received my doctoral degree, I walked around the business school corridors, holding my new diploma conspicuously in my hand. I was feeling very accomplished indeed when a group of students who had just finished taking their qualifying exam began to pour out of a classroom. They were about two years behind me in the doctoral program. I asked one of them if I could see the exam and realized, to my embarrassment, that I would have failed it. The very day I was awarded my doctoral degree, I was already obsolete.

I knew then that the devil was right behind me. I could never stop. I had to be in motion, moving ahead, learning something new, working just a little harder, just a little longer. To never stop asking questions and to never cease challenging my own convictions.

Even today, after writing many books and lecturing in over fifty countries, I feel ignorant. There is so much more to learn, so much more to know, and so much more to tell. There is no light at the end of the tunnel. There is no end. Instead, I have had to learn to enjoy being in the tunnel itself.

By the late sixties, industrial democracy had become very much in vogue among left-leaning politicians and well-meaning liberal students and faculty, especially in the fields of sociology and political science. Columbia recognized my thesis as distinguished and published it as a book titled *Industrial Democracy: Yugoslav Style.*[4]

Suddenly, my writing and ideas were branching out into fields that stretched far beyond management and business schools. I was invited to become a member of the International Academy of Sociology, although I had never even taken a course in sociology. I also became a member of the Academy of Political Science.

The Swedish government invited me to speak before parliament, together with Olof Palme, who later became prime minister. At the time, the county was exploring autonomous working teams and the field of industrial democracy. Volvo asked me to give a lecture to its top management. I was asked to consult and lecture in Peru, where the country's leaders were attempting to establish industrial communities. I was invited to Chile just as Salvador Allende was elected to power. I was invited to

---

4 Ichak Adizes, *Industrial Democracy: Yugoslav Style* (New York: Free Press, 1971). Reprinted by Adizes Institute Publications, 2006.

Japan, where my dissertation was translated and published in Japanese, and to Mexico, where it was translated into Spanish.

I was even recognized by the Yugoslavs as an authority on the subject. I considered this the real success: those who knew best how the system worked thought that I had something of value to say. I corresponded with President Tito's deputy, Edvard Kardelj, who was considered the theoretician and designer behind the self-management system. Without planning, I had made an international multidisciplinary career out of industrial democracy. I should have further capitalized on my budding fame. Instead, I found a new field to explore.

BEING FIRST

I had been an acting assistant professor at UCLA for less than a year when Charles Mark reappeared in my life. I'd first met him when I was living with the Cortinovis family in St. Louis. He had been the director of one of the city's leading arts organizations, and he welcomed the Experiment fellows. During the month I lived in the city we became friendly, spent many evenings drinking beer on his porch, debating what life was all about.

By the time we reconnected in Los Angeles, Charles had become a director at the newly formed National Endowment for the Arts in Washington, D.C. He was staying at the Biltmore Hotel in downtown Los Angeles. Would I stop by to say hello? I raced downtown, and when I arrived, he was still in his pajamas.

He told me his role was to approve and award money to states arts organizations across the country. He had come to California to assess which arts institutions and projects in the state deserved funding.

"You've got it easy, Charles," I told him. "All you have to do is dish out money!"

"That's not true. Giving out money is difficult."

"Why?" I asked, surprised.

"The people running cultural organizations don't know how to put together a budget, much less how to use one."

I couldn't believe they didn't know the practice of managing their organizations.

"Believe it," he reassured me. The typical course of events went like this: An opera singer who had lost her voice or a dancer who had become too old to perform became the director of their performing arts company. Only an artist, it was believed, could run an arts company. They understood the intricacies of the art and were accepted by their fellow artists, but they were often unaware of what was involved in the business side of running an arts organization.

Alright, I thought. I knew management theory. Now I had discovered a field with unresolved problems I could use my knowledge to address. Here is something for me to take on.

"Let's start a program to teach arts management at UCLA," I suggested. The idea just popped out.

Charles demurred. It would not be easy, there would be too much opposition. "Arts organizations do not believe arts administration can be taught," he explained. "We need first to convince them that it should be done."

"But it needs to be done, and we should be the ones to do it." I was too excited to abandon the proposition.

He became pensive. Without knowledge of management, many arts organizations were already losing ground. Symphonic orchestras, for example, were folding left and right. Opera houses were in deep financial trouble, and most of the museums, Charles laughed, had reluctantly begun to admit wealthy Jewish benefactors to their boards of directors in order to survive. Necessity was calling for a change.

His enthusiasm began to catch up with mine. "What we should do first is bring together all the leading arts administrators to discuss whether such a program is desirable, and if so, how to go about creating it." He stressed the need to bring them on board rather than hand them a new blueprint that lacked their voice or signature.

Over the following year, with five thousand dollars from the National Endowment of the Arts, I organized two conferences: one at UCLA and the other at Lincoln Center in New York. With Charles, the government's moneyman, in my corner, everyone would accept the invitation. The leaders of philharmonic orchestras in New York and Los Angeles, the head of the Los Angeles Music Center, representatives of the New York City Ballet, the directors of the Rockefeller Foundation and Ford Foundation, and the heads of LACMA and MoMA all came. It was a gathering of arts royalty, and I, a lowly acting assistant professor, was hosting them all.

This fact was not lost on my academic colleagues. Those who were friends warned me that organizing conferences would not get me tenure. "You should sit in the library and do research. Stop running around," they said, but organizing something new, bold, got my blood pumping again. I was past saving.

But the deans of the School of Business and College of Fine Arts didn't exactly complain about having the leaders of the country's most prestigious arts organizations meet on their doorstep. Newspapers from *The New York Times* to *The Christian Science Monitor* to the *Los Angeles Times* covered the event. Never before had directors of museums, ballets, national opera companies, and symphonic orchestras come together like this.[5]

The conferences were a good start, but in order to start a new program, we first needed to identify the unique managerial problems performing arts organizations faced. With a five thousand dollar grant from the Ford Foundation, I set out across the country to interview the administrators of the leading arts organizations in the country.

---

5 Ichak Adizes, "Establishing a Program for Arts Administration," *Management in the Arts Research Publication Series,* no. 1 (working paper, University of California, Los Angeles, 1969). Available from the Adizes Institute.

One of my first meetings was with Lincoln Kirstein, who, with Georges Balanchine, founded the New York City Ballet. He was a tall, self-possessed man but modest. He was the product of a Harvard education and a lifetime spent using his wealth to acquire knowledge. He did not have to work for a living, so he had made culture in all its forms his life's work. Balanchine had been the creative master of ballet in America, but without Kirstein, there would be no Balanchine in America, no New York City Ballet.

"How do you motivate dancers?" I asked him.

"You step on their toes just before they go on stage. Hurt, they want to perform their best," he said, without a hint of a smile. I was shocked by his response. Nowhere in all the books on motivation I had read for my classes was a solution like this presented.

He was pulling my leg, I thought, but years later, I listened to an interview with the leading Russian gymnastics coach. When asked how he motivated his gymnasts, the coach replied, "I tell them they are terrible and cannot perform. I humiliate them. Hurt, they try to prove me wrong." Maybe Kirstein was not joking after all.

Was it a message for me, too? Was I working like a lunatic trying to prove wrong all those who had humiliated me?

In my interview with the music director and conductor of the Seattle Philharmonic Orchestra, I learned why he objected to summer pops orchestras like the Boston Pops, which played in parks and beer halls.

"You do not train a violinist to play Paganini during the winter season and then, when summer arrives, ask him to play Sousa. He will have difficulty going back to playing Paganini. At least, he will have difficulty playing him well," he claimed.

I understood then that the most difficult and inflexible components of an organization were its people. The more professional they were, the less flexible their behavior. That insight served me well in my consulting years later.

Glynn Ross of the Seattle Opera became my model of an arts administrator. He was a "social animator," as the French novelist and cultural leader André Malraux described arts leaders. Ross took a city that conductor Eugene Ormandy called "the cultural dustbin of America" and brought opera to its citizens, turning Seattle into a world-renowned opera center.[6]

I followed my field study by writing a textbook on arts management. My fellow Yugoslavs printed a Serbian language edition, but it was never published in English. I was told there was not a big enough market. Indeed, market forces can be as oppressive as political censorship.[7]

And that is what is happening today. The media follows the market to get the maximum number of eyeballs, which brings maximum revenues. The more sensational the material, the better. The result: fake news.

I knew that starting a brand-new master's degree program in a university, in a nonexistent field of knowledge, would take a great deal of skill. Academicians are very conservative and not readily prone to innovation. I would need to use all of my knowledge of management to carry this out. Using the model of coalesced authority, power, and influence I developed in Yugoslavia, I recruited a handful of professors from both the business school and the College of Fine Arts, finding the people who brought complementary backgrounds and skill sets to the table.

---

6 Ichak Adizes, "Seattle Opera Association," in W. Glueck, ed., *Business Policy: Strategy Formation and Management Action,* 2nd ed. (New York: McGraw-Hill, 1976), pp. 610–634; Ichak Adizes, "The Cost of Being an Artist: An Argument for the Public Support of the Arts," *California Management Review* (summer 1975); Ichak Adizes and Will McWhinney, "Arts, Society and Administration," *Arts and Society* (1973); Ichak Adizes, "Administering for the Arts: Introduction and Overview," *California Management Review* (winter 1972); Ichak Adizes, "Boards of Directors in the Performing Arts: A Managerial Analysis," *California Management Review* (winter 1972).

7 Ichak Adizes, "Menadžment za Kulturu," 2nd rev. ed (Adizes Southeast Europe, 2006), adizesbooks.com.

I reached out to each person who would have to be involved in the decision-making process, one by one, level by level, until I had included everyone necessary to approve the program. No one was excluded. And I "bribed" them with autographed posters from arts organizations I visited and with tickets to Music Center performances. I spent nights and long dinners talking and mobilizing faculty around the idea that training and developing social entrepreneurs via the arts is necessary in light of the acceleration of societal change.

Building the program took a year, which for universities is record time. I had convinced the deans of the business school and the College of Fine Arts to start a joint master's program to train arts administrators. It was the first program of its kind in America and, indeed, the world.

For six months after my tour of the United States' leading arts organizations, we assembled class descriptions, including courses in marketing, finance, and accounting from the School of Business, as well as courses like theater production from the College of Fine Arts. Voilà! The program was approved, but the courses were assembled from existing courses, and we needed new ones particular to this new field. And then the question was who was going to teach them when so little was known about the field?

At first, only one class in the program was brand new: it was a course I cotaught with Charles called arts management. I would teach management theory, and Charles would discuss how it applied or did not apply to arts organizations. An academic and a practitioner from the field coteaching—what could be better? I knew management, and he knew the reality that underlay the performing arts. It was hilarious. Since we did not always agree, most of our time in class was spent debating each other, with the students watching. We were all learning.

But what about other teachers?

The recording mogul and entrepreneur David Geffen was excited by the program and offered to teach a class on the music industry for one dollar a year.

"Wonderful," I said. But the politics of academia began to assert themselves: David Geffen had no academic background—how could he teach at UCLA? The deans rejected him, and they dismissed Charles after our first course concluded. He also had no PhD.

The academic establishment ignored the fact that the field was completely new and needed people with experience more than it needed people with degrees. Anyway, there were no people with degrees in the field because the field did not exist yet.

Managing performing arts was the second theoretical earthquake that shook my knowledge and convictions about management. It challenged the theories I learned at school. One cannot manage artists as though they are coal miners. The goals are different, as are the financing and the culture. Therefore, leadership styles have to be different, too. We had to redefine the organizations' end goals. What is the goal of an opera? Of a ballet? Of any fine arts organization? How do you structure things to reach that goal? How do you manage creative people? Again, my knowledge of management theory and practice did not give me a satisfactory answer. I had to create new answers, and I dared to do so. Artists were coming to see me. The manager of the Vienna State Opera visited. He wanted to spend time with me, not with members of the music department.

I already knew from my studies of industrial democracy that there is no ideal executive who can perform all the roles necessary to make an organization effective and efficient in the short and long term. While studying performing arts organizations, I realized what to do about it. The administrative director of the New York City Opera, Julius Rudel, was the man who gave me the idea. He explained how he and Rudolph Bing, the artistic director, served as two wings of the Austro-Hungarian eagle. The eagle cannot fly on one wing, he said. It needs two wings to propel itself through the air successfully, just as the opera company needs two leaders to carry out its artistic and administrative functions—a complementary team to provide collaborative leadership.

This concept feels revolutionary even today, almost fifty years later. The current fad in management is to look for an excellent leader, and I say there is no such thing. No one is perfect. Every leader must have a complementary person as a collaborator. This individual might not be recognized as a leader by the organization, but the chief executive will not perform well without such a person in the copilot's seat.

In 1974, an Australian named Alan Bond decided to challenge the US for the America's Cup sailing competition. America had never lost the Cup to a foreign country before. "Everyone believes that the Australian team's advantage is their secret keel," Bond told me. "Not so. It is your methodology."

He explained that there is always conflict between the skipper and the tactician in these twelve-meter sailboats. The tactician at the front of the boat is deciding if they should tack or not, looking at what the other boats are doing, checking the wind and other conditions. The skipper is monitoring the computer so that his sails are used optimally. The tactician might say they should tack, and the skipper might refuse because it would reduce the efficiency of the sails. A moment of hesitation is one boat-length lost in the competition.

"I spent a year testing for the best complementary team, a skipper and a tactician who trust and respect each other, so it only takes them a split second, just one look, to agree on what to do. That is thanks to your methodology for building complementary teams. And the sailors who were in training for a year, living in close quarters, had to practice respect and trust in their daily interactions. Whoever broke the rules had to wear a sign for a day saying, 'I broke the rules.' "

At Alan's invitation, I was there to watch Australia win the America's Cup that year. After their win, Alan and his boat were featured on a *Time* magazine cover with the title "The Aussies Are Coming." He sent me a signed copy with the inscription, "Thank you, Dr. Adizes."

Universities are small ponds populated by large, proud sharks: administrators and professors with substantial egos. Political life in academia tends to breed fierce battles. Opinions are legitimized by academic research, but that research is often influenced by an academic's self-serving pursuit of academic promotion, ego gratification, and dominating power struggles within the field of study. In fact, resistance to change and entrenched power are the norms, as is a certain competitive envy.

Managing the program, I had to fight on two frontiers simultaneously. I was dealing with two faculties. Jealousy soon became a major problem. Some faculty insisted on calling the program Management *of* the Arts. I fought back. It should be Management *for* the Arts and its artists. Even better, Arts Administration since the word to *administer* means *to serve.* You do not manage artists, I claimed. You serve them. In the business world, a manager brings the product that the market wants. In the arts, the administrator brings the audience that the artist wants. The orientation is different. The focus is different. The measurements of success are different. But it was like selling pork to Orthodox Jews.

Business professors resented me because I criticized their approach. We weren't selling shoes or cars here. The course on business strategy had to be adapted to a different kind of organization and a different set of participants. How do you build an annual program of operas or plays or ballets with casts and costumes and stage designs? Stage designs and costumes are too expensive for one season. Why not share them later with other opera companies? How do you establish the volunteer organization necessary to raise funds and promote the opera, the ballet, or the museum?

Arts professors considered me to be a Trojan horse that had somehow slipped inside their formidable gates. I was viewed as someone who was going to demean the arts by teaching the subject as a business. "That was what destroyed Broadway," one of them argued. "The moment we aim for profits, art is out of the room."

I was outnumbered and out-influenced. And I was only an assistant professor without tenure. One day, my dean pulled me aside and informed me that I was out. I could still teach the usual business policy and management theory classes, but Hy Fine, the head of the musician's union in New York, would be appointed the head of the program. Today, there are forty-nine master's programs in arts administration at universities across America. At UCLA, the program did not survive.

Where did I find the courage to explore unknown territories? To go to Yugoslavia and study something the West knew nothing about. To start a new field of arts administration? I have no idea, but I get excited anytime someone tells me there is a problem with no solution. It is like a red cloth in front of a bull. I will go at it, even if my career, my well-being, my life might be endangered by it.

SOMEONE WANTS ME

In a matter of just three years, I had abandoned my career in industrial democracy to become an activist in the field of arts administration, and just as arts administration began to look viable, I left for Israel. Instead of capitalizing on my success in either of those areas (which would have been the smart move), I took a leave of absence from UCLA in 1970, returned home, and discontinued my efforts in both.

I had convinced myself that Israel was where I truly belonged. It was where my parents and my sister lived. It was where my closest friends were. It was where my roots were, or at least a significant portion of them. And maybe it was where I could find a wife. But just in case I did not fit in, I had a backup plan. My plan was to build myself a home in Israel but keep my options open in the United States. To borrow the Yiddish expression, I thought I could dance at two weddings.

And I was right. Upon my return, all the old apprehensions about life in Israel came back into focus. For every one idea, there were three dissenting opinions. Those opinions were considered to be facts, reinforced by the volume at which they were spoken. I was especially bothered by people who had never visited Los Angeles but claimed that they knew what Los Angeles was all about because of something they had read.

I was asked to deliver a keynote speech at a celebration of the department of business administration at Hebrew University Jerusalem, where I was once a student, and not a good one, either. Preparing for the event was stressful for me. I had to shine. My former professors were going to be in the front row. It felt like taking oral exams all over again, but this time with the whole faculty watching and ready to pounce. I did not sleep the night before; I stayed up rehearsing every word I would say.

Climbing up to the podium to speak, I felt like I was being led to the guillotine. It wasn't until the applause at the end of the lecture that I began to breathe. It was a real applause, not done out of politeness. Apparently, I did well.

In the audience, I could see a friend of mine from high school—a good friend—who came up to greet me afterward.

"Yitz!" he said, using my high school nickname. "I'm sorry to admit it, but I really enjoyed your lecture."

He had been looking for flaws and points to criticize and only reluctantly acknowledged that he had been bested. My lecture had been that good. He was *sorry to admit* that I had done well. Only in Israel!

I understood, and not for the first time, that it is difficult for many Israelis to acknowledge pleasure, to offer a laudatory word. They are always looking for the fault, for the hole in the argument. It is a Talmudic practice honed over thousands of years. They are judgmental of everything.

The hypercritical culture makes Israelis very smart and competitive. You have to be on your toes constantly as others are seeking to catch you in a mistake. It makes you work hard. It sharpens your mind. You have to excel, nonstop. It is a highly stressful environment, terrific training for learning and growing—and terrific for heart attacks, too.

When the time came, I returned to UCLA as planned by the rotation. Still, I felt the pull of family, and, wary but determined to give it another try, I returned to Israel in 1972, as a visiting professor at Tel Aviv University, after building myself a home there and furnishing it. I bought a car, which is a big expense in Israel, as I was still hoping I would be able to stay permanently. But, by the year's end, it was clear that I would not. The faculty declined to grant me tenure. I was being considered for tenure at UCLA, so I could easily go back. But I had another reason to return to California: I had met someone who would eventually become my wife.

I met her through Rafi, a friend from my high school days who had become the personal physician of Shimon Peres, the president of Israel. Like me, he had been a student leader and volunteered to lead the German student group during the summer of 1959, even though his father had been murdered in Auschwitz. During that summer of touring with the German high school students, we became very, very close friends.

Rafi invited me to celebrate his birthday with him, suggesting we take my car and spend the day driving to Jericho. He was going to bring along Yael, his former girlfriend, and he suggested I bring a friend, too.

I asked someone I hardly knew to join me. She and I sat in the front as I drove. Rafi and his former girlfriend were in the backseat, talking and giggling. She was cute and petite, with a small nose and green eyes. Her hair was tied behind her head in a ponytail. She had an easy laugh that was infectious. I could not stop watching her in the rearview mirror.

At one of the stops, I took Rafi aside and asked him what was the story with Yael? Why was she a "former" girlfriend?

Well, he told me, he was seriously involved with Shimon Peres's daughter Tzvia now. (Within a year, Rafi and Tzvia were married.)

So I could make a pass at her?

"Sure," he encouraged me, laughing. "Be my guest."

Yael was a student at Hebrew University. But I was not interested in her only because she was attractive and intelligent—she was also from a family that had settled in Israel as pioneers and started one of the country's first kibbutzim. They were the salt of the Israeli earth and just the kind of people I wanted to belong to.

She was interested in me, too. I could tell from the way she met my eyes when she saw me staring at her, from the way she talked with Rafi but made sure that I was part of the conversation. When the day was over, we decided to see each other again the next time I was in Jerusalem.

Yael wanted to study for her doctorate in America. Since UCLA was at least considering me for tenure, she could do her doctoral studies at UCLA and she wouldn't be alone. She came, and we moved into an apartment together. After a year, we got married, and within a few years, we became the parents of two sons: Topaz and Shoham, which means "onyx" in Hebrew. Both boys were named for gemstones in honor of my mother, whose name means "diamond."

We were both very busy and not spending much time together, almost like roommates who came and went on our own schedules. Yael was a

My sons Topaz and Shoham as young boys at home in Los Angeles. They were both named for gemstones in honor of my mother, whose name means diamond.

very dedicated student and worked day and night on her studies. A live-in maid took care of the house and the family. When I wasn't on campus, preparing course material, or grading papers, I was building my consulting business. I was a one-man band, working over the phone across a dozen time zones from our kitchen table, traveling to meet and work with those clients, or refining reports late into the night. Here I was, finally, with a family to call my own, and I could barely slow down enough to enjoy the ride.

WOULD I MAKE IT?

I bought my first house in Los Angeles from the ex-wife of Sanford Rothenberg, a neurosurgeon who divorced her to marry Faye Wray, the actress from *King Kong*. The house was at the entrance to Mandeville Canyon, where many movie actors had their homes. Not a poor professor's neighborhood. Shirley Temple grew up one street over.

The house had a room for each child and a space I converted into an office. Next to the kitchen we built a room for the live-in maid. To me, it was a villa; in Israel or Serbia it would have been considered a mansion. It had a pool. And a garage. And a yard. The house cost $150,000—for me at the time, a scary fortune. How would I manage on an assistant professor's salary, even with the consulting work I was doing on the side? A friend of mine at UCLA calmed me down, "Ichak, you're at the beginning of your life, not the end. You will make it."

In six years, I had gone from starving graduate student to lecturing around the world, advising companies from Northrop to Equifax, and being considered for tenure at one of the top business schools in the country. But would I make it? After all, I had strayed from the carefully marked university path of publish or perish.

I had published, but mostly in Yugoslavia, since so much of my research focused on the Yugoslav system of self-management. I had started and run a new program in arts administration, but administrative leadership didn't count toward tenure. If anything, my entrepreneurial approach had worked against me, breeding animosity among my colleagues. My speaking engagements got me, and therefore the university, attention in the media; but this only intensified the political will against me from others within the business school, as did my growing list of private clients. So it was no surprise that when the staffing committee met, it voted seven-to-one against awarding me tenure. I had a year to finish up my classes and move on.

In American academic circles, being denied tenure is considered to be a polite rejection—embarrassing but not disgraceful. Those rejected were expected to accept the decision and fade off into the sunset. But I did not. I could not. What was I going to do, leave America in disgrace? Tel Aviv University had already denied me tenure. Would I move to Belgrade and teach there? It was one thing to be a Tito Pioneer as a nine-year-old, but it was quite another to live under a Communist dictatorship as a man almost forty years of age, no matter how well-known an academic figure I might be there. Not to mention, there was no chance of my wife following me. She was still in the doctoral program at UCLA, and even if that wasn't the case, she and the children would not be coming with me to Yugoslavia. She did not speak the language. She had no affinity for that country, and the economic conditions were far from acceptable to her. We had to stay in Los Angeles. In an act of sheer chutzpah, I asked to meet with the staffing committee to argue my case. The committee was taken aback—*no one* had ever made that request, at least in their memory. It broke with protocol. But, yes, they would meet with me and grant me the right to speak for thirty minutes.

I did not stay up all night in a state of anxiety, crafting my every word. I kissed my children goodnight, got into bed, and read whatever happened to be on my nightstand before turning out the lights. I drove to campus the next morning, taking my time around every curve of Sunset Boulevard. No rush. I wanted to be as relaxed as possible, not to project panic.

I parked in my usual parking place, strolled across the sculpture garden outside the business school building, and slowly walked up the stairs to the third floor to meet the staffing committee.

Why was I so calm? I had been practicing yoga and noticed that when I got into a painful posture, I would stop breathing, and my face would grimace, broadcasting my displeasure with the posture. My entire body would tighten, and that would make me hurt even more. If, however, I relaxed my body and continued to breathe, the pain would subside. I could go deeper into the pose. I could bend more. I was learning that the more threatening the situation, the more relaxed I need to be if I want to overcome the threat and reduce the pain.

The committee members convened, all eight of them seated around a table in classroom normally reserved for seminars. I took my place at the head of the table as I had when teaching classes over the years. With only a short hello, I began with the importance of arts management: "As materialistic needs decline in importance, the value of social needs will increase. We have an opportunity to train future social entrepreneurs." The concept of "social entrepreneurs" didn't really exist at the time. I just said it, assuming it would be understood. We had a chance to provide leadership, to be innovative, the first in the world.

All eyes were on me. I could tell I had their attention. "It's not only true that art imitates life." I went on. "Life imitates art, too."

If this was true, we had a moral responsibility to help mold the next generation of social, artistic leaders who would build the future culture of the country. I stood up and began to pace. Then I started a new subject: "The new generation is not willing to put up with hierarchy where they feel disempowered. They are more educated. And not starving like we were. They have different needs for self-actualization. They need to feel empowered. Let us be not blind to the future coming our way." The future of management was industrial democracy, and I knew more about it than just about anyone else in the world. I did not plead or appear desperate. On the contrary. I told them my truth and left the rest to destiny. Perhaps the school needed me as much as I needed the school?

When I finished, there was silence in the room. No questions. They thanked me, and I left. Later that day, I got word that the vote had shifted: it was seven to one in favor of granting me tenure. That had never happened before. How could a thirty-minute presentation flip the outcome so dramatically?

Whatever the case, the decision was an embarrassment for the administration, bringing into question the whole tenure approval process. The chairman of the department sent around a memo that the rules had

Selected among the ten most effective communicators in the world, 2017. The last three voted the worst communicators.

changed. No candidate would be allowed to make a personal presentation to the committee ever again.

Now that I had tenure, I could relax. I was free from the pressure to publish. I could stop working hard and pay more attention to my family. Only a major moral or professional violation of the academic code could remove my lifetime appointment. Yet I continued laboring around the clock, even more obsessively than before. I was trying desperately to get somewhere, although I could not tell where that somewhere was. Was I trying to prove to the world, or maybe to myself, that I was worthy and not a useless person to be rejected?

I did not know then—and to be honest, I still do not know now—how to relax. It is in my DNA to work nonstop. Even on a vacation, I cannot enjoy a casual conversation with the hotel manager. Within minutes, I'm suggesting how to improve operations.

Do people who starve in life, those who know what real hardship is, behave like I do? Do they work nonstop for fear their world will fall apart if they stop moving?

At the time, the answer was too deep-seated for me to try to figure it out. I knew, though, that I was unable to channel my energy from work into my personal life. Personal interactions meant intimacy, and intimacy scared me, although I was yearning, yearning badly, for it. In the professional sphere, I found my desire for love satisfied by working with clients, by speaking to audiences, noticing a spark of insight light up in the eyes. My work gratified me. It provided me the love I ached for, but it was a love I had to earn.

HELPING OTHERS WHILE FAILING MYSELF

In 1973, I took a sabbatical from UCLA and accepted a visiting fellowship at the Center for the Study of Democratic Institutions in Santa Barbara, California.

Robert Maynard Hutchins was the founder and president of the Center, a born leader and a profound man. When Hutchins graduated from Yale Law School, the professors elected him dean, even though he was only twenty-eight years old. His term papers had influenced US Supreme Court decisions. At the age of thirty, he became the president of the University of Chicago. During the McCarthy era, Hutchins became concerned that democracy was in danger and established the Center for the Study of Democratic Institutions.

In addition to Hutchins, there were six full-time associates at the center. One of them was Elisabeth Mann Borgese, the daughter of Thomas Mann. We coedited a book.[8]

---

8 Ichak Adizes and Elisabeth Mann Borgese, *Self-Management: New Dimensions to Democracy* (Santa Barbara, CA: ABC-CLIO, 1975; reprinted by Adizes Institute Publications, 2020).

Every morning at the center, from ten to noon, someone (usually a visiting intellectual star from around the world) would present a paper and everyone would sit around the table and have a discussion that would be taped, edited, and published in *The Center Magazine,* which was read by thought leaders around the world.

The fellows in residence at the time were the poet and politician Eugene McCarthy, a former senator and the antiwar candidate who challenged Lyndon Johnson for the presidency of the United States in 1968; the Czech literary scholar Eduard Goldstücker; and me.

I was immediately drawn to Eduard. When he was the Czechoslovak ambassador to the emerging nation of Israel in 1948, he provided the Czechoslovak rifles to Israel during the Israeli War of Independence. He was convicted of treason during Stalin's infamous Slánský trials, and his death sentence was later commuted to a life sentence of hard labor in a uranium mine—without protection from the radiation. For all intents and purposes, he was gone, but his wife never gave up on him.

When Khrushchev came to power and denounced Stalin, Goldstücker was released and reunited with his loyal wife. He became rector of the leading university in the country, lecturing on literature, including the works of Franz Kafka, which had been banned by the Communists for essentially describing how a totalitarian system suffocates society. It was thanks to his teachings that a theater was founded in Prague to perform Kafka's plays, and the seed was planted for the democratic change to begin in that country. In 1968, during the Prague Spring, Goldstücker was the intellectual leader of the movement and was asked to become the country's president. He declined. When I asked him why, his answer was: "If this revolution failed, they'd say the Jews were to blame, and then we'd all be in trouble."

When the Soviet tanks entered Prague in 1968, he fled to England. He was scared that this time it would not be exile to a gulag, but execution.

Why did the Czechoslovak uprising of 1968 fail? I asked him. "Because we did not cascade it down to the grassroots fast enough. When there is a revolution in a banana republic, the revolutionaries take over the radio and

TV stations and announce that the revolution succeeded. Then the counterrevolutionaries take back the TV and radio stations, and the revolution is over," he replied, and went on to compare it to Mao Zedong's strategy. Chairman Mao started the revolution in the villages, then slowly moved closer and closer to the capital. He took over the TV and radio stations last. By that time, the whole country was on his side. It was difficult, if not impossible, for the counterrevolutionaries to stop the revolution.

Years later, I knew Goldstücker was right, from my experience with a client. The participative system I developed was working like a charm: complementary teams making decisions, constructive conflict, and disciplined meetings were thriving. The company did well, the president was promoted, and a new president was hired from the outside. But since my managerial processes were only applied to top management, it took the new president less than a month to destroy everything we had built over three years. He canceled all teamwork. Back to command and control.

I was in Goldstücker's office at the center one day when he received some mail from his daughter, who lived in Prague. When he opened it, his eyes filled with tears. I asked why he was crying, and he showed me a lock of hair from his grandson, whom he had never seen and probably never would.

His daughter had sent it to him, she wrote, so he would at least feel, perhaps even smell, his grandson. This touched my heart. It was an experience many of us who had lived through those haunted years under communism or tyranny knew only too well.

The center was a place of powerful connection, and it organized forums with exciting writers, scholars, and intellectuals from all over the world.

Belgrade University's dean of political science and chairman of the Serbian parliament, Najdan Pašić, attended one of the gatherings. Hearing that my middle name was Kalderon, he asked if I knew someone named Yosef Kalderon. Yosef had been his best friend in high school, Pašić said, and he was brilliant. There was no record that he lived in Serbia today. Since I had lived in Israel after the war, Pašić asked, maybe I had met him there?

It was my beloved uncle.

I started to answer and began to remember my uncle playing his violin in the living room of my grandparents' house as I, a child of three or four, was captivated by the sound and his attention. His smile lit up whenever he saw me. He let me touch the violin and pluck a few sounds from its strings. Whenever he called for me, I would run to hold his hand. I knew he would always take me for a walk. And now this stranger was asking me about him.

I stood there, paralyzed, the mountains behind me, the sea holding us transfixed as it fell away from the golden hills below. I wanted to say something—anything—but I felt my lips trembling. Then, standing in front of this stranger, struggling to tell him that the Nazis had burned Yosef alive in Treblinka, I began to weep.

Soon after I left Santa Barbara, Robert Hutchins informed me that he had leukemia. He knew that he held the Center for the Study of Democratic Institutions together, intellectually and financially, and without a successor, there would be no center. Wanting to help save this place, I volunteered my time to write a plan of succession to ensure its survival without him.

Everyone, including Hutchins himself, agreed with my diagnosis and recommendation. I was thrilled. A bit breathlessly, I waited for the next move, but no one took action. For God's sake, I thought, how can it be that such an intelligent man cannot or will not act on a proposal he personally assured me he agreed with? I wondered whether I had gotten it all wrong. But everything I predicted came true. When Hutchins died, there was no one to take over. It became part of the University of California, Santa Barbara, and there it died, too.

HEALING ORGANIZATIONS

Why would Hutchins not act on the plan when he told me he agreed with it?

Was I failing as a consultant? I wondered. I felt like an imposter professor of management, teaching concepts that were not carried out. I happened to meet a partner from the McKinsey consulting firm and told him about my self-doubt. He looked at me with amusement. "Welcome to the club," he said. "Most of our recommendations do not get put into practice or get implemented badly or very painfully, firing lots of people to enable change."

There was not one management course on how to make implementation a reality. All the classes at UCLA and the Columbia University Business School Executive Program, where I also taught, were on how to make good decisions–whether in finance or marketing or human resources management–but they stopped there. We were all assuming that if the decision was a good one, it would be implemented.

There is something for me to do, I said to myself.

When Christopher Columbus set sail for India, he found America instead. Penicillin was discovered unintentionally; Alexander Fleming found it in his lab when he returned from a two-week vacation. Innovation is often recognized by being open to see what you're not looking for.

One night, working late in my office at UCLA on an article for a Yugoslavian management journal, my mind wandered back to the implementation riddle. I had to crack it. When I started advising companies, I did what management consultants did at the time: write reports. But I noticed that reports or oral recommendations often had little, if any, impact in the end, so I tried to find new ways to make change happen and not just pull recommendations off the shelf. Joseph Schumpeter had already proposed that entrepreneurship is a necessary variable for economic growth. That however, is not enough, I thought. I developed a model by trial and error: what is the DNA of an organization, that makes it healthy, *effective,* and *efficient,* profitable, in the *short* and *long run*? I came to a conclusion that I thought was a paradigm shift in the theory of leadership.

I thought back to my research in arts administration. Arts organizations need both the artistic director and the administrative director. Without one of them, there is a high likelihood of failure. Similarly, a marriage is a complementary relationship. It is difficult to raise a child as a single parent because the single parent must assume both father and mother roles, provide both masculine and feminine energies. And this applies to a healthy country.

As a prime minister once told me, "You Americans are smart. You have the Republican Party to build the economy for the Democratic Party to share the benefits with the people. If only one party ran the country, there would be either an increasing disparity in wealth or an almost equal distribution of poverty."

But a complementary team—a team of people with different styles, parties with different ideologies—will inevitably be in conflict. Marriage has its conflicts. Opposites attract, which is exciting when those individuals are courting each other and there are no tasks to accomplish. But, once married and confronted with problems and tasks, those same differences become a source of conflict.[9]

It was after midnight. The ideas were flowing one after the other and I was writing frantically. If I was right, then the entire premise of management education was wrong. We were all trying to develop *the* leader. But no one is capable of leading perfectly well by him- or herself. We needed to train for teamwork, collaborative leadership, and how to manage conflicts constructively.

My mind began to wander beyond how these ideas applied to business or even marriage. I thought of political systems. One way to stop conflict is to prohibit diversity, and that is what racism, communism, and religious fanaticism do. They forbid and suffocate diversity, and what happens? Change stops. There is no cross-fertilization. Look at a desert. Same sand everywhere. Nothing grows there. But a desert might contain an oasis, and what is an oasis if not diversity? Look at a jungle. Diversity galore. Growth galore.

It follows, then, that if we want a complementary team we need to accept conflict, but we must prevent it from becoming destructive. Partnerships fall apart. In countries like Yugoslavia, where there was diversity of religions and cultures, the country fell apart.

As I was working "out there" with clients, it started to dawn on me that marriages fall apart, too. Since no one is perfect, it had to be okay that I was not perfect. Neither was my wife. Conflict is normal. What is abnormal, dysfunctional, is not the conflict itself, which comes with the territory, but *how* is this conflict handled. We should not forbid conflict but convert it to be constructive. But how?

One of my students would enlighten me.

It takes mutual respect, she wrote in a seminar paper. According to

9 Ichak Kalderon Adizes with Yechetzkel Madanes and Ruth Madanes, *The Power of Opposites: How to Succeed in Your Marriage and Family Not in Spite of, but Because of, Your Differences* (Santa Barbara, CA: Adizes Institute Publications, 2015).

Immanuel Kant, she said, respect is recognizing the sovereignty of the other person to be free to think differently. If there is mutual respect, people's minds are open to learn from each other's differences of opinion and, voilà, they will make better decisions than one single individual can make alone.

Now the question was, how do you *build* mutual respect?

Observing the world around me offered an unexpected solution. I was invited to give a lecture in Toronto. It was ten o'clock at night when I finally arrived. I was met by the CEO of the company, who suggested that we go to the hospitality room, where everyone was expecting me. Although it was late, I agreed to join them.

In the hospitality room, I saw the vice presidents of the company playing poker. I don't play cards, but I watched the game anyway. I found it fascinating. A lot of money was changing hands. There were conflicts because of competing interests, but the players weren't fighting. There was no tension around the table despite the competition and the fact that lots of money was at stake.

What was going on? If this had been a management meeting where these same people had to decide how to budget their resources, there would have been a lot of destructive conflict. Here, however, even though some players were losing money, the entire group couldn't have been having a better time.

What was the difference between a poker game and a committee meeting? Suddenly it dawned on me: the difference was that there are rules of the game that everyone agrees to follow and honor. Aha! You cannot have constructive diversified participation without mutual respect, and there is no mutual respect without up-front rules that everyone agrees to honor. In all interactions, even in war, people have rules about what is acceptable behavior and what is not. That night after the game, I went back to my room and wrote all night, drafting protocols on how to run meetings effectively with mutual respect, what rules to follow.

Now I knew there must be rules for how a meeting should be run in order to create a safe environment for people to participate. But who should participate? What should they discuss, and how? I was still in the dark.

Luckily, at that time I was going through psychotherapy. It helped show me the way.

WHAT TO ASK AND WHEN

I first sought out Dr. David Shapiro, a professor in the department of psychiatry and biobehavioral sciences at UCLA's medical school because I realized I was unhappy. It was not just the traumas of my youth. I had difficulty communicating with people who disagreed with me, and I would be overcome by anger. I was having trouble adjusting to the social changes of the era, to the shifting dynamics between men and women out in the world. I was having problems in my marriage. A woman in my folk dancing group told me about her troubles and how she was in treatment with Dr. Shapiro. I decided to go to him as well.

In my line of business, the client traditionally has the problems, and the consultant traditionally has the answers. In talk therapy, I observed, it is the reverse. The doctor has the questions, and the patient has the answers. The probability of implementation is higher because the decision arrived at is the client's, not the consultant's.

I said to myself, companies don't need consulting, and they don't need advice. Companies need someone to ask them the right questions and help them arrive at their own answers, which they can actually implement over

The organization that started at my kitchen table now has certified organziational therapists working from ten offices around the world. Photo at the 31st Annual Adizes International Convention. Las Vegas, Nevada, 2009.

time. They need *organizational therapy.* Now the challenge was what questions to ask, of whom, and in what order.

The order is crucial to getting it right: Imagine the sexual act. Your body is present, but your mind is on something else. You have to bring your mind where your body is. In a meeting, the Adizes protocol is the same. For the first five minutes, participants meditate or ask one another how they feel about the meeting—something to bring each person's mind to where their body is. Once their minds and bodies are together, the protocol leads them in a very structured way, step-by-step, to final agreement

where they reinforce and express how they feel about the meeting and the decision taken. This last step I learned from the sex expert Dr. Ruth Westheimer, who said that what you do after an orgasm is extremely important. You have to touch and kiss as much as you did in the leadup to climax. It's a preparation for the next sexual act. The end should be like the beginning.

But what about implementation? I already knew that deciding is not enough. The cooperation of the stakeholders is needed for efficient implementation.

But they have their own diverse interests. The workers on the line want higher salaries and better working conditions. And those with the know-how want the best learning and growth experiences. Managers representing owners want the highest profits and, thus, the greatest return on investment. It's a recipe for conflict.

It took me a few years to figure out how to address these competing interests.

At that time, I used to say in my lectures that handling conflicts of interest requires a culture of give and take—like in a good, solid marriage. I give in to your demands when your needs are stronger than mine, and you reciprocate when my interests are more important than yours.

Give and take.

Once, during the break in a lecture I gave in Istanbul, an executive came to me with a smile on his face and said, "In Turkey we don't say 'give and take.' We say, 'take and give.' We reverse the order."

This made me consider: what is the difference between "give and take" and "take and give"?

In give and take, there is trust: I give in to you because I trust that you—you or the system—will reciprocate. In take and give, there is no trust. I first take.

The essence of the Adizes Methodology for organizational therapy was starting to take shape. People in companies I was advising, or those who came to my lectures, wanted to learn more—as much as possible—and asked to join me. I began to build the company that would become the Adizes Institute, which today has over seventy certified organizational therapists working out of ten offices worldwide.

With mutual trust and respect, conflict is constructive. Without it, it is destructive. In a company. In a country. In a marriage. And how about in a person? We need self-trust and self-respect. Self-esteem.

That is what I was missing. My father missed it, too. We were trying to find it "out there," he as a fake doctor and me with my clients and in my lectures. I traveled to fifty-two countries and was still searching for it. What I didn't realize is that it wasn't "out there" that I needed to look, it was "in here."

The theme of mutual trust and respect occupied me throughout my professional life, and it still does. Maybe being denied respect and trust while I was growing up made me addicted to finding out what they are and how one gets them.

I could see its importance for companies and countries. What has made America so successful? It is not its size. Other countries are even bigger. Not its physical resources. Others have no less. It is the diversity of its population, the culture of tolerance and respect for differences, and trust in the open market to benefit all those who contribute to the country's well-being. Once America starts losing this culture, it will start to lose its dominance in the world. But what about self-respect and trust in personal life. Late in life, but not too late, I found the answer.

WHAT KEPT ME GOING

I used to teach CEOs management and leadership principles through the practice of yoga. I would describe a pose, then stand back and observe. By watching how each individual approached the challenge, I could tell how they managed their company—what was working and what was not.

One of my favorites was a standing head-to-knee posture. "Stand on one foot and *do not bend the knee of that leg,*" I began. "Lift the other leg parallel to the ground, then grab your toes and bring your head to the lifted knee *without bending it.*"

This is a very difficult posture and to master it takes years of practice.

What do people do? To reach the toes, they *bend the knee* of the standing foot and to reach the lifted knee with their head they *bend the lifted knee,* too; although the instruction was clear not to bend either knee. To reach the goal they violated the rules.

Did they achieve the goal bending the knees? Some did. But not for long. As soon as they touched the knee with their head, they lost their balance and fell.

"You can reach your goals," I'd say, "bending rules and values. But for how long? To have sustainable success you need to stick to your values and do your best. Doing your best might not be enough right now to reach the goal. It might take time to reach the goal but then it is sustainable. So? Do you want short-term profitability or long-term sustainable profitability?"

There is another difficult posture with another message: "Stand on one foot and, again, *do not bend the knee.* With the other leg straight behind you, hinge forward at the hip and stretch your hands in front of your head until your torso and back leg are parallel to the ground. Your body will take the shape of the letter *T.*"

"What will increase the chance of holding the posture a bit longer?" I would ask, usually once most participants had lost their balance.

"First, you must learn to *relax.* Getting into this strange posture is a change, so your body tenses up, wasting all its energy on fighting the posture. Love the pose instead to make the change successful.

"Second, do not stop breathing. When there is change of major proportions, some leaders stop doing what they used to do and focus totally on the changes they are involved in. Wrong! You still need to breathe to keep the business running.

"And third"—most people would raise an eyebrow on this one—"do not lift your big toe of the standing foot off the ground. If you lift it, you will lose balance and fall. Look at your company: who is the big toe of the organization? We all know who the head is, right? But the toe? Well, who is on the ground delivering your vision?"

I learned this early on as a consultant to the United States Postal Service when it became an independent agency in the early 1970s. The postmaster general had become a professional appointment (rather than a political one) and was charged with making the service work in a more businesslike way. I was hired to help change the organization's bureaucratic culture.

I started at the main post office in San Francisco to learn how the mail was processed. How did a letter sent from Los Angeles reach its destination in New York? How did this miracle happen for a billion pieces of mail a year?

At that time, they all had to go through a machine called a Blind Belinda. Envelopes were placed on a conveyor belt that fed to a person who looked at the zip code and punched it into a computer keyboard. A magnetic stamp followed the keyboard instruction, and the mail would be properly sorted by zip code. This task was boring and stressful because the mail moved quickly on that track. Because of the stress, people working the Belindas took breaks frequently.

Now, I asked myself what makes the person—and there were twenty of them with twenty Blind Belindas—what makes this person type in the correct zip code? Why not just click at random and mail destined for Hawaii goes to Mississippi?

"How do you know that employees are doing the job right, that they are clicking the right zip codes?" I asked the supervisor who walked me around the facility.

"We sample the zip code sacks and check for mistakes," was the answer.

"How do you know which worker did it wrong?" I continued.

"Well, we know which Blind Belinda processed it from the stamp, but not which worker clicked the wrong zip code, since more than one person will be operating the machine in any given day."

Whoa, I thought. That means if the mail arrived, it was because those "toes," those workers on the ground, did their job accurately. The toe sticks to the ground, anchors itself to the floor, so the organization does not fail.

I discovered there were over hundred reasons mail did not to arrive to its intended destination if the "toe" was not committed. The mail collector misses collecting it from the delivery box. Or it gets the wrong zip code assigned by the Belinda. Or it gets stuck at the bottom of the sack. Or, or, or . . . In Argentina, I discovered, the mail carriers at the time sometimes took the mail, dropped it in a garbage can, and went home early. This was so common that if you wanted to send business mail to Argentina, you better sent it by messenger.

It is the worker on the line, the salesperson knocking on doors, and the clerk ensuring the right product is shipped to the right address, that make a company shine or fail. So, I tell the business leaders I work with, pay attention to the toe. Listen to the toe. We experienced it more than once.

One of my early clients was Equifax (at the time called Retail Credit). I was initially hired to work with a division called Credit Bureaus. The company was in the aging part of the lifecycle, searching for answers on how to rejuvenate itself.

Early on, I convinced top management they needed to "listen to the toe" and visit the people who worked on the ground, processing credit checkups. We flew to Washington, D.C., to visit the branch of the company there.

To break the ice, I mixed top management with the workers, in pairs. The instruction was for the executive to tell the worker what he or she liked about their job. Then the worker shared the same. Next, the protocol was repeated for what they hated about their jobs. The exercise was very successful. Top management got to know what was actually happening on the ground level, and we took off back to Atlanta.

I sat next to Jeff White, the CEO, on the flight. He looked pensive, so I asked what was wrong.

"You son of a bitch, you really set me up," he said.

"What are you talking about?" I asked, a bit alarmed.

"It's that file clerk you paired me up with."

"What about her?" I remembered she had been an older heavyset woman.

"I told her how much I hate the stress of meeting budgets and battling the competition. When her turn came, she told me how much she hates getting on her knees most of the working day, dealing with the lowest file box of the file cabinet. How painful it was for her.

"I started in this company as a file clerk, and I remember how I hated getting on my knees day after day to handle those f—ing files, and how I swore that if I ever became a manager I would change those file cabinets and make them high enough that no one would have to get on their knees."

"I forgot, Ichak, I forgot my promise."

I conducted the identical exercise with Domino's Pizza when it was a client of the Adizes Institute, bringing top management to listen to the workers on the line. We began with the same warmup. One employee said that he hated working there because every time he moved around, the hot oven burned his elbow.

It turned out that an architect designed the restaurant for efficiency, but never visited the location to see how it was working out. This is what I call the Kremlin syndrome. Management sits in its exclusive offices, with its exclusive elevators to its exclusive floor, and decides what should happen on the ground floor without visiting or listening to the "toes."

How many disasters could have been prevented if the "toes" had access to the brain? The ability to relay feedback and information so they can stick to the ground and do their job honestly and well? Hundreds of people would never have died in the Boeing 737 MAX crashes. Workers who built the planes knew they were designed wrong. According to newspaper reports, many said they would not fly their own families on these planes. But top management never got this information because the "toe" had no way to communicate to the brain and anchor itself to the ground.

What about managing by just walking around as recommended by the authors of the best-selling *In Search of Excellence*. Great idea but how much walking around can top management do if the company has ten thousand employees? Or is a multinational with locations all over the world? How about suggestion boxes? It usually collects cigarette butts.

In the Adizes methodology, we create a safe environment. No witch hunts, no accusations, no judgements, just facts—with a very strict protocol on how to manage a diagnostic forum where all problems are disclosed and recorded digitally. This information is made available to management, and management has a system to deal with and solve the problems. We open channels for energy to flow from bottom up and from top down. An organism is sick when the energy gets stuck. When it flows in its normal flow the organism is healthy. That is why we call ourselves organizational therapists.

In the 1980s, I was working with the Outrigger Hotels chain in Hawaii. We were in a team process trying to stretch the budget and see where we could cut costs. According to the protocol, whoever could contribute was invited, regardless of status or rank.

A member of the housekeeping staff said, "We spend a lot of money washing towels every day. Why don't we ask our guests if, maybe, they would not mind keeping a towel for more than one day."

Someone else jumped in and said, "It would be good for the environment, too. We could save water and stop polluting the groundwater with detergents." And that is how those little signs you see in hotels asking if you want to keep or change your towels started to appear and spread worldwide.

Another time I was in Houston delivering a systemic participative diagnosis with the top management of an engineering company. At the close of the workshop, everyone was asked to say how they felt about the experience. One engineer, an emigrant from Russia, started crying. It was uncomfortable because none of us knew what was wrong, so I asked him.

Through tears, he said, "This is what I came from Russia for."

THE ONE-EYED MAN

The first time I lectured at the Los Angeles chapter of Young Presidents Organization—the same group that had awarded me the scholarship at Columbia—it was as if my whole life was coming full circle from my days as a poor student. So when the group asked me to speak at their annual global summit in Brazil in 1976, I jumped at the chance.

The entire car ride from the Rio airport, I could not stop pinching myself. My wife sat beside me in the backseat, and when we arrived at the hotel and the driver opened the door for us, I knew I had arrived. My days of lecturing to middle management or owners of midsize companies were over. I would be speaking to the leaders of some of the largest companies on earth.

At YPO International Universities, there are always several lectures going on at once, so an unknown speaker could find themself speaking to an empty room. My first lecture was in a small hall with a few dozen people and a lot of empty seats. I felt like a horse before a race and couldn't wait to prove myself.

By the second day, the room was completely full. Word had circulated that I had something to say. On the third day, they moved me to the largest hall at the conference, which filled up. On the fourth day, the hall was standing room only; people lined the walls, and others peered in through the open door. I closed my remarks on the edge of tears, thanking YPO for its support when I was a student, support that had kept me from the brink of starvation.

An American man with a small brokerage firm was in the audience that day. He bought one of my books and applied my methodology as best as he could while he built the massive company that carried his name: Charles Schwab.[10]

In 1982, the company was bought out by Bank of America, and Schwab encountered enormous bureaucracy within the bank.

Schwab believed that if Bank of America was going to remain competitive in what had become a rapidly changing industry, it would first have to undergo radical change. He gave the bank's president Sam Armacost a recording of my YPO lecture in Rio from several years earlier. Armacost liked what he heard and called my office.

"The president of Bank of America wants to talk to you!" my secretary practically screamed. At the time, Bank of America was the largest bank in the United States, with a hundred and twenty billion dollars in assets.

We made an appointment.

When I arrived in San Francisco and approached the bank's headquarters, my mind was spinning like a revolving door. The headquarters were located in a fifty-two-floor glass high-rise that took up almost the entire block. The lobby was enormous, luxurious, intimidating. It projected wealth and, even more than that, power. I tried to slow down my breathing.

---

10 Charles Schwab, *Invested: Changing Forever the Way Americans Invest* (New York: Currency, 2019).

Who was I, a Jewish hick from Macedonia, to advise the biggest bank in the United States?

I calmed my breathing and thought of the Mexican expression "In the land of the blind, the one-eyed man is king." Maybe I am the man with one eye, I thought. I did not know much, but perhaps I knew something others did not. Then it occurred to me that I actually was a man with only one good eye.

I reached the executive floor and was led down a hallway lined with art to the president's office. He rose from his chair to greet me. The first thing he said to me was that the bank was losing market share. Management was not aggressive enough, and there was no flexibility, no innovation. "We've got to change the corporate culture," he said, but he was not sure how to go about it.

"Have you tried any change programs so far?" I asked.

"We did an exercise on values and how our values have to change." He hesitated for a moment. "Nothing much really happened thereafter."

"What about other consulting firms?"

"We use the Boston Consulting Group but only as our outsourced research arm. They don't deal with change. And, I must warn you," he said, "as the largest bank in America, our culture here is very elitist. We do not use consultants. We consider ourselves the best and feel we do not need anyone to tell us what to do or how to do it."

This is the culture typical of companies that have reached what I call the aristocratic stage of their lifecycle. It is like some aristocrats in Europe who live in big castles they refuse to let go of, proud of their name and heritage but freezing from the cold because they have no money to heat the place.

I understood it would be my role to convince the top management that the bank needed to change its culture and become more aggressive in the marketplace.

"Can you get me all your top managers in one room at the same time and give me at least three hours?" I asked. "No more than thirty of the movers and shakers?"

CORPORATE PERFORMANCE

Spearheading *BankAmerica's effort to alter its culture, management consultant Ichak Adizes has spent two years trying to move decision-making down to the company's lower ranks.*

Adizes, a Yugoslavian-born management consultant from Santa Monica, California, to coax top managers to contribute ideas for restructuring the bank. Adizes, who has helped restructure other companies but no large banks, was an unusual choice. But outside help of some sort seemed imperative. "The painful part of the process," says Armacost, "is that the existing culture would have preferred to sit back and let me make all those decisions: 'Tell us what to do and we'll do it.' That was fine, but you're not going to develop people that way, you're not going to develop any innovative entrepreneurial approach, and you're not going to develop feedback."

Adizes spent two years in the hard slog of building a consensus about how best to redesign the company. It proved frustrating and time-consuming, with Adizes bringing together almost 2,000 executives and other employees for what amounted to a series of corporate encounter groups.

In the past two months the company has begun revealing to the public the first fruits of this process. In February the bank unveiled its biggest change: a new organization called Global Consumer Markets, under Vice Chairman Wiesler, which realigns consumer banking into four specialized lines—the mass market, affluent consumers, not-so-affluent customers who want personalized service, and small business. A revamping of the world banking group, which serves large corporations and overseas customers, will come later.

Many outsiders scoff at these changes. "It took them two years, and they're just playing musical chairs," snorts a former Bank of America executive. "That won't solve their problems." But along with the reshufflings have come striking changes in the company's ways of doing things, starting with pay. In the past Bank of America employees were graded much like civil servants, with narrow pay bands for those within the same grade. Now the bank pays top performers in a grade up to 60% more than poor performers.

The California branch system, meanwhile, is in the midst of a serious shakeup. In the past, Bank of America's branch managers were rewarded on the basis of size: the bigger the branch in assets and employees, the higher the pay. But in a deregulated world, size is less important than bringing in profitable business, and the branch managers have been told to get more.

"We started telling them that they are salespeople," says Wiesler, and the compensation formula now encourages salesmanship as well as cost control. Armacost has wrung big savings out of the branch system, closing 132 branches in the U.S. last year and trimming the size of 42. Some 8,000 jobs have been eliminated in the California network alone.

But Armacost has yet to launch a companywide assault on costs. Stark figures on assets per employee show the magnitude of the job that still lies largely ahead. BankAmerica ranks dead last among the top ten banks, with $1.4 million of assets per employee to Citicorp's $2.1 million. Richard Fredericks, a partner with the San Francisco brokerage firm Montgomery Securities, says, "Costs are much too high for BankAmerica's base of business."

Armacost's heavy spending on technology virtually dictates that he offset the costs with savings elsewhere. BankAmerica has spent $105 million on ATMs. And it's getting ready to spend as much as $1 billion a year, including salaries, equipment, and overhead, building one of the most sophisticated worldwide electronic networks in banking.

BANKAMERICA's overhead expenses—including rent and headquarters staff salaries—zoomed 19% in 1984 alone. To suggestions that he's too timid to sail into the problem, Armacost counters: "I could lay off 10,000 people. But who would deliver the services? Why should I be frantic to make a change that would destroy a lot of the inherently good parts of the cultural values of the company? To drive away most of my customers?"

The other stain on Armacost's record is the bank's bumper crop of snafus. Some stem from poor decisions, others from the failure of internal controls. Among the dreadful

My involvement in the dramatic restructure of Bank of America was catnip to the business media. *Fortune,* April 1, 1985.

He thought for a moment. "Yes. We are planning a top management retreat in Napa Valley. All will be there, heads of all divisions, heads of countries where we operate, and key members of the board. I can give you three hours in the program but not as a consultant. It's too touchy a subject. We will present you as a professor giving a lecture."

Two months later, I was standing in an elegant room at the Silverado Resort in front of forty people seated in a semicircle, as I had requested. All of Bank of America's vice presidents and country managers and some of its board members in their bank "uniforms"—the darker the suit, the more official, the better. I imagined them thinking: Who is this short guy with the heavy accent from Albania or Macedonia or Israel or wherever? What can he teach us? I do not know where I got the chutzpah to speak with confidence, but I did.

Unlike my personal life, where I felt timid, when it came to performing professionally I was unshakable. All I needed to do was create a safe environment for my clients to think, recognize their problems, share them with one another, and find their own solution. The challenge was how to create that safe environment. I felt that my intuition would guide me. I would find the solution by listening to my clients and making them do the work as if I was playing the accordion and trying to get them to sing along.

I began by explaining my concept of the corporate lifecycle and the problems an organization faces at each stage of the lifecycle—which of the problems were typical and which defied the odds.[11]

About thirty minutes in, I had their total attention and asked, "Would you like to know where Bank of America is on the lifecycle and which of your problems are normal and which are abnormal?" The president nodded his head.

---

11 Ichak Adizes, *Managing Corporate Lifecycles,* 2004.

"Okay, everyone take five index cards and write down the top five problems that confront the bank today. But here are the rules:

"First, the problems have to be solvable by the people in this room. Do not tell me that it is raining outside. You cannot control rain. That's God's problem, not yours. Your problem is that you have no umbrella or that you did not listen to the weather forecast or that your roof is leaking. By the same token, do not tell me interest rates are unpredictable. Instead say, 'We have no strategy to deal with unpredictable interest rates.' The problem must be written in a way that makes it clear that the participants in this room can solve it.

"Second, do not mention any names—not yours, not anyone else's. We are not interested in *who* is at fault but in *what* can and should be improved." (That way we avoided oversimplifying problems by laying them at the feet of one person, which leads to a sacrificial lamb, if not to a witch hunt.)

"Third, do not attribute problems or use the word 'because.' If you need to do that, separate the problems and write each one on its own card." (Complex problems have multiple causes, and we needed to avoid coming to a premature conclusion that one issue was to blame.)

"Finally, the most important rule, the fourth one: You are not allowed to show anyone what you have written on your cards. You won't have to read those cards to me or to anyone else, either. When you finish, you can tear them apart, chew them up, and swallow them. No one will know what you have written, and that's okay.

"All I ask," I continued, raising my voice a bit, "is that you be honest with yourself." I hoped that once they wrote the problems honestly on their cards (and they would be honest because no one would read what they wrote), and once they realized no names were being mentioned and no single individual could solve the problems alone, they would feel safe. They would not be able to resist. They would give me their cards.

I gave them fifteen minutes to write. When the allotted time was up, I asked, "Of the current problems you identified, how many of them did you have last year? Do not tell me what they are, just how many."

"All of them!" came the answer.

"How many two years ago?"

"All!" was the answer again. It was loud and enveloping.

"How many three years ago?"

It faded to an embarrassed whisper, "Most."

"So let me ask you this: if you have had those problems for the last three years, what is the chance you will have them three years from now, too?"

Silence. An uncomfortable silence.

"Now, let me tell you why you have had those problems for three years and why you will have them for at least the next three years." They seemed frozen with anticipation. I went on, "Among the many problems that you are holding in your hand—*and I do not know what you have written*—could any single individual in the company solve any single problem working alone?"

They were quiet. "Very few," someone finally said.

I expected this answer. If a problem can be solved by an individual at the level of the participants in the room, it is usually solved. Obviously, several members of the group were needed to address the issues spelled out on those cards.

An aging system disintegrates like an old person: the different organs do not cooperate as well as they did in their youth. The problems were caused by disintegration, so the solution could be found in integration.

"How many of the problems could be solved if I gave each of you a magic pill that, after you swallowed it, made you all agree on a solution?"

The room was absolutely still. All eyes looked as if they were waiting for me to pull a rabbit out of a hat.

"I set you up," I said, raising my voice for drama. "I told you to write down only problems all of you in this room could control if you can work together. So if you were to agree on the solutions, how many of the problems could you solve? By definition, all of them, right?"

They nodded their heads in support.

"So the problems you have are not the ones you have written down.

The problems you have written down are manifestations that you are falling apart. Instead of one manager chasing ten problems all at once, you should have ten managers chasing one problem at a time. The task that confronts you is deciding which of the problems you have in your hands should be the one addressed first and which should be placed on the back burner. There is simply no chance you can handle and solve all your problems simultaneously. You have to let go of what you *want* to solve and instead dedicate your focus and energy to addressing what you as a team *should* solve."

"The right sequence is critical." I was speaking with the energy and movements of a preacher. "To sneeze, then wipe one's nose is the right sequence. Too many managers first wipe their nose, then sneeze, and do not understand why they look ridiculous." I paused, hesitating for a second before I very quietly asked, rather than commanded, "If you allow me to see the problems, I can outline the right sequence for you."

Because the problems *did not have any individual names attached to the cards* and because I had convinced them that none of the problems were the burden of any single person in the room, they gave me their cards. There was no blame and no responsibility, no threat of losing face. It was safe.

"Go and have a break," I instructed them. During the break, I sorted the problems in a chain of causality using the attribution analysis chart I had developed over the years with clients.

I invited the crowd back in and read them their cards, proceeding from causes to symptoms to manifestations. I added nothing of my own: I just organized the sequence of their cards.

Their challenge was finding a way to break the chain of causality, to choose what to work on and in what sequence. "By the way," I told them, "I am available to show you how to do it."

The bank offered me a three-year contract.

A CHANGE HAS A PRICE

To make change in the life of a person or a company or a country there must be commitment. Many have tried to lose weight with no commitment. It does not work.

There is no commitment without a price to pay. You cannot get into a new set of shoes without getting out of a set of old shoes. You cannot go on a diet without suffering from some hunger or depriving yourself of some tasty sugary desserts. That is the price.

Many initiatives of change fail because there is not enough commitment, because those that need to change are not willing to pay the price.

Changing the bureaucratic culture of a bank with almost a hundred thousand employees was an enormous undertaking. I was not going to study the organization, interview the corporate leaders, and write a report, as consultants would. This was not consulting, not writing reports; it was working mano a mano with the top managers of Bank of America, the challenge of a lifetime. Taking one day a week off from teaching (the maximum the university allowed its professors to take) wouldn't cut it. I needed three years off.

When I asked the chairman of UCLA's Graduate School of Management for time off without pay, I thought he would congratulate me. I assumed he might feel a twinge of envy as he did so but then acknowledge what a feather in the department's cap my work would be. I thought he might even be a little excited.

But he wouldn't hear of it. How could I even contemplate such an action? Where was my sense of commitment to teaching and conducting *true* research? He was adamant. He did not beat around the bush. "Either leave consulting for good or leave the university!" he said. "Teaching and academic research are what we're about, not consulting out in the marketplace." Then, so there would be no misunderstanding, he took it a step further: he threatened to assign me a four-day-week teaching load if I failed to stop consulting. With that schedule, it would be next to impossible to function as a consultant.

I felt crushed. I mumbled something about thinking it over and left the room.

When I returned from San Francisco the following week, I found my office closed. I went downstairs to ask the department secretary what was wrong.

"Oh, you were moved to another room," she said.

"Which one?"

"The one next to the bathroom." The chairman had made the decision. I took the keys to my new office. When I opened the door, I could not believe my eyes. Someone had emptied all the cabinets from my old office and piled the contents on the floor. All my notes were scattered everywhere.

I got the hint. I handed in my resignation the next day and left the university. I gave up my tenure, a lifetime appointment—or maybe a lifetime of intellectual imprisonment.

I began my treatment of Bank of America by asking the leaders a deceptively simple question: what business are you in? I asked the question as if

I did not know what a bank was. They were incredulous. It was, in a sense, a rude question for a highly paid consultant to ask, but I asked it with a specific purpose in mind. I explained gently, "We cannot find a solution if we don't know what we're talking about. We need to define the words we use. Can we agree on what a bank is?"

In order to understand a concept, it needs to be simplified. It is very easy to make concepts complicated, and very complicated to make them simple. If it is not simple, it is too complicated to be understood or implemented. I believe that you do not know what you claim to know until you can make it simple enough to explain to anyone, even a child.

They had the patience to explain to me: a bank collects savings (on which it pays interest) and gives loans (on which it charges interest). The difference between the amount of interest the bank pays on savings and the amount it charges on loans is its operating profit. Sounds obvious, right? Yet when we finished formulating our definition, we came across a startling discovery: banking, according to this definition, was a dying industry. This proved to be true few years later when many savings-and-loan banks failed.

Banking managers and executives were going through the motions of propping up a dying business. This worked in the distant past and might still work in some developing countries, but not anymore in developed countries. Who in the United States or Western Europe would place most of their money in a savings account today? There are so many better alternatives: shares, bonds, real estate—even art, if you're willing to gamble.

There was also competition on the demand side. There were many opportunities for mobilizing capital. A company does not necessarily need a loan from a bank; it could go to the stock market or insurance companies or private investment funds. Banks faced major competition from sectors other than traditional banking. To stay in business, a bank had to become a provider of fee-based services and generate revenue from those services.

Bank of America had to stop being a bank and become a financial services institution. That's how the revolution of fee-based services started at Bank of America. To actualize the new strategy, we had to change the company's structure. That meant reorganizing parts of the power structure at the bank. But none of that could be done easily. The structure Bank of America had in place was dominated by retail banking because that was how the company began.

With me serving as an integrator and providing tools on how to structure the company, a selected team of top management including the CEO and the chairman of the bank designed a new organizational structure, in an atmosphere of mutual trust and respect. And I had the tools to make that happen.

At one point during the process, I was asked if an advisor from the Boston Consulting Group could attend one of the reorganization sessions I was leading. He was on a retainer and had developed a strategy for them to provide payment services. Briefly, I wondered if this request was an indirect way of reining me in. Don't be afraid, I told myself. Be a true professional. If it helps the client, let it be. Even if it means you lose.

The day the observer arrived, we were working on realigning the structure. I noticed he was uncomfortable. He could not sit still in his chair. Surprise and disapproval were written all over his face.

During the break, he asked to speak to me in private. We went to a corner, and he asked me in a very polite way, "Professor Adizes, are you not rearranging the chairs on a sinking *Titanic*? You are dealing with the structure before you have a strategy. Does it make sense?" Apparently, the decision to go after fee-based services was not sufficient strategic planning for him. He was probably wondering where the study of the market and competition was. Where were the tables and the numbers BCG is famous for?

He certainly had a point. I was designing the structure before the strategy was fully articulated. The professional literature says that form follows function. Alfred Chandler's 1962 book *Strategy and Structure,*[12] the bible in business schools and consulting firms at the time, states that

---

12 A. D. Chandler Jr., *Strategy and Structure: Chapters in the History of the American Industrial Enterprise* (Cambridge, MA: MIT Press, 1962).

structure follows strategy. Why was I operating in reverse order? I admit I did not sleep that night.

Then, in the early hours of the morning, I woke in my hotel room remembering a trip I had taken with a high school student delegation, paid for by the Ministry of Education of Israel. As the president of the student union of the high schools of Tel Aviv, I had been selected to go to France.

On a night train to Paris, a group of about fifteen of us attempted to sleep in a compartment designed for ten travelers. We were almost sitting on top of one another; it took us an hour to finally fall asleep. Then someone wanted to go to the bathroom. Change! There was total commotion. We screamed at him for not going earlier. Why was he waking us all up?

In poorly structured organizations, it is easier to pee in your pants than to go to the bathroom and cause turmoil. You have to decide if the change you need to make is worth the rejection, criticism, anger, and suspicion that making that change will arouse in the rest of the organization.

Just imagine, I said to myself, lying awake at four in the morning, as I mulled over why I was doing what I was doing at Bank of America, the consultant sitting happily in his office writing a well-documented, logical report. Imagine he makes a proposal—which is the result of careful study and for which he will charge a tidy sum—that the travelers should go to Rome instead of Paris. Do you think they will move, change their behavior, and adopt the new strategy? Most probably not. If they could not even go to the bathroom (make small changes) easily, why would they believe that they could make any major, disruptive change at all?

In an organizational structure, people are interdependent. When the interdependency is poorly aligned, people duplicate each other's responsibilities and second-guess each other. Each wants to move but is scared of the political repercussions, so everyone tends to stand still. That is why it is said that you know the innovators in a bureaucracy by the arrows in their backs.

No, I said to myself. You are doing the right thing. Start with the structure. First, rearrange the seats in that compartment. Make sure everyone has their own space. Make sure the participants realize that they are interdependent. First develop a structure that is amenable to change (what I would call a first-draft structure), then develop the strategy. Then, and only then, adapt or change the structure to reflect the strategy. No structure should be final, ever. It should be continuously changing because strategy might be changing, and it should be changing because the environment is changing.

Changing the company's structure creates ripples in the power structure. Some (probably many) of the company's leaders feel threatened by the process and want to throw the agent of change out—in this case, me. But, I said to myself, if I am not willing to be thrown out when I am doing the right thing, I do not deserve to be an organizational therapist. No fear, I used to remind myself, and it worked. The company made the necessary changes under my coaching. I did not recommend; I simply gave the company the tools to use, and they decided what to do.

As people found their place in the new structure, my enemies became my friends. Some thanked me. They lost a job they could hardly perform but, with a new and clearer understanding of their position, found the energy to recommit themselves to the company. Nevertheless, the reorganization of Bank of America had its price: me.

In 1983, the real estate market was faltering, as was the energy sector. As for developing countries, they were not responding promptly to calls to repay their loans, and Sam Armacost inherited an enormous portfolio of nonperforming loans. The restructuring's focus on transparency and accountability unveiled the toxic portfolio. He had to clean up the portfolio and increase the reserves. This called for another radical shift in thinking: a bank is the services it provides, not the real estate it possesses. Selling the Bank of America building in Singapore was not enough. The famous building housing their headquarters in San Francisco needed to be sold as well.

That touched a nerve with Claire Giannini Hoffman, a member of the board and the daughter of Amadeo Giannini, the man who founded Bank of America at the turn of the twentieth century. His bust was prominently displayed in the bank's entrance. His picture was everywhere. The building was named after him. His presence was still felt, even though he had died many years prior.

Claire Giannini Hoffman fought tooth and nail against the proposal. She wanted to know who this "communist consultant" the bank had hired was. That was only the start of my challenges. The media sensed that something was wrong at Bank of America. There were whispers and press leaks. Why did the bank suddenly have so many nonperforming loans? If Bank of America went down, the fall would affect the whole worldwide financial industry. Thirty years later, following the 2008 financial crisis, this notion came to be known as the "too big to fail" principle.

The Wall Street Journal eagerly wrote about the bank's difficulties,[13] as did *Fortune* magazine, which ran an article about my intervention at the bank.[14] The comptroller of the currency in Washington, D.C., who supervises banks across the country, was getting nervous, and he insisted that he attend all top management meetings to review their decisions. Armacost, a man of great integrity and very strong beliefs about the independence of the market economy from government interference, absolutely refused to let that happen.

I tried to convince him to relent. "You cannot fight Washington," I told him.

"The day government starts managing private businesses is the end of our free enterprise system as we know it," he said quietly. "If fighting it means my head will roll, so be it." It became a question of honor for him.

---

13 Christian Hill and Mike Tharp, "Stumbling Giant: Bank America Stunned," *Wall Street Journal,* July 18, 1985; Victor F. Zonana, "Bank of America Considers Sale of Headquarters," *Wall Street Journal,* November 19, 1984; Gary Hector, *Breaking the Bank: The Decline of BankAmerica* (New York: Little, Brown & Company, 1988).

14 Gary Hector, "More than Mortgage Ails Bank of America," *Fortune,* April 1, 1985.

Washington was not going to tell Bank of America what to do, not on his watch.

But he had to do something. He called me into his office. “Ichak,” he told me, “it’s nothing personal, but you’ve become a political liability. I’m going to have to let you go.” Someone had to be sacrificed. It was done so effortlessly, without forced regret or bonhomie. It was just the way things were. There were no hard feelings. He shook my hand warmly and walked away.

Soon after I was fired, it was Armacost’s turn to go. The comptroller of the currency has the right by law to approve or disapprove the CEOs of American banks, and he gave the board of directors a list of acceptable candidates to choose from. Armacost’s name was not on the list.

THE PRICE TO PAY FOR SUCCESS

The corporate executives I worked with were friends with political leaders around the world, and they introduced me to the heads of state. In Mexico I advised President-elect Vicente Fox on how to reorganize the executive branch of government during his transition. In Ghana I designed the country's health delivery system during Ignatius Kutu Acheampong's administration in the 1970s.[15]

Clóvis Carvalho, who I trained and certified, used the Adizes Methodology to curb inflation in Brazil when he became the *Ministro Chefe da Casa Civil* (a de facto prime minister) during Henrique Cardoso's administration. When I asked Clóvis how he did it, he said that inflation is not an economic problem. Many books are written on what it is and what to do. It is a political problem. Following the Adizes protocols, he developed coalesced authority, power, and influence by making the ministry of finance, the Central Bank, and the trade unions cooperate.

---

15 Ichak Adizes and Paul Zukin, "Management Approach to Health Planning in Developing Countries," *Health Care Management Review* 2, no. 1 (winter 1977).

With Nobel Laureate Shimon Peres, who was then Deputy Prime Minister of Israel, and his wife Sonia. In the mid-1980s, Peres invited me for consultations to analyze the health of the Labor Party.

In the mid-1980s, Shimon Peres read a paper that I coauthored with Bob Haldeman, chief of staff of President Nixon's White House, which we sent to Mikhail Gorbachev. It outlined what was wrong with the way he was leading change in the Soviet Union.[16] Peres was apparently impressed and invited me to diagnose the Israeli Labor Party (HaAvoda) with the top leaders of the party, and the conclusions we arrived at were startling. The party was dying. It had more members than voters. Why?

One of the reasons was that the leadership was not united. To rejuvenate the Labor Party, we agreed to compose a team of party leaders

---

16 Ichak Adizes and Robert Haldeman, *Leading Change in the Soviet Union,* Adizes Institute working paper.

headed by Peres and Yitzhak Rabin, then prime minister of Israel. The two men, who had competing agendas, needed to join forces and design a cohesive, united, attractive political platform if the party was going to be rejuvenated.

What happened? Nothing. The party was distracted by the other political and national demands.

Researching and applying the methodology, building the institute—it was easy to get swept up in my success. But after each lecture or consultation I would go to my hotel room, miserable, depleted. There were nights I would walk the hotel corridors for hours, unable to sleep. I was deadly tired.

When I was on the road, I ate my breakfast and dinners alone. Sometime I would go out, also alone, to some bar. I would come back to my

room more depressed than when I went out. Bars were not my scene. Sometimes I would buy a ticket to a performance, but there was no one to share the experience with. I did not socialize with clients, as getting too close undermined the professional distance I had to maintain.

I was never home and when I was, I was not there for my family mentally or emotionally. One day, my wife moved out, took the kids with her, and said that she would not come back unless I changed.

Change? I wondered. Into what?

All the knowledge and self-confidence I had gained from my academic and professional experiences and from my success in solving managerial problems disappeared. The losses from my childhood came crashing in on me. I felt abandoned again, utterly alone. I tried to convince my wife to come back. I will change, I said, but she didn't buy it.

She claimed that I did not understand how to relate to women. Was I a male chauvinist? My parents and grandparents were my behavioral models. My grandmother never ate with my grandfather. She would eat before he came home, to be ready to serve him—yes, serve him—when he arrived. She was proud of it. It was her role, she said. She never disagreed with him, at least not in public. She always spoke to him using the formal "you" in Ladino, the royal "you."

My parents did not relate to each other like this, but when the extended family got together, the women hung out in the kitchen, cleaned up after a meal, and stayed in there, knitting or embroidering and talking. If it was an afternoon event, the men would often take a nap; or if it was an evening event, they would play cards and laugh. They never showed up in the kitchen to help. If they wandered in, they would be chased out. It was exclusively a woman's domain. No one openly complained about the arrangement.

When I was growing up, I was taught that women were not supposed to work outside the house. Even when there was no food at home and my father was lying in bed with broken legs, he would not let my mother find a job. To him, this would be the utmost humiliation as a man and head of the family. He insisted that I (although I was only eleven years old) should work and earn the bread for the family.

The women in my family received all the income the men earned and then gave their husbands and children allowances, but the men had the last word on everything. My father had final say over where we would live and the budget of the house. He made all the important decisions, and my mother had to abide.

I admit that I did not know what to do or how to behave as a husband in the new reality where women had careers and the same decision-making power as their spouses.

I was lecturing to the Icelandic government, the president in the front, in 1991, when an urgent phone call came in from the prime minister of Serbia. Yugoslavia was falling apart. Would I come to Belgrade at once?

SYMBOLS THAT IMPRISON

Word had gotten around about the work I had done advising governments when, in August 1991, I received a telephone call from Dragutin Zelenović, prime minister of Serbia. He was brief and to the point. He told me, "Please come as soon as possible."

I was in Iceland working with a large corporation and giving a presentation to the cabinet and the president when Zelenović called. My two sons, in their early teens, had come there with me on a vacation I had long promised them. The company's CEO had arranged for us to experience a day of fly-fishing and to ride the small Icelandic ponies across the landscape for a week after that.

I told Topaz and Shoham that I was sorry to cut their vacation short, but we had to go. There was a war in the offing. Maybe I could do something. They understood. My cousins were in Belgrade, so they would not be alone. Yugoslavia was not just another country for them to experience. I wanted them to see where I grew up. To know their roots.

Since Tito's death in 1980, the Socialist Federal Republic of Yugoslavia had begun to unravel. Different cultures. Different religions. And the different entities were looking for a way out of the federation. Tito had created a nation-state out of the assorted entities of Serbia and Montenegro, Macedonia, Bosnia and Herzegovina, Croatia, and Slovenia: a jumble of languages, nationalities, and religions with little common interest or shared affection. He had united them with an iron fist.

With Tito gone, unrest in Kosovo, a region on the southern border of Serbia, had become a tipping point. The minority Christian Serbian population was under siege from the impoverished Albian Muslim population, which had increased from one hundred thousand to around two million since the end of the Second World War. They wanted autonomy, and when Serbia denied it, a stream of terror attacks against the Serbian minority began. Milošević had unilaterally raided the federal treasury and sent a billion dollars of support to Kosovo. The wealthier regions of Croatia and Slovenia had no interest in shouldering the financial burden—it was not their national cradle and they wanted to secede. And Dragutin Zelenović had asked for my help.

I was on the next plane to Belgrade with my boys. We were met at the airport by a delegation from the prime minister's office. Several black Mercedes sedans were waiting and drove us to a villa reserved for foreign dignitaries. It had a personal chef and bodyguards, everything we could dream of. Even more impressive to me, it was next door to the mausoleum with Tito's tomb.

The next morning, when I arrived at Prime Minister Zelenović's office, he wasted no time in briefing me. Yugoslavia was coming apart.

What could I do to help? I began by examining the facts and figures. Kosovo had a very high unemployment rate. Because the Yugoslav federation was dissolving, if Kosovo did not secede, Serbia would bear the burden of financially supporting the region alone. It would cost Serbia over a billion dollars a year to keep Kosovo's health and educational services going. Instead of investing in itself, Serbia's scarce resources would go to support the Albanians of Kosovo, who did not want to be a part of Serbia in the first place. But there was more, another reason it made sense strategically to let Kosovo secede: the Albanians had one of the highest reproduction rates in Europe, and if they kept expanding their population, in twenty years at most, they would become a majority in Serbia, too.

Prime Minister Zelenović and I sat in his office debating the subject. Initially, he was reluctant to discuss Kosovo. It was a dangerous choice for him, with painful political consequences. Even discussing the issue of Kosovo was taboo.

I challenged Zelenović: "If you don't let go, they will squeeze the Serbs not only out of Kosovo but eventually out of Belgrade, too. The Albanian media claimed already that Kosovo will win the war against Serbia in bed. What choice do you have?

"Can you create a culture like in America, where different nationalities, religions, and races still live together in peace?" I continued. "Is there mutual trust and respect in the Balkans? If not, can it be developed in time to solve the problem?"

At a certain point, Zelenović decided we needed to take the proposal to Milošević, who had come to power on the slogan "Kosovo Is Ours." Everyone knew, however, that Milošević's wife was even fiercer in her Serbian nationalism than himself.

Zelenović and I were driven to the presidential compound. His sprawling office overflowed with heavy, carved wood furniture, books, and large pictures of Serbian fields and forests on the wall. Milošević rose from his chair and greeted us with a handshake.

Turkish coffee, cold water, and a little cube of Turkish delight were served. We were asked if we wanted any Vinjak or Shlivovitz. I accepted.

More than seventy years after Albanian villagers protected my family from falling into the hands of the Nazis, I was awarded the "Grand Master" title by President Ilir Meta.

It is a Serbian custom to have at least one drink of brandy (as it is the custom in Russia to have a glass of vodka) before starting any serious talks.

In the Serb culture, there is a ritual one goes through to develop intimacy. First, the parties communicate using the formal "you," like the French *vous* or the Spanish *usted.* Whenever the person with higher status (in title or in age) decides to increase intimacy, he will move to the familiar "you." That is the custom in many other cultures, too, such as in the French and the Spanish, but the Serbs go one step further. When the higher-ranking person curses you—or, better yet, curses your mother—it means you have become intimate friends and can say whatever you wish.

That's how the conversation unfolded. Milošević began with the formal "you." After some talk, when I asked him about the Serbian economy, he used *kurac* (a dick) to refer to it. I knew we could speak openly.

I tried to reason with him. It was one thing to gain political strength, but it was another, much harder thing, to maintain political strength. "You got the position you have because of Kosovo, but can you keep it with the Kosovo problem, its costs, the terrorism ongoing?"

His eyes narrowed. He heard me well and apparently did not like the question.

"What can you do to make Kosovo Serb again?" I asked. "Will you wake up one morning to find these two million Albanians have disappeared. Where would they go? To Albania? People are starving there. To Macedonia? Would it not change the composition of the population there, make it a Muslim country? Would Greece allow it to happen? The Greeks already have Turkish Muslims to the south; would they allow a Macedonia full of Albanian Muslims to the north? They have a history of struggle with the Albanians anyway. Greece is a member of NATO. Pushing Albanians to Macedonia would be asking NATO to intervene, no?"

He smiled. "We took on the Turks. We took on the Germans. We can take on NATO, too.

"Would you give up Jerusalem?" he asked, knowing I was Jewish and had immigrated to Israel. "Kosovo is our Jerusalem."

"Israel can probably afford to hold on to Jerusalem," I explained. "Its economy is strong, and America supports Israel with billions of dollars. Serbia is not in the same position. The billion and a half dollars a year you send to Kosovo could be spent on Serbia. Serbia has no medicine in its hospitals, yet you send money to support Albanians who do not want to be part of Serbia. How does that make sense?" I dared to ask.

It was then that I realized the genuine and visceral difference between heading a nation and running a company—the emotional ingredient is of a vastly different order.

Milošević was quiet for a few seconds. He looked at Zelenović and asked me to provide a possible solution. I spoke quickly, suggesting that a qualified international commission should be formed, headed by former president of the United States Jimmy Carter. The commission would carry out a referendum in Yugoslavia and find out who wanted to remain in the Yugoslav federation and who wanted to become independent.

"The Serbs in Bosnia will join Serbia, and Kosovo will secede, and, voilà, you have the greater Serbia without war. You unite the big Serbian nation and let go of the Kosovar economic and security liability."

He nodded for me to continue.

"The world will support this plan because the world understands and supports self-determination."

Milošević challenged my argument. "What about our monasteries in Kosovo?"

"Who goes to visit them?" I asked. "The Jewish people had no access to the Western Wall, the ancient wall of their temple in Jerusalem, for two thousand years. What happened? Symbols maintain their power no matter what. Or," I continued, "split Metohija, where many of the monasteries are."

He turned to Zelenović and asked his opinion.

"I think," Zelenović said, hesitating, "I think Isak is right."

"Get a map made," Milošević told him. "Mark out where the new border should be!"

To me, he said, "Speak to the American ambassador about the plan, and see if the Americans agree." He was not speaking with the American ambassador at the time.

The next day, I telephoned Warren Zimmerman, the American ambassador to Serbia, and told him I was coming with a proposal after a meeting with Milošević. He agreed to see me and took me into a soundproofed room so no one could overhear us. I told him what I'd suggested to Milošević. We would quietly encourage the Albanians in Kosovo to vote for independence and the Bosnian Serbs to vote to remain in the Yugoslav federation.

Zimmerman smiled. "If you manage to pull that off, you'll get the

Nobel Peace Prize," he said. "I'll back the proposal. However," he continued, "I wouldn't trust a word Milošević says."

I decided to wait for Milošević to contact me. The last thing I wanted was to appear to be pushing the president. So, I held back. Which was a grave mistake.

After two weeks, I could wait no longer for Milošević's call. I was scheduled to lecture in South Africa, which was also going through a cataclysmic political change as a result of the collapse of apartheid. I told Zelenović, "If Milošević calls for me, tell him that I saw Zimmerman, that he agreed to the plan, and that I'm ready to come back and help implement it." But it never happened.

Months later, after I left Serbia, I called a senior member of the cabinet and asked him what happened with the Kosovo project in light of my recommendations.

He told me in no uncertain terms, "You're an idiot! As soon as you left, Milošević fired Zelenović, mostly because he brought you on board and agreed with your Kosovo solution. Milošević won't give up Kosovo—not on his mother's life!"

"But what about our meeting? He agreed with me. He even assigned Zelenović to draw the map."

"Milošević used Tito's old strategy," the former cabinet member explained. "Water the field to see which weeds sprout, and then cut off their heads. He acted as if he agreed with your proposal to see where Zelenović stood. Then he fired him."

Milošević was not going to let go of Kosovo no matter what. It didn't hurt that his wife, who had critical influence over him, was even fiercer in her Serbian nationalism than Milošević himself. I found this phenomenon more than once, where the spouses of very powerful leaders have an outsized influence over them. Bibi Netanyahu is another one. And it is said that the first lady of Mexico has an enormous effect on Andrés Manuel

López Obrador's decisions. It's often the same with CEOs of major corporations. When I consult with them, I sometimes insist on having their spouse in the room. Otherwise, whatever we decide will be undermined during the pillow talk that night.

A while after that visit, I was talking to a member of the cabinet of Serbia and asking him why the Kosovo issue is still not solved. "It is a political liability," he said. "No politician can afford to let go of Kosovo. It is a political suicide."

It appeared to me that what the history books will say drove Milošević's decision. He could not let go of Kosovo, just as Netanyahu would not let go of Jerusalem or the Saudi royals of Mecca. Symbols have a tremendous power in the consciousness of nations.

Milošević pushed the Kosovo Albanians into Macedonia in a move the West labeled ethnic cleansing. NATO intervened and bombed Belgrade. Later, Milošević was tried by the International Court in The Hague for crimes against humanity. According to the official announcement, he died there from a heart attack. I believe he committed suicide, as did many members of his family before him.

Many years later, I met with the head of the Serbian intelligence agency and told him about my experience with Milošević. He told me I was totally wrong about what happened. "Do you know that NATO built Europe's biggest military airport in Kosovo? Do you know that it was NATO that told the Albanians to move out of Kosovo? We did not push them out. They told them to move because they were going to bomb the region."

"Why," I asked him, surprised.

"The wall between communism and capitalism has fallen down. There is a new wall being built between Muslims and Judeo-Christian nations. Why do you think the Russians were in Afghanistan? Why are you in Afghanistan? Look at the map. The wall being built is American forces in Afghanistan, in Iraq, now in Kosovo, and the biggest American embassy you can imagine in Bosnia. That is the new wall the Americans are building. We were just puppets in the American show. In a meeting in France that I attended, where negotiations were supposed to take place between us and the Kosovo-Albanian leadership, we wanted to have direct negotiations. The Americans would not allow us."

I was speechless. I did not believe him and asked the minister of defense of Macedonia, Blagoje Handjisky, if it was true that there was a large military airport in Kosovo. He said, "Sure."

I asked Kiro Gligorov, the president of Macedonia, what happened in Kosovo. He said, "I told President Clinton we cannot allow NATO forces from Greece through Macedonia into Kosovo to fight the Serbs. Our Serb brothers will never forgive us. My request was ignored. NATO forces moved through Macedonia without permission."

I did not and don't have the capability to validate those claims. Kosovo is still in limbo, as Serbia will not recognize it as an independent state.

WHAT'S IN A NAME?

Years ago, I was invited by a top executive at a major corporation to speak to its staff at an annual conference. I stood in the wings of the stage as he introduced me to the crowd, rattling off a list of accomplishments and accolades. That I had consulted not only to Fortune 500 companies but to the governments of Iceland and Israel, Montenegro and Mesopotamia. Well, my grandchildren may think I'm old, but I'm not that old. He was of course referring to Macedonia.

When my American friends ask me about Macedonia—a country sandwiched between Greece and Kosovo and Serbia, in the heart of the Balkans—I tell them about Alexander the Great, who was king of Macedonia. He was tutored as a boy by none other than Aristotle and set out to conquer the world in the fourth century BCE. I tell them that Mother Teresa was born in Skopje, the capital and the place of my birth.

The country then known as the Republic of Macedonia was locked in a dispute with Greece for decades over its name, which the Greeks felt was theirs. For Greece, the name Macedonia was deadly serious. They feared that the establishment of a sovereign Macedonian state in the north might ignite nationalistic sentiments among the large population of ethnic

Macedonians inhabiting northern Greece, a region the Greeks *also* called Macedonia. Greece placed an embargo on Macedonia in 1991, and the country's economy was in trouble.

When I was brought in to consult with the prime minister, Branko Crvenkovski, it did not take long for me to diagnose the big first issue. "Why," I asked, "couldn't you change the name? The economy is in trouble, unemployment is high. Why suffer just for a name?"

"You Americans," he responded, "will do anything for money. That is the only thing you care for. Why don't we call it Coca-Cola Country? We could make a fortune in royalties, but what about our identity? Our pride?

"Macedonia is not just a name," the prime minister continued. "People died for our right to call ourselves Macedonians. We sing songs about Mother Macedonia, not about Coca-Cola."

I should have known better. One of the painful points in my divorce was that my first wife insisted the children have her family name as their middle name. I was scared. My two sons were the last to carry the name Adizes. My cousins had only daughters. All other members of the Adizes family were ashes in Treblinka. If my sons had a middle name, maybe it would be considered their family name as it is in Mexico, and the Adizes name would disappear forever. In retrospect, this was an unnecessary fight, even more so since it played out publicly in court, but the legacy of the Holocaust, the fear that my family name would disappear altogether, was haunting me.

Nevertheless, Crvenkovski did not discourage me when I suggested taking a stab at mediation between the two countries. I had access to the leading members of the Greek cabinet through some corporate clients and thought maybe I could help resolve the issue.

I traveled to Greece and met with George Papandreou, the future prime minister and son of the current prime minister, Andreas Papandreou, who was very ill and often incoherent. Nobody could speak with him except his son and his wife, a former airline hostess, who seemed to be making policy by default as she interpreted her husband's wishes to the cabinet.

In 1991, I worked closely with Macedonia's President Kiro Gligorov and other high ranking officials to help end the dispute with Greece over the country's use of their country's name.

After a long conversation, George and I put together the following plan: if Macedonia changed its name and calls itself Nova Macedonia, or "New Macedonia," the change would sufficiently prove that Macedonia had no claim on the territory with the same name in the north of Greece. If the country also changed its flag, which the Greeks believed featured uniquely Greek symbols, Greece would champion Nova Macedonia's acceptance into NATO, which would probably stop Milošević's threat.

George Papandreou took our plan to his father, who agreed to it, and I went back to Macedonia to relay this to Crvenkovski. To my astonishment, he rejected the name change. "Never," he said. "There'll be a civil war in Macedonia."

Not willing to take no for an answer, I made a pitch to Kiro Gligorov, Macedonia's president. Gligorov also refused to consider a name change. "We'll change the flag," he said, "but that's it." A new design for the flag was drawn, a sun in the center surrounded by eight light rays that still flies high in Macedonia today.

Almost immediately after the new flag was unveiled, a car bomb nearly took President Gligorov's life. My cultural perceptions had been way off. It seemed that with all my time in America I had lost my connection to the nationalistic way of thinking that governs the Balkans—and much of the world.

In time, the issue of Macedonia's name came up again when it sought to join the European Union in 2004. But to join the EU or NATO, as long as Greece found Macedonia's name unacceptable, Greece could, would, and did veto every one of Macedonia's attempts to gain membership.

So I went back to work to see if I could broker a solution, working with Greek and Macedonia officials across the power structure of government and across the political spectrum. I failed, leaving with my tail between my legs. But the seed had been planted. In 2019, Macedonia changed its name to North Macedonia, and the following year EU leaders approved both North Macedonia and Albania to begin the process of accession.

Working with presidents and prime ministers fed my ego. But there was a dimension to my work that touched me so deeply I was not even able to fully appreciate or understand it at the time.

I had lost my childhood to the war and built a shield to protect myself from love and intimacy and the pain that could come with them. My defense against reliving that personal trauma was to channel everything into my work. It is this attempt to escape from my personal pain that explains, in large part, my professional success.

Toward the end of my time working with Equifax, one of the vice presidents offered to drive me to the airport after a session. I was surprised.

He had been diagnosed with terminal cancer but refused to stay at home waiting for the end. I thought he should spend his limited time on something more important, but he insisted, and we got into the car.

"Listen," he said, once we were on the road, "I have been working at this company for thirty years," he said, "trying to make changes and getting nowhere. You are making change happen before I die, and I wanted to thank you somehow."

I took a deep breath. When we came to a stoplight, he looked my way and continued. "I pray for you in church every Sunday." He was the one who was dying. He was the one who needed prayers. But here he was praying for me. I really could make a difference. It is this scene that keeps me going for fifty years now, teaching, training, consulting, working hard to make a difference. But it had its price. Was it worth it?

Once my divorce from Yael was finalized, the custody agreement stipulated that I would have the children half the time; they would change homes every Wednesday. In order to be home to receive them every second Wednesday, I went to great lengths to rearrange my international travel. I would fly to Australia for a week, fly back to California to be with the children for a week, then fly back to Australia for another week to continue working. I developed chronic jet lag.

But my sons were not happy. They complained that I did not love them.

"What do you mean, I don't love you?" I would ask, irritated. "I travel across the globe to be with you. I coach your soccer on Saturdays."

"No, you don't love us," they would answer.

I could not understand what they wanted. Of course, I loved them. What did they mean? What did they see that I failed to understand? I had to do something but what? I could heal corporations (and to a lesser degree solve problems on national level), but as for what to do on my personal level, I was lost.

What was blocking my happiness? What was making my family feel I did not love them?

Was it that I was scared to love? Whoever I loved, it seemed, disappeared. I developed a protective mechanism to deal with it. "There is no such thing as love," I used to say to those who would listen. "There is only commitment," and I truly believed in what I was saying.

In the years during and following the war, my parents and I were without a steady home, work, or food. I had watched the people whom I loved the most, and who had loved me the most, sent to their deaths. Yet, somehow, there we were, alive. Except for my one blind eye and my mother's periodic fainting spells, we had no visible wounds or scars. But the hidden costs were everywhere. I was scared. Whoever I loved, it seemed, disappeared.

PART III

OPENING THE CAGE

I played at the KotorArt Festival in Montenegro in 2018 with my son Sapphire Adizes, who performed in his concert with a symphonic orchestra choir and electronic music.

Fifty thousand people attended my lecture in Saint Petersburg at the Gazprom Arena in 2019. Speaking to or playing for a crowd gave me more pleasure and happiness than any other activity I was involved in.

MAKING A WISH

I have led a divided life and been a divided self for most of my first seventy years. While my personal life was not a happy one, my professional life was exceptionally functional—some might say high-powered. Discipline, focus, and creativity in operation, with all cylinders going full blast. Perhaps my career worked so well because my emotional self was closed off. I was like a man who, having lost his sight, discovers that his other senses have sharpened and perform well beyond the bounds of normal.

My whole life has been a constant struggle to be open and trusting, to allow fear to leave my heart and love to enter. It hurt so deeply when my own children would say, "Daddy, you do not love us," or when my wife Nurit would cry because she felt unloved.

There were moments when I found a way to express something like love: playing the accordion. It began in my childhood. Whenever I was feeling lonely and rejected, the accordion was my companion. Whenever I played it, I was myself. Whenever I led community singing, I felt included. I seemed to belong. I remember on the *Kefalos,* the boat that carried us to Israel, I would play the Montenegrin song "Three Meadows, Three Meadows, and No Shade in Sight" at night when they let us on deck. The people around me would break into song, and I would feel like I was part of something.

In my professional life, I have often adopted the same role, the same gestures, of the accordion player. When I move onstage to give a lecture or when I lead my organizational therapy sessions, I am still, in a manner of speaking, performing with my instrument. I use the same techniques in my lectures and professional practice that I learned leading community singing. When leading a group of people in song, or when I lead collaborative change management sessions, I watch the audience carefully. I feel their presence and intuitively feel their mood. I get the process started, but my clients do all the necessary work. I lead, but they sing.

Playing the accordion enabled me to feel, but how could I feel love without holding an accordion? How could I feel love while holding my wife and children?

In the summer of 1991, after meeting with Milošević, my sons came with me to Cape Town, where I was scheduled to lecture. South Africa was at a crossroads: what was the country going to do about the apartheid system and the revolutionary rise of its Black population? Once again, my sons were watching history up close. I had brought them halfway around the globe so they could witness the birth of the twenty-first century. What better gift could I offer them?

The South African YPO chapter had invited me to lecture on how to manage change without destructive conflict. This was my area of expertise and a subject that was about to confront the country as it attempted to integrate its people: the Black members of the African National Congress (ANC); their rivals, the Zulus of the Inkatha Freedom Party (IFP); the white Afrikaners; the liberal white British; the Indians; and the Pakistanis.

A prominent South African businessman, Nick Frangos, who was a certified Adizes Associate at the time, was advising Prime Minister F. W. de Klerk as he handed over the reins of government to Nelson Mandela.

Nick had written a hundred-page plan for the transition following the Adizes Methodology for managing change.

YPO hired a couple to organize the logistics of the event. I had trouble taking my eyes off them as they went about their work. They were a marvel to watch. They exhibited an enviable intimacy in their relationship: they worked in complete unison, whether setting the table for a meal (placing the glasses in the identical spots above the plates) or organizing the public event (without one tense word spoken). I could see the affection when they were in a room together; indeed, I could feel it. How had they managed that? It looked like a perfect marriage.

I had never witnessed that kind of relationship up close before. And I was envious. I suddenly realized that what I wanted was a wife and a family with that kind of intimacy.

One evening, during a safari we took before my lecture, we sat around a campfire. Everyone was asked to describe their greatest wish. My firstborn son, Topaz, said something that touched me deeply. He said, "I would like to have a family again." He did not like living in a divorced one.

It hurt me to hear him say that. Wasn't I offering him the world? He was only fourteen years old. What other boy his age had been given such a rich introduction to politics and power? And yet his desire was to live as part of an intact family. I was up half the night, his words running through my head; his greatest wish was also mine.

Marriage is like a chicken coop, my father used to say. Those who are out want in, and those who are in want out. I hated being single.

I had signed up with a matchmaking service that kept my evenings busy whenever I was home in Los Angeles. At first, I was like a kid in a candy store. I liked this one and that one and that one and this one. Any time I wanted a date I had one. Freedom.

After a while, I tired of telling my life story every time I went out with a new woman. I had enough uncertainty and stress in my profession. I craved stability at home and believed that meant having a wife to come home to.

How would I go about finding a new wife? I started by researching our host couple, whose marriage had so impressed me. How did they meet? Maybe I could learn something from them.

The husband told me his story. He had been single for a long time and realized it was not what he wanted out of life. He visualized exactly how he would meet his future wife, what she would look like, and what would happen when they met. Since he was a religious man, he prayed to God to help make that vision a reality.

The prayer led to a precise vision, a set of images in his mind. There she was, singing in the church choir, a tall, blonde woman. He would approach her after the service and invite her to dinner. She would accept, and they would have a long, intimate conversation. They would talk to each other on several levels, connecting on all of them, and at that instant they would each recognize their future together.

The next Sunday, he went to church. There she was in the choir, the tall, blonde woman he had visualized and prayed for. He invited her to dinner. They had a great conversation that went deeper as the night went on. Two weeks later, they announced their engagement.

"Make your wish, and it will be granted," he said. "Pray."

Pray? To what? To whom? I am not a religious person, so I decided instead to write a personal ad. I would never dream of publishing it, but it would serve as a secular sort of prayer. I would spell out for myself what I was looking for, what I wanted in a wife.

I stayed up all night thinking about it and finally wrote it down for fear of forgetting. She would be a widow with children, I wrote. Why a widow? So I would not have to deal with an ex-husband. Why with children? Because I adored children and wanted to raise as many as I could. I wanted someone from Israel. There it was again: my dream of belonging. She would have lived in a moshav, an agricultural settlement in Israel. Why? I wanted someone who had lived close to the earth, someone genuine. Finally, she would be a journalist or a photographer so she could pursue her own interests while traveling with me on my professional assignments.

Notice the one item that my list did not include: love. I still did not believe that there was such a thing. But I had my list.

⸻

From Cape Town, my sons and I flew to Tel Aviv to visit my parents. While there, I consulted with an astrologer recommended to me by a friend. "Which sign should my future wife be born under?" I asked her. "What kind of woman would be best suited for me?" She said someone born around sunrise and in the first week in January.

In Israel a true friend is a friend for life. So whenever I am there, I call my old friends and we continue our conversations as if we had never parted company. On that trip, I called Ami, my roommate from my army days, to say hello.

"It's good you called," he said. "My daughter is visiting from Canada and wants to speak with you." He handed her the phone.

"I know who your wife should be," Essi said, not wasting any time. She knew I was divorced and assumed I wanted to remarry. She had a friend in Montreal: a widow, Israeli, with three kids. Her name was Nurit, and she was perfect for me, she said. "Promise me that you will call her," she requested.

I told Essi that I was not interested. Her friend was geographically undesirable. "I live in Los Angeles and travel the world fifty percent of the time," I explained. "It's not possible."

"I will bring you her picture, and then you can decide," she insisted.

Later that day, she came to my parents' house with the picture in hand. Nurit had big, beautiful brown eyes that were loving, warm, and captivating—my mother's eyes.

"I will make the call when I get back to Los Angeles," I promised, "but that is all."

⸻

That photograph had piqued my curiosity, but I went into the call with no expectations. Chitchat eventually gave way to questions, my questions for her.

I saw Nurit's photo before agreeing to meet with her.
Her eyes were big, beautiful, captivating, like my mother's.
It wasn't long before we were married.

I remember starting with something like "So have you been married?"

"I'm a widow," she replied, "with three kids."

Wait, I said to myself. Where is my list?

"What do you do for a living?" I continued.

"I am a journalist."

"Where were you born?"

"In Kfar Bilu, do you know it?" I did. It was an agricultural settlement south of Tel Aviv.

"When were you born?"

"The seventh of January."

"What time?"

"Six in the morning."

It was like a clap of thunder. My ad had been answered.

Was she the one? She had to be.

Nurit and I talked on the phone for hours every day. I liked talking to her. She was interesting, open, honest, not trying to hide anything. She was real. She was twenty years younger than me. I wondered if she would look like the photograph when we finally met in person.

The Jewish High Holidays arrived, and my kids were going to their mother's, so I would be alone for Rosh Hashanah, the Jewish New Year celebrations. I hate being alone at that time of year, so I asked Nurit if I could come and be with her in Montreal instead.

"Sure, come over," she said. "You are welcome to celebrate with me, my children, and my brother's family."

To my surprise, I later discovered that Nurit had seen a video of my friend's daughter's wedding, a wedding that I had attended. I was a divorced man then, and weddings were a perfect place to meet new women. I danced with most of the single women in attendance and took everyone's phone number, which they willingly gave me. I did not know that the camera was following me and recording my charm offensive. When Nurit saw the video, she had asked to meet me.

When my son Shoham was a boy, I taught him about music, but was it real love? "There is no such thing as love," I used to say to those who would listen. "There is only commitment."

ON THE SPUR OF THE MOMENT

When I landed, Nurit was waiting for me at the airport, and my mind immediately took over, looking for the white spots. I usually went for simply dressed women, not too fashionable, and she was dressed to kill. I liked petite women, and she was not. When we celebrated the Jewish New Year, she wanted to dance with me but would not let me lead. I am a good dancer, so this annoyed me, and I stopped dancing.

I liked her children, though, and the little ones sought my company. When I hugged her youngest daughter, Cnaan, from the word *go* I felt she was like my daughter. Her son, Nimrod, was reserved but played with me. Her elder daughter, Atalia, was going back to Israel to serve in the army, so it was more difficult to connect with her. But my mind wouldn't stop chattering, blocking me from the chance to connect with Nurit, heart to heart. I felt as if I were wearing armor all the time. After just two days, I cut the trip short and headed back to California with no intention of continuing the relationship.

But this was not the end.

Two weeks later, I received a call that my mother was in the hospital.

Commemoration for the Jewish community of Macedonia that perished in the Holocaust. To the right are Prime Minister Branko Crvenkovski and Prime Minister and President Kiro Gligorov.

She had high blood pressure and a weak heart. A stroke had left her paralyzed. Now she was hospitalized again, and my sister said it was serious, giving me no explanations. I called Nurit in Montreal. Why? I do not know, but I did.

She did not ask why I had left early, or why I hadn't called since. She was all love and support. "Go be with your mother," she said. "You will regret it later if she dies and you did not say good-bye."

I took her advice.

My father and sister were waiting for me at the hospital. My mother's hair, normally a deep brown, trimmed to just above her shoulders, was ringed in a halo of gray. My father looked thin. His face was covered in stubble. He had been caring for my mother since her stroke, doing all the cooking, washing the dishes, things he had never done before in his life. "Still, it was not enough to please her," he said. After her stroke she could not talk, but her eyes "talked," and she would look at him with anger. Maybe in the last years of her life she dared to show her displeasure for how he had treated her in the marriage. One night a year earlier, he broke down while I was visiting them. "She does not love me," he wailed. "I do not want to live. Let me jump off the terrace." I had never seen him like this before. My tough, macho father, it turned out, needed love, too. Very much so. He never got it from his parents. He never got it from his brother Leon, who used him almost like a servant. And he suspected not even his wife loved him.

We approached the bed. "Duka, Izi is here," my father said, reaching to stroke her cheek.

She looked at me with sad eyes. She could not talk, but I could see how deeply she loved me. My God, I said to myself, where have I been all these years? Working. Working, but never having time to be with her. To take her out anywhere. Or to just sit and talk. I gave them financial support. I was willing to help them but would not give them the most valuable asset I had. I never had time for her. Not for my wife, nor my children. Whenever I came to Israel, I was busy talking to members of parliament and to major corporations and lecturing and being interviewed and . . . No time to have dinner with my parents or sister. My mother never complained. She let me be. But now I felt the loss.

She will be gone. The past cannot be relived. Sitting next to her and looking into her eyes, I knew it was too late. The most valuable things in life we know by their absence. We do not know the value of health till we are sick. The value of democracy till we live in a dictatorship. And the value of life till we are dying.

I kissed her hand, and—remembering Topaz and his wish to belong to a family again, and the personal ad I had written after the trip to South Africa—looking into my mother's beautiful honey-colored eyes, so like Nurit's eyes, wanting to please her before she departed to the next life, I made a decision.

"Mom," I announced, without a second thought, "I have good news: I am getting married." I wanted with all of my heart for her to leave this world at peace, to give her the sense that I would be okay. That I would not be alone. That someone would take care of me.

I showed her Nurit's picture, and she took a long, hard look before turning her eyes to meet mine as if she was trying to tell me something.

A few days later, her doctor took me aside and told me my mother would have to be put on life support. He asked me what I wanted done because she would not recuperate. "It will be just keeping her alive," he said. Like a vegetable, I thought. I took a deep breath and made the decision. It was time for her to stop suffering. She had suffered enough in this life.

A few hours later, my mother lost consciousness, but her eyes were still open, looking straight at me. I believed that she was struggling to see me for just one more minute. One more minute to be alive with the one she loved. We take life for granted because it is too scary to admit that we will die. So we abuse time as if we will live forever. Only when confronted with the experience of dying do we realize that we would give everything we had worked so hard to possess just one more minute, just one more minute alive with someone we love.

I watched her breath as it began to slow. Her eyes looked in my direction but were cloudy and expressionless. Eventually, I had to use the bathroom, so I left for few minutes. When I came back, she was gone.

For years after, when I asked people about those they had lost, I found the same phenomenon over and over again. Their loved ones died when there was no one in the room who loved them. When they were alone.

I stayed in Israel for seven days to sit shiva for my mother. Nurit asked me if I wanted her to come be with me, and I said yes. She flew from Montreal to be with me in my sorrow. She was warm, loving, supportive.

Once she returned to Montreal, we resumed our long phone calls. One evening—thinking of how much I liked her children, how kind she had been to me in Israel, and how I had promised my mother I would marry her—I asked Nurit, "Why don't you come and live with me in Los Angeles?"

Without hesitation, she said yes. She sold all of her furniture, took her children out of school, and moved in. I was touched. If she cared enough to give up everything and come to the other side of the continent to be with me, then she must be the one. I married Nurit, adopted her children, and two years later we had a son together, Sapphire Moshe, named after my mother, Diamanta, a precious gemstone, and my grandfather Mushon Kalderon.

Was it love? I do not know. All I knew was working hard to bring money home. That was how I expressed love. Not feeling it.

My mind had been one of my greatest assets. But where was my heart? Whenever Nurit would tell me she loved me, I would say, “Thank you.”

“Thank you! That is all you have to say?” She was infuriated that I did not reciprocate and tell her that I loved her, too. She did not understand the reasons that I was saying “thank you.” I thanked her for loving me because I did not believe any woman could love me. I had to earn it. I had to fulfill her wishes and the wishes of her children. Otherwise, I felt I did not deserve to be loved.

I actually did not believe there was such a “thing” as *love.* I argued with people that it did not exist. The only thing that existed was commitment.

As I write these lines, I cannot believe myself that that was who I was at the time. I really, truly believed that there is no such thing called love. And Nurit needed a constant shower of love. She was a woman who could not live without it: hugging, kissing, holding hands, and telling each other how much we loved each other. What she wanted, I could not give. I feared it as I feared fire.

No wonder the marriage wasn’t easy.

In spite of Nurit’s efforts, I felt lonely in my marriage. The more she tried, the more scared I grew, and the more I rejected her. She was miserable, but so was I. I desperately wanted what I continually rejected. And she, herself, was not easy. I wanted an Israeli wife. I got one. Tough. Independent. Opinionated. Affectionately sarcastic and cheeky. She periodically put me down to keep me in check, to make sure I didn’t let my success go to my head, pushing all of my buttons, triggering all of my fears that my father was right: that I was no good, that no woman could truly love me.

The atmosphere in our house was tense. She would scream at me, I would react with rage, and our son Sapphire would hide in the housekeeper's room, where she would hug him and try to calm him down.

Nurit would tell me, "If you are so unhappy with me, why don't you divorce me? You do not love me. You do not see me."

"What do you mean I do not love you?" I would say. "Don't I bring home food and give you a roof over your head? Don't I finance your children's education and provide you with a live-in housekeeper and a palace? What is that? Is that all nothing?"

"I want you to see me," she would say through her tears.

"I am looking at you right now. What do you want?" I did not understand.

She was unhappy, and I was unhappy that I could not make her happy. What the hell did she want?

She wanted me. But I was not available, not even to myself.

There is a Mexican song with the lyrics *El tiempo que te quede libre si te es posible, dedícalo a mí.* (The free time you have, if it is only possible, dedicate it to me.) I would get very emotional whenever I heard that song. I identified with the lyrics. I longed to give some time, even a few minutes, to myself—but where was I? Who was the person inhabiting my skin? I had no idea. I was busy serving the world, but not my wife, my children, or myself.

I had to do something. Where should I start?

FACING THE WOUNDS

In 2013, when I was seventy-five years old, I returned to Kiryat Motzkin, Israel, to search for my old elementary school, face my past, close the loop, and free myself from those painful childhood memories.

I found the school. The main entrance had been moved to another location, but the old door was still there. I knocked on the door, and a woman opened it. "How did you know about this entrance?" she asked.

I walked past her and saw another door to the right.

"This is the principal's office, right?" I asked her.

"Yes, how do you know?"

I was standing at the exact same spot where I had stood sixty-five years before, waiting for the principal to come out so I could beg him to let me attend the school. The place had not changed.

I went to my old classroom and found my chair. I walked out into the corridor where Ehud used to kick me. I closed my eyes and breathed deeply. Time to release my pain, I said to myself. Time to let go.

The principal of the school wanted to know who I was. When I told her I was an alumnus, she gave me files of pictures to find my class graduation photo. There I was. Next to mine was a picture of Ehud. I paused for a very long moment.

"Do you have his address, maybe?" I asked in a low voice.

"No, I don't, but let's try the Internet. Maybe we can find him." The principal took the lead to help me find my old classmate. I lacked the courage to do it. We found a man by the same name, a lawyer.

The phone rang. A secretary answered.

"This is the principal of Ahdut Elementary School in Kiryat Motzkin. We are organizing an alumni get-together," she lied. "I wonder if Ehud Artzi is an alumnus of our school?"

"He's in court," replied the secretary. "When he comes back, I will ask him and call you back."

I was nervous. Was it him? What would I say to him? Could I even face him?

I was tense waiting for the call. When it came, we learned that this Ehud was from Tel Aviv and much too young to be my classmate.

A few years later, one of my best friends in the United States, an Israeli, was looking through my pictures when she came across that class photo from elementary school.

"Whoa," she said. "This is my aunt's husband." She recognized the name under the picture. My body froze.

"He joined a kibbutz. He fought with everyone there and died from a heart attack years ago."

Next, we drove to Tzur Shalom to look for the house where I had lived. We took the long road I had walked to and from school sixty years ago. It used to have fields on both sides—there were high-rises now. The view was different, but the distance was the same. I could direct the driver where to turn. I could tell him in advance where the road would encounter the plaza. I retraced the indignities of each step of that walk along the way.

I found our home easily, although the entire neighborhood had changed. From a distance, I could see the palm tree my father had planted. There was the garage where he kept the pickup truck and, beside it, the place where I had to dry the truck and suffer his scathing put-downs. I took deep breaths and told myself to let go.

I returned to Kiryat Motzkin years later, when a classmate organized our class reunion for our sixty-year anniversary. At the reunion, I told my old classmates about my suffering. They were incredulous.

They'd had no idea what I was going through. Some even wondered if I was making it all up.

My attachment to Israel was never in doubt, but I remember the days when I felt it as deeply as can one feel anything. One of them was when I was driving from Tel Aviv to Haifa. I stopped the car somewhere off the road

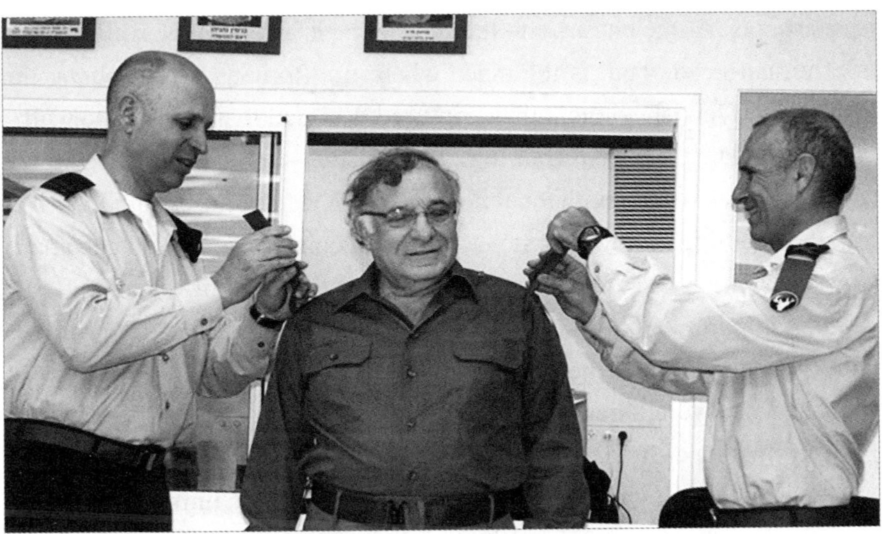

Even after half a century living in America, my attachment to Israel still runs deep. In the early 2000s, I was awarded the honorary rank of lieutenant colonel by the Israeli Defense Forces.

where I could see the shoreline of the Mediterranean. I stood there in silence, watching the waves wash ashore and the seagulls flying overhead. I stood there on the coast south of Tel Aviv, watching the waves crash on an ordinary strip of sand. In my travels, I have seen some of the most beautiful beaches in the world, but I never felt that sensation watching any other waves. Those are my waters; that is my sea. We have history. We have memories. It was an ordinary beach, but it was mine.

My mind flooded with a series of memories. I remembered standing beneath the Arch of Titus when I was in Rome with my youth delegation the summer after I'd graduated from high school. The emperor Titus erected the arch after conquering Judea, the Jewish state that had rebelled against the Roman Empire. On the columns of the arch is an engraving of enslaved Jewish people carrying to Rome the menorah, the candelabrum Israel uses today as its national symbol.

I was moved. There we were, high school graduates to be recruited into the Israeli army upon returning home. Israel was still alive. Where was the Roman Empire? I felt so proud to be Jewish, to be Israeli. A survivor.

I remembered visiting the catacombs in Rome where they kept the Jewish prisoners. At the entrance to the catacombs is a dent in the wall the size of a human head. That is the place where the Romans used to bang the heads of the Jewish soldiers they captured. I kissed that dent in the wall.

As a soldier, I was in training, walking the sands of Ashkelon in the south of Israel, when another soldier walking ahead of me shouted. He had found something in the sand. It was a Roman coin made when the Romans won the war against Judea. On one side was the head of the conquering Roman emperor; on the other side was a woman sitting under a broken palm tree, a symbol of the conquered Judea, crying.

There we were, Israeli soldiers, living proof that although the Roman Empire was gone, Judea was still alive.

Yes, Israel is my emotional home. Good, bad, or indifferent. Home is home no matter what. I love the country with all of my heart. Unfortunately, Israel has gone far too much to the right for me to feel comfortable. Well, you like because of. You love in spite of.

MY ENEMIES, MY FRIENDS

When we emerged from hiding at the end of the Second World War, my father promised the people of Bërdicë that he would come back and build them a well so that they would not need to walk to the river to fetch water. For fifty years, Albania was closed to foreigners, and we were unable to return. The country was ruled by a paranoid Communist dictator, Enver Hoxha, who believed Albania was surrounded by enemies waiting to attack and seize control. He constructed thousands of bunkers all across the countryside—one per family. It was the poorest nation in Europe, with a border closed to outsiders, but with more bunkers per capita than any other country in the world.

In 1995, fifty years after the end of the war, Enver Hoxha died, and Albania's borders finally opened. My father was eighty-three years old, and I told him that time was running out—the moment had come to fulfill his promise.

But would the village even be there? Would anyone we knew still be alive? How would we locate the family who had taken us in?

At that time, I was consulting to Branko Crvenkovski, prime minister of Macedonia. I asked him for help. He contacted the prime minister of

I spent my career healing corporations. When I realized I needed to heal myself, I began returning to the sites of childhood trauma. In 1995, a film crew followed me and father back to Bërdicë.

Albania, who in turn instructed the Albanian Ministry of Internal Affairs to provide all the information and assistance we needed. They found the village and the Brahimi family with whom we had stayed during the war. Visas and passage were quickly made available to us.

Then the leading Israeli television channel discovered that we were making the trip and decided to film our journey.[1]

My father could barely walk. Age had seen to that. My mother was

1 Eitan Oren, dir., *I Want to Remember, He Wants to Forget* (Israeli New Fund for Cinema and TV, the Israeli Broadcasting Authority, the Adizes Institute, 1996), YouTube video, 1:02:10, https://www.youtube.com/watch?v=YcCq-uSeDSY.

not alive anymore, and he had since married a woman who had heard our stories so many times that she felt she herself had lived in Bërdicë. She joined us on the trip. I wanted Nurit to see where I had spent my childhood years in hiding, so she and our son Sapphire, who was one at the time, made the trip as well.

First, we visited the Monopol concentration camp in Skopje. It had not changed: the same cramped, flat bunks, the same smells. The same wood planks we had slept on were still there. A section of the train tracks remained, too. I closed my eyes and could hear the sounds of shuffling feet. Of people crying. Of the doors to the cattle cars slamming closed. I was surprised by how much I remembered. My father wanted to leave the place. He refused to relive memories. He wanted to forget it all.

In Albania, we were met by a representative of the Ministry of Interior Affairs, who took us directly to Bërdicë. There was no horse-drawn cart this time: we rode to the village in a motorcade of Mercedes limousines provided by the Macedonian prime minister's office.

When we arrived at the house where we had hidden in the midst of a wedding celebration, it was as though history was repeating itself. Fifty years earlier, when we had first sought shelter in this village, a stray bullet at a wedding had hit a guest in the neck, and my father had become a medical doctor. Gunshots rang out once again at this wedding. Random bullets punctured the air. My body responded in the same way it had so many years before. I began to sweat and had to make an effort to control my breathing. This time no one was hurt.

I was a grown man at ease with corporate executives and heads of state, but as I watched the Brahimi brothers walk toward us, the thought cycled through my mind over and over that these were the people I had feared. These were the people I had believed would kill us if they discovered who we were. I felt my body shaking.

Ali was the first to appear, an old man dragging his feet. His brother followed behind him with his wife. We had been told Rajib was dying of cancer, and he looked frail. The brothers and my father hugged each other for a long time.

These were the men I was told to beware of? These were the dangerous Muslims who would kill us without a second thought?

My father asked Ali about the gun he always had worn. He laughed, "No more."

"Where is the baby?" my father asked. Ali's wife had been pregnant during the war. He pointed to a man standing next to him. The "baby" was fifty years old.

"And Philip?" The names of the people he remembered from those days in the village came flooding back to my father.

"They are all dead," Rajib told him. My father, the survivor, began to wail. When he finally regained his composure, he pointed at me and said, "This is Ishuk," using my Muslim name from during the war. Obviously, they did not recognize me. I was sixty-some years old, bald, and somewhat heavyset—no longer the little, skinny, sickly kid they remembered, who had come upstairs to play during Ramadan.

As we strolled to the village community center for lunch, my father turned jovial. He started singing Albanian songs, the ones he remembered from those wartime days. There was lots of laughter and singing. Everyone seemed happy.

But not me. I was still terrified. Would they finally discover who we really were?

Then it happened. The director of the documentary asked the brothers if they had believed that we were Muslims.

Oh my God, I thought. What now?

"Of course, we knew they were Jewish," the older brother replied. "They ate during Ramadan."

What!? I could not believe my ears. They had known we were eating. They had known we were Jews. And the whole time I had believed they would behead us if they found out we were Jews. And I was hallucinating for days and nights out of fear that they would kill us if they ever discovered who we really were.

"The qadi who brought them to us told us they were Jewish. We put our lives in danger to keep them safe," Ali continued.

No wonder the qadi had been so tense on that bridge: he was putting his life on the line as well.

"Did you believe that he was a medical doctor?" asked the director, pointing to my father.

Now it was my father's turn to feel uncomfortable. "Do not destroy my image," he said, laughing, but it was not his normal laugh. "Do not destroy my reputation," he said, still clinging to those best years of his life, when he had been a man of substance, with considerable prestige, who for one brief moment in time had mattered.

Ali wagged his finger from left to right, as if to say, "Yes and no." With a big smile on his face, he said, "a doctor, but with no diploma."

Many Albanians belong to the Bektashi Order of Islam, a small sect that teaches tolerance of other religions. An important feature of the Bektashi culture is the duty to protect anyone whose life is in danger. Anyone who comes seeking shelter will be protected. When the war was over, they hid German soldiers from the Partisans.

The generosity of the Albanian villagers who hid us, fed us, and defended our dignity had a great impact on my way of thinking, particularly on my understanding of what the words *progress* and *development* really mean. By the standards of what we call developed countries, those Albanian villagers were simple people. They had no running water, no electricity, or higher education. But they had huge hearts and warm souls, which many of us in the developed world have lost despite, or perhaps because of, our technological progress. It is quite possible to live in a culture with a high level of technological development and a complete lack of spirituality. Who is the primitive now? Think of the Nazis.

Oh, the Nazis. They needed to be faced.

Decades of travel to Eastern Europe for business often took me within range of the Treblinka extermination camp, but it was a place I had long avoided, perhaps because I did not want to face my pain. It was only in 2011, when I was invited to lecture in nearby Warsaw, that I summoned the courage to go. I wanted to recite the Kaddish, the Jewish prayer for the dead for my grandparents, uncles, aunts, and cousins. For the Jewish community of Macedonia that was lost forever.

The ride from Warsaw to Treblinka is a little over an hour by highway. I sat with my thoughts in the back of a car, and I felt almost dead inside. Scared to feel. Scared of falling apart when we arrived.

What would I learn? I wondered. I had been to *Auschwitz*. I saw the barracks. I saw the ovens. What would Treblinka look like?

As we entered the camp, I saw the railroad tracks, the tracks that brought my grandparents, uncles, aunts, and cousins to their death.

At the end of the tracks was a building.

On the side of the building were memorial stones for the different communities that had perished there. One of them was Macedonia.

I stood frozen. Unable to move. Unable to cry.

It was on this visit that I discovered how they had died. I had assumed that everyone had been gassed, just as they had been in Auschwitz. I was wrong. The Macedonian Jews were given no food or water, other than tins of salted fish, during the six-day trip from Skopje. Many died of dehydration before reaching the camp. Our guide told us that those who were still alive were taken from the train directly to the gas chamber.[2] The gas employed at Treblinka was only carbon monoxide. Instead of killing the victims, the gas rendered them unconscious. Still alive, they were removed from the chamber and flipped one atop another, stacked like logs, each body placed across the one below it. Gasoline was poured over all the bodies and ignited. They burned for hours until all were reduced to ash.

When I visited Treblinka, the fire pits and the earth around them were

2 The full story is even more gruesome than what our guide revealed. See https://muzeumtreblinka.eu/en/informacje/method-of-killing/.

When I visited Treblinka, the fire pits and earth around them were still black with ashes. This was how I first learned how my family perished there: they were burned alive.

still black with ashes. I picked up one pebble, or perhaps a bone, black from that fire set sixty-eight years ago, to carry home. I prayed Kaddish for their souls and said good-bye to my family forever.

Since none of my grandfather's Kalderon family survived—his name was one our family has used for six hundred years—I took Kalderon as my middle name. At least while I am still alive, the Kalderon memory lives. Upon my death, some of my ashes will join them in Treblinka. It is written into my will.

I closed my heart in the concentration camp. I needed to open it.

HEAVEN AND HELL

Back when I was at UCLA, Dr. Shapiro had gotten me hooked on therapy. Working with him revealed that I had a problem—probably more than one. To begin with, I had a problem with wanting. If I wanted anything outside of my professional life, I would not reach for it. Even the smallest things seemed too dangerous. For instance, if an article in the newspaper seemed interesting, I would not read it. If I wanted to sleep, I would stay awake. And if I truly liked a certain woman, I would run away as fast and as far as possible.

In therapy I discovered why. My father had denied me whatever I wanted. If I asked for something, he would deprive me of it—with pleasure. He would physically abuse me if I persisted in asking for things I desired. So wanting anything seemed dangerous to me. As an adult, especially in my marriage, whenever I wanted anything, I would raise my voice and make angry demands, as if I assumed a priori it would be denied.

But apparently it was not just my father causing this.

My mother once told me that I was a very demanding baby. I would not stop asking to nurse. When she had no more milk to give, I would cry for hours. I discovered the rest of the story in a Tony Robbins workshop years later: that it wasn't just me crying. He asked us to close our eyes and recall our earliest life experience, and I remembered crying for more milk. "Now," he continued, "look around the room. Who else is there?" I saw I wasn't the only one in tears. My mother was crying, too. Apparently, she was crying because she felt that she had failed as a mother—she could not satisfy me? At the time there was no bottled baby milk. I realized that this was my repetitive pattern in life. I always wanted more than what people could give me. But I was not asking one hundred and fifty percent only of others. I was asking the same of myself. I needed to change. I was not the only one miserable. I was making others miserable.

I sought out treatment with Dr. Barry Morguelan, known as Dr. B, a world-renowned energy healer.

The rules were simple: for the three days of the treatment process, I was not allowed to work, even a little bit. I was not to touch an iPhone, a computer, or even a writing pad. "Go to the botanical garden," he said. "Watch flowers grow. Feel them. Go to the Norton Simon Museum, spend at least four hours there, and get close to the pictures. Feel them. Go to a nice open restaurant on a promenade, sit at a table, eat, or have a cup of coffee, and just watch people pass by. Feel them."

I had never done any of that before. Sit at a restaurant? Of course, I had gone to plenty of restaurants, but do nothing? I went to eat or have a meeting and leave as soon as possible. I had too much to do to sit very long. I went to museums, but I saw nothing. My mind was always on my work, on the tools and concepts needed to change organizations.

I spent the three days as instructed. I watched the people and the art and the flowers. I enjoyed just sitting at a table in a restaurant doing "nothing." But at the same time, it was not "nothing." My time was full of excitement. It was fascinating to notice flowers and children playing and couples hugging. How come I had never seen any of this before? I looked at them but had not seen any of it. It is like hearing but not listening.

After those three days, I started to see my wife—not just physically, but emotionally. I started seeing myself as well.

I remember a 108-year-old woman giving the prescription for longevity: “Love what you do and love the one you are with.”

I obviously loved what I did, but who was it that I was with all day long? Who spoke to me endlessly? Who criticized me incessantly? Who kept me up at night? It was me. I needed to love myself.

I had heard this expression many times before, but I did not know what it meant to love myself. The answer finally occurred to me. I love my children more than life itself. Would I let them eat junk food? No. Would I let them be in destructive relationships? No. If I love myself, the same should apply to me. What became clear to me was that those of us who have never had a functional parent need to become a parent to ourselves, to take care of ourselves as a caring parent would. *How?* was the question.

A healer named Uri taught me to tap on my meridians while repeating words symbolic of my behaviors. Then I went to a life coach, and then to a hypnotist. Nada. The different techniques didn’t seem to make much difference in how I felt about myself, or in my behavior.

So I began a search for healing in other methodologies. I was determined. I promised myself that I would open my heart, I would love and be loved before leaving this earth. It led me to breathing therapy, yoga, meditation, the Himalayas, Indian ashrams, a shaman, and a conduit. Each contributed to my healing.

I call him a shaman because that is what he called himself. He was a healer who treated people with weeds, plants, and pills. I later discovered that some of those plants were psychotropic mushrooms and that some of those pills were Ecstasy, which I took only twice. It allowed me to relax to the point that I could take in the world without being defensive and enjoy being alive. I discovered a sensation I believed was love. I tried to replicate the feeling without the pill but did not succeed, so I continued seeing the shaman.

Once a month for the next two years I took pills that made me hallucinate, scream, vomit, and sweat. The tea I drank according to the shaman's directions was a brew with psychedelic effects not unlike those of LSD. One day, the shaman looked at me and said, "Your problem is not just your inability to open your heart but also your fear of death."

I felt the truth of that sentence sink in and take hold of me. I was scared to die.

I had recently read *The Denial of Death,* in which the author, Ernest Becker, claims that people who deny their death do not enjoy their life. Instead, they spend their lives trying to immortalize themselves with creations that will survive them.[3] It all seemed a reflection of how I felt. When I asked the shaman how I could address this problem, his answer was simple.

"You have to experience death."

His prescription was not easy to swallow. To experience death? I was hallucinating for forty days fearing death, and now he wants me to experience it? But I said yes, I will do it. I was willing to do whatever it took to open my heart.

At the time, I owned a thirty-two-foot powerboat. We decided to conduct the session there, far up in the marina where no one could interrupt or wonder what we were doing. The shaman brought along his fiancée, Kelly, to help with the process. Once we were out on the water, he asked me to lie down, then told me, "I am going to give you an injection typically administered in hospitals to paralyze psychiatric patients when they lose control.

---

3 Ernest Becker, *The Denial of Death* (New York: Free Press, 1973).

You will become paralyzed, and you will experience death for an hour. When you come out of it, you will know what life all is about."

I was sweating from fear, but I was desperate. I wanted to solve my emotional problems at any cost, even if it killed me. (I did not tell my wife, who surely would have killed me if I had revealed the plan to her in advance.) I accepted everything he said calmly and agreed to go through with it. He injected the fluid.

Within a few minutes, I closed my eyes. I felt my whole body become stiff. For a moment, I panicked. I could not move a muscle. I had absolutely no control. A white tunnel came into focus, with light at the end that seemed to invite me in.

Then something interesting happened. While I was lying there "dead," I was unable to move or hear or see, but I could feel. I could feel the energy of the shaman and his fiancée, and I felt cared for. I felt safe although I could not move a limb, not even an eyelash. Nothing. I did not feel my body. Nothing. But I could feel the atmosphere. The people. I remember a sense of wonder: did I need to die to feel alive?

When I emerged from the episode, I began to wail like a deeply hurt baby. I clung to Kelly like a fearful child, begging, "I need love."

Then I asked if I could hug Kelly. She drew me closer and stroked my hair, and I pretended to nurse from her breast. I just simulated it. I was reenacting the scene of my infancy and was holding her tight until I was spent. When I stopped "nursing," I felt relieved. I felt reborn.

I realized then what heaven and hell must be like. Imagine that you have died, and people are gathered for your funeral. You are dead, but you still feel, and what you feel is hate. You have committed so many offenses that the people at your funeral hate you. Those people are happy that you are gone, and there is nothing you can do about it anymore. You cannot ask for their forgiveness. You cannot repair what you have done. That is hell. It became clear to me why people are supposed to forgive the dead—so that their souls can leave the earth and go wherever souls go. If you do not forgive, the soul drifts around, asking forgiveness.

Now imagine that people are gathered for your funeral, and all you feel from them is love. You are surrounded by love, lots of love. You gave all you could give. You can leave now. That is heaven.

I set a goal for myself: I would love and be loved before I died. I would tell people—my wife, my children, my employees—that I loved them. I would say it and feel it, say it and mean it. But how should a loving person actually behave? I had no idea.

SEEK THE LIGHT IN YOUR HEART

I learned about love from meeting a master of meditation.

I had tried for years to meditate, without success. Just as I would settle in, my legs would start to fidget, or I would scratch myself.

I just could not sit still. I had given up on meditation when my associate Sunil told me that he had discovered a form of meditation that worked for him.

"What's different about it?" I asked. I had already tried about ten approaches to meditation, so how different could this one be?

"It focuses on the heart," he said.

The heart? That was the magic word for me. "Please teach me."

"Come to our ashram in Denmark," he said.

I was going to visit the Adizes office in Silkeborg at the same time that Shri Parthasarathi Rajagopalachari, also known as Chariji, was scheduled to be at the ashram nearby. On the last night of the trip, Sunil drove me through the Jutland countryside to get there. Hundreds of people gathered around the little building, peering through the windows in the hope of catching a glimpse of the master.

"Go in," said Sunil.

Master Chariji, the founder of Heartfulness Meditation, India, taught me that loving is a choice we can make. It is a muscle we need to develop. It was the beginning of the opening of my heart.

"How can I?" I asked, irritated. "All these people are blocking the way."

"Go, go," Sunil insisted.

I approached the building, and the crowd separated to give me passage without my asking for anyone to move. I came to the door, where a man was guarding the entrance so no one could go in uninvited. I was not invited, so I wondered how I would get in to see the master. It's probably time to retreat, I thought. But as I approached the door, the guard opened it for me without asking any questions.

I walked into the dining room. Chariji and six disciples were having dinner. One chair was unoccupied.

"Please sit down," the master said. "Join us."

It looked as though they had been expecting me. I assumed Sunil had made all this happen, but Sunil swears by everything dear to him that he made absolutely no arrangements whatsoever.

I sat, but I did not eat. Instead, I boldly began to ask the master questions: What is God? What is love? I wanted to find the passageway to love.

He answered, but still today I cannot recall what he said. I believe I was blocking his answers.

At a certain point, I said that I would like to meditate but that I was unable to find my way. I never seemed to succeed. He asked everyone to leave the room and gave me a personal sitting.

That started a long-term relationship with Master Chariji and Heartfulness Meditation. Over time, I had long conversations with the master and visited him several times in India.

Once, when I was visiting the master at the Satkhol Ashram at the foot of the Himalayas, I told him a theory I had developed about love. While life is give and take, love is when the giving *is* the taking. They are simultaneous.

I tried to explain, "Why do you take your little children to the circus? Not because they will pay you back when you are old and feeble. You take them because their happiness is your happiness. The reward—the taking—is in the giving." That is why the Buddhists say, "Thank you for allowing me to serve you." In the serving is the reward.

He disagreed. He said that I was still living in my head, that I was still a divided self. That I was doing a profit-and-loss accounting in my relations. My heart was still closed.

"Love is not in the head," he told me. "There is no computation in love, no profit-and-loss statement, no cost-value balancing act. Love is absolute. It is what we are. How we are. No thinking. It is automatic. Like breathing."

"To love is a choice we make." He went on, "Love is like a muscle. You need to exercise it, to nourish, to develop it. If you do not use it, you will lose it.

I asked Chariji a new question. "Is hate the opposite of love?"

"They are the different parts of the same 'pie,'" he said. "Hate is the absence of love. The less love, the more hate. And by the same token, the more love, the less hate. It is like light and darkness. As the Chinese proverb says, 'Do not curse the darkness. Light a candle.' So do not hate *hate*. Just love. Just love, and hate will fade like the fog when sun shines."

I could see that it was fear that was blocking my ability to love: fear of being abandoned, fear of being unworthy. I was always acting quickly to keep out those fears. Immersing myself in endless challenging work was my way to avoid confronting my fears. I had to find a way to put this into practice.

In Heartfulness Meditation, you seek the light in your heart. In my case, I decided that the light I sought would be the experience of love. It goes like this: just close your eyes, relax, take a few deep breaths, and feel love. If you have difficulty, think about a child you love dearly, or anyone or anything you have a deep emotional connection to. You love the child without expecting anything. Now hold on to that feeling and start loving every part of your body, even those that give you pain. Do not let the pain undermine your feeling of love. As thoughts come into your mind, don't let them distract you. Love them, too.

To love is to feel, and to feel you have to stop thinking. You try to have "constant remembrance," to feel love during the day. Continue the feeling of loving you started in the meditation, practice it throughout the day, and if you do this for some time, you do not *try* to love anymore. Love becomes who you are. Just repeat what you do and it becomes a habit, and if you continue, it becomes your personality and eventually it determines your destiny.

I am meditating daily, and I believe it is working. I am more tolerant, less demanding. And this translates, I hope, to being more loving: you cannot love without being tolerant. You like because of; you love in spite of.

A few years ago, I was invited to speak at the American Academy of Anti-Aging Medicine in Las Vegas. Over five thousand medical doctors convened to listen to the latest in biology, chemistry, medicine, and physiology on how to slow down aging. I was surprised at the invitation. I am not an MD. Nevertheless, they wanted to hear what I had to say, so I showed up.

My message was *love*. Look at people who are in love. Shining eyes. Full of energy. They look and feel younger. Look at people who hate. They resemble a squeezed lemon. Old. No energy. Energy is fixed. Hating depletes energy, leading to a shorter life.

You want to stay young? Surround yourself with love. How much do you love your spouse? Your family? Your community? Your work? Your car, house, neighborhood, country? Air, water, and vegetation? Even love the people who hurt you, and they won't hurt you anymore. The more you love, the younger you will feel and the less energy you will waste. And the longer you may live.

With my parents Diamanta (Duka) and Salamon (Moni) Adizes.

KISSING THE MARBLE

Much earlier on my journey to understand everything I could about love, I attended a workshop devoted to the subject at Kripalu, a yoga center in the Berkshires, in Massachusetts. In the workshop, we were divided into pairs, with an assignment: tell your partner something you resent about someone in your life. No names. Simple.

My partner went first. He spoke about a certain person who gave him a hard time for leaving his socks on the floor and not clearing the table after eating. Obviously, it was his wife, and he looked a little relieved to get the complaint off his chest. The sounds of similar conversations around us kept the energy of the room warm and welcoming.

When it was my turn, I spoke about how I disliked the coldness and unresponsiveness of a certain person in my life. How harsh that person could be, how emotionally unavailable, especially when I was in need.

"I see," my partner said. "Is your resentment directed toward your father?"

"My father?" I was shocked. I had been telling him about my first wife. What did my father have to do with it? As I asked myself the question, I began to shake and I started to cry, and then weep. I lost all control.

I began screaming, and two leaders of the workshop came over and put their arms around me. If I was falling apart, they were there to hold me together. They did not say a word; they just held me for as long as I needed. Their embrace was the reassurance I needed to understand I was loved. By the time I opened my eyes, everyone else but them had left the room.

That night alone in my bed, I sat with myself and tried to understand what had happened. It dawned on me that I had married a person whose communication style resembled that of my father. By working through my relationship with her, I was reliving my problems with him. That was sometimes true with my second wife, too. When she gets upset, the rhythm of her words forms patterns like those of my father. I feel it in my body, the tempo and intonation of her voice. I feel it in my body, and my body reacts.

For as long as I can remember I feared my father. I learned early on that if he felt I had disobeyed or disrespected him, I would pay dearly for it. I was beaten up, continually rejected, shamed, and called a parasite or, even worse, "shorty." He knew I felt inferior for being short. Years later in business, I surrounded myself with employees who were tall. I needed to manage those who had what I did not have.

When my father got angry, he used to tell me that he would kill me. He said in Ladino that he would feed me *vidru pizadu* (ground glass), and I believed him. Until I left home for military service, I would eat everything with a fork to check my food for broken glass. As a teenager, I would cry at night and beg God to take him away. My mother was unable to protect me. She feared him, too.

Many parents in the Serbian and Israeli cultures that I come from threaten to kill their children in moments of anger or despair, without ever intending any actual harm. But I believed my father. Why? Perhaps because I have no memory of him ever hugging me or kissing me—of taking delight in my mere being. In his defense, it was not the custom in the Sephardic culture to show physical affection. Hugging and kissing on the cheeks are recent developments. Nor was it Serbian custom to display fondness toward your children. My old mentor, Vlastimir Matejic, once told me that his father admonished him, "Stop kissing your children. If you feel like doing so, wait until they go to sleep, then do it. Otherwise, you are spoiling them."

For years, I believed that I had resolved my relationship with my father during my freshman year at Hebrew University through the Moral Re-Armament movement. MRA had enabled me to forgive him, at least outwardly. Later, I realized that his emotional distance throughout much of my childhood had taught me how to be alone with myself. As a child, I invented imaginary worlds with kitchen cutlery, lost myself in books, and took it upon myself to see that I went to school. As an adult, I siphoned all of my energy into my profession, a world in which my father could neither dominate nor control me. But he basked in my achievements without knowing what I do.

As I became prominent in my field and articles were written about me, I discovered that my father would carry newspaper or magazine articles about me around with him and tell people, "This is my son." He had no idea why people were writing about me or what I did for a living, but he was proud of me. When my first wife and I divorced, he and my mother came to Los Angeles to be with me. He was seventy-one years old, but he joined me in my yoga practice, studied English, and then took up the guitar. He tried to get closer.

Forgiving him would be relatively easy. Or so I thought.

I was at home when my father died. My sister called me in the middle of the night and told me to hurry. He had been taken to the hospital with pneumonia, unconscious, and would not have much time to live. I had a severe ear infection, however, and could not fly anywhere. It cleared just in time for me to bury him.

At his funeral, I tried to connect with my emotions. This man had dominated me all my life. I tried to feel love, anger, relief—something. But I was numb. I could not even cry.

Yet somehow, I missed him, and I miss him still. I think of him almost daily: what he would have said, what he would have done.

People who knew my father knew a man who loved life, who loved to sing and joke. At age eighty-two, he started taking classes to learn English and to play a guitar and sing. A man who would flirt with any woman of any age, nonstop and to my embarrassment. He was uncontrollable. He had no boundaries. Whoever he was with was overwhelmed by his quick and fantastic capability to observe and analyze situations. This was, after all, the man who had saved our lives many times over during the war.

When we were still newcomers to Israel, living in Haifa, he would sometimes drag me along on weekend errands to Tel Aviv. Around the time we would pass Atlit, a little village by the sea where the illegal immigrants used to disembark before Israel was established, the show would inevitably begin. He would move to the front of the bus, stand there, turn around, and start singing a folk song, usually a Serbian one, to get warmed up. Then he'd switch to a popular song everyone would know, like "Arrivederci, Roma," and before I knew it, everyone on the bus was singing along, laughing, and clapping their hands.

He was like a different person, full of life, *bigger* than life, lovable. Later, once he got his truck, he would regularly pick up hitchhikers. At that time, people were supportive of one another; it was a common way to get around. My father, before letting them in the truck, would inform them they were welcome only if they were going to sing with him till arriving at their destination. He was serious about this. Once a hitchhiker mistook the request for a joke and refused to sing along. My father stopped the truck and asked him to find another ride. Life is beautiful, he used to say. Enjoy it. And he would criticize me for not doing so.

Now, when I look in the mirror, I see my father. I can see his expressions on my face. When I laugh, I laugh like him. I flirt with women like he did. And there have been times when I took my anger out on my children like he did. Yes, I am ashamed to say I even used force on them the way he did with me.

He casts a long shadow over my personal life—my marriages, my relationship with my children, and my relationship with myself. He was and still is with me all the time. So much of what I resented him for I find in myself. So much of my life has been a reaction to him or an impersonation of him.

I find this strange, as for many years I wondered if he was my father at all. When I was a child, he used to tell me with a big smile on his face that I was adopted. And it hurt. He denied his paternity. He lied, but I believed him.

I realized I had to free myself of my father's shadow. I wanted to be the gentle person my mother was, supportive, loving—not the macho man my father was. But how?

I accidentally stumbled across one of the major steps in my healing. During a massage, a masseuse kneaded a spot at the top of my rib cage called the heart key, and I suddenly started to sob. I didn't know what was happening. She told me that the spot she'd touched was where I had accumulated my sorrow. I learned that we store different information in different parts of our bodies.

I listened, and then hired a breathing therapist, who taught me how to breathe in a way that released the built-up pressure in my body. When I breathed in that specific way, I would cry a lot, and then my body would relax, I would stop fidgeting my feet, and I could lie down peacefully.

In one of my breathing sessions, the image of my father appeared in front of me. I started screaming. Then I flailed at him. I could not stop. I begged him to go away, to leave me alone. Please, please, leave me alone. In a flash of recognition, I saw that I was behaving the way I had wanted to as a child but had been too afraid to. As a child, I had been paralyzed by fear. I had not dared to utter even a word. But now I was pushing him away, again and again. I was crying and yelling. I was exorcising that powerful man who had been my father until I was spent.

Finally, his picture receded and then disappeared.

On one of my trips to Israel, I came across a conduit, a woman I knew and trusted. She could communicate with the souls of people who had physically died. I took a three-day workshop with her and learned how to recall energy, scenes, and deceased people from the past. On the third day of the workshop, the conduit came with a large piece of paper in her hand, on which something was written in longhand.

"Who in your life called you *azno*?" she asked. *Azno* means "ass" or "donkey" in Ladino. The conduit was an Ashkenazi Jew; she did not know Ladino. The word had no meaning for her at all.

"My father," I said.

"Okay. That means we have a sign that it was him."

"What do you mean?" I asked.

"Last night at 3:00 a.m., your father woke me up from my sleep and dictated this long message. I wrote it down," she told me.

I was incredulous, speechless—but curious.

"Go on," I said. "Read it to me, please."

"He said that from the day you were born he did not like you," she began.

My father dictated to her, "My wife, the woman I loved, gave him all the love I wanted. I realized she was capable of loving, but not of loving me. I hated him. I know I mistreated him. Only after he left for the United States did I realize there was nothing I could do to win his mother's love.

It was not his fault she did not show me love. I tried to establish a relationship with him. But it was too late."

His letter to me continued:

"Tell him I am doing my best to open his heart and help him stop suffering, but he has to make that decision himself. But I know him. He is an *azno.* He won't listen."

The next day, I went to my father's burial place in Tel Aviv and brought flowers. It was the first time I had been to his grave since he had died and been buried. I stood there and told him, "I forgive you. Thank you for saving our lives. I truly forgive you. Go in peace to the world you belong to now."

And I kissed his name on the marble.

Our blended family c. 2000. Seated from left: Atalia, Nurit, Sapphire, me, and Topaz. Standing from left: Nimrod, Cnaan, and Shoham.

EPILOGUE

There is a Serbian expression: "*Behind* every successful man there is a surprised wife." Nurit taught me that it should have been: "*Beside* every successful man there is a supportive wife." I could not have made my career without her support. She let me have all the time I needed and wanted to build the Adizes organizational therapy methodology by working non nonstop around the globe.

That reminds me of a story told about Bob Hope's wife. On their fifty years of marriage celebration, she had a toast thanking him for the twenty minutes they had together.

I work hard, and once I have a goal, I am like a bulldog; I do not let go. I stick tenaciously to my objective and in the process expect maximum performance from myself and others. I expect a lot and Nurit exorcised this tenet of mine. Painfully so.

Nurit is a very independent woman. If I make a demand and expect performance (what I do as a manager), there is a high probability that she will not do it. I have to ask her whether she is willing to do whatever I need. I have to handle her with love and not with demands.

Nurit trained me not to expect. It is okay to express my need, but not as a demand. She is a free woman. I learned that *expecting* is a barrier to love. Why is that? Because when you expect, you get on the first step on the ladder of rejection, and eventually hate.

I learned a lot about this through Heartfulness Meditation. The first step is to wish. *Wish* is not a loaded word. You just wish. When a wish is not accomplished, it escalates to a want. Wanting is not a problem as long as you stay on that first step of the ladder, but when what you want is not fulfilled, you might move one step higher and expect. In expecting, there is an ingredient of control. You believe it should happen; that is why you expect it.

When your expectation is not realized, it might escalate to a demand, and when that does not happen, you might move on to the next stage and feel that you are entitled to what it is you desire. And when your belief in your entitlement is not met, you become rebellious and hateful.

There you have it. It all starts with a simple wish. If you allow it to grow, and you start expecting, and then go even further, love evaporates and hate takes its place.

The second healing contribution my dear wife gave to me was to never stop expressing her love, no matter how mad or resentful I became when my demands or expectations were not met.

She was there for me even when I was not there for her.

It would be misleading and irresponsible to leave with the impression that all is well and dandy. I cannot stand anyone raising their voice at me. Especially my wife. It makes me sick. Is it the tone of voice of my father? Am I really in deep, continuous love with my wife? She deserves it. But the chatter in my head continues. I still have not got rid of it; I'm still finding issues, still seeking those white spots.

Did I open my heart? I believe so. How do I know? I suffer more than ever. When my heart was closed and I could not feel, I did not suffer. I made others suffer. Now that I seek to love and feel loved, I am vulnerable. At the slightest sign that love is not real, or that it is slipping through my fingers, I am in deep pain. Love without depending. I had to master that.

Nurit found a health center in Northern California called TrueNorth, which uses water fasting to help patients with diabetes, high blood pressure, and other immunological diseases. She attended their program, lost a lot of weight, and left feeling great. She convinced me to go, too.

In one of the lectures I attended there, the resident doctor taught us how to interpret our blood test results. He said, "If your creatinine is high, it means you have kidney disease."

I looked at my blood test results. Creatinine: four.

I raised my hand. "I have a four," I said. "Does that mean I have kidney disease?"

"Yes," he said.

I was dumbfounded. Incredulous. How the hell did I get kidney disease?

Then I thought about it for a minute. I spent years traveling and staying up all night, changing time zones, eating out, and being overweight. To heal the Shaman gave me psychoactive drugs and herbs and pills that made me hallucinate and scream. I was so desperate for love that I was willing to do anything, and so I did everything. Learning to love had its price. These frenzied attempts combined with the stresses of working with demanding clients and building an institute led to chronic high blood pressure, but I was too preoccupied with my career to address it. So my kidney failed.

I went to a nephrologist. He did not beat around the bush. "You need to get a kidney transplant," he said, raising his voice, "and preferably before you start dialysis. Dialysis will make you weak." He made an appointment for me at UCLA's hospital right there and then.

Now I needed potential donors. When I asked for donors, I discovered something my lifelong fear of love had blinded me to: I am loved. Twenty-four friends, clients, associates, and family members were willing to give me a kidney.

Unfortunately, UCLA does not take chances if there is the smallest

With my boys: from front left to back,
Nimmy, Topaz, Shoham, and Sapphire.

indication that the operation might not be successful. The hospital rejected every one of my donors. Some were too old; some were too young. Some had diabetes, and some had diabetes in their family. Some were overweight, and some were underweight. The reasons were endless.

I was put on dialysis for two years while I continued searching the world for a donor. Through it all, my email inbox remained flooded with messages from people asking how they could help, until one of my clients finally found me the right donor.

I had the surgery, and then spent six months recuperating. Someone had to take care of me all that time, which isn't a small undertaking. Nurit was with me for it all.

Because of the dialysis and the surgery, I could not travel for two years, and I spent more time at home. God gave me a present. He gave me kidney disease so I could find the love and life I never knew I had. With all the therapy and experiences, I discovered that I loved myself, too.

One day I looked at my hands and discovered that my nails had grown in fully. Unconsciously, without any attempt, I had stopped biting my nails. People began to tell me that I looked great, better than they'd seen me look before. How strange! I always thought myself to be on the verge of being unattractive. How did my appearance change? I have lost weight without trying too hard to go on a diet. I simply eat less and started exercising regularly. As my self-esteem improved, my need to make myself feel better changed. I feel fine as is. And I can look women in the eye and not blink. I noticed I am more tolerant. My wife tells me so. More patient. More forgiving. I have more faith, less fear. I feel I am more in control of my destiny. Less of a victim.

Aha! Changing the inside changes the outside. If you truly love yourself, if you truly walk the walk and care for yourself, no one can take the love from you. When you work to earn love, you work as though love is scarce. You are needy; you depend on others to give you love, so you can experience love. When you love yourself, love is abundant. When you love, you do not need to get love: you are love. You are full and happy as you are.

I appreciate my family more and more each day. My children exhibit endless love for me. I am eighty-five years old, and I am happier now than ever. I love, I know I am loved, and I am not scared to love.

My maternal grandparents' ashes are in Treblinka, Poland.

My paternal grandmother is buried in a communal grave in Skopje, Macedonia.

My paternal grandfather is buried in Belgrade, Serbia.

My parents are buried in Tel Aviv, Israel.

Where will I be buried?

This is the wrong question.

What counts is not where you will be buried, but how you will live:
Speak without offending,
Listen without defending,
Live without pretending,
and
LOVE WITHOUT DEPENDING.

I am loved for who I am, not for what I will become.
Love is here, not there.
Love is like breathing.
Just breathe, just love.
Today, not tomorrow.

With love,
Ichak K. Adizes

Santa Barbara County, California,
and Tel Aviv, Israel

POSTSCRIPT

Nurit and I reside at our ranch in Carpinteria, California, but we maintain an apartment in Israel, where we spend as much time as possible. Despite my age, I still travel to teach and consult, write my blog, and try to publish one new book a year. Nurit, with her love and knowledge of art, created an outstanding collection of contemporary art. A journalist by profession, she's a talented writer and documentary filmmaker. She is in the process of writing a book. The world deserves to hear her stories.

Our blended family has six children. Atalia Omer and her husband, Jason Springs, are professors at Notre Dame. Topaz Adizes is a filmmaker, and his wife, Icari, is a singer. Shoham Adizes joined me in leading the Institute. Cnaan Omer Hamburger is a mother, first of all, and a very gifted painter. Cnaan's husband, Philip Hamburger, is a law professor at Columbia University. Nimmy Omer is a philosopher and into computers. Sapphire Adizes is a composer and jazz saxophonist.

We are blessed with grandchildren: Yehonathan Daniele Omer-Springs and Pnei'el Alois Omer-Springs; Joseph, Zosha, and Isaiah Hamburger; and Cosmos Ilan Adizes Gomez and Laila Oceana Diamanta Adizes Gomez.

Most of the extended Adizes family at our home in California, c. 2018.
From bottom left: Icari, Topaz, Nurit, Sapphire, Jason, Atalia, me,
Nimrod (cooking), Shoham, Pnei'el, and Yehonathan.

DOCUMENTARY

Many of the stories and the content contained in this book can be experienced in the 1996 documentary film from the Israeli Broadcasting Authority called *I Want to Remember, He Wants to Forget.* This film is available to stream on YouTube: https://www.youtube.com/watch?v=YcCq-uSeDSY.

AFTERWORD

I survived the Holocaust as a hidden child in Poland and Lithuania. As I grew older, I failed to understand why it was I survived. At first, I asked many questions—why did it happen to us, the Jewish people? Why was the world silent? Why did not the Almighty intervene? Why did children perish? Why did I survive, and the other Jewish boys and girls didn't?

Jews risked their lives to leave a record so that the world would know and hopefully remember. That is why Ichak Adizes's autobiography is important on many levels. First, as a memory, a memory of the Holocaust. Second, Ichak Adizes honestly shares the trauma that haunts almost all of us survivors, a feeling of guilt for surviving, a trauma that never really leaves us. Many of us cover it up, deny it. But Ichak Adizes courageously shares it in this inspiring story of success, creativity, ingenuity, and overcoming challenges of all types.

Ichak Adizes's drive and smarts made a major contribution to better understanding human nature, especially human beings in personal and corporate environments. He developed a blueprint, a strategy, a process to improve human relations while at the same time increasing productivity and respect. Thank God that Ichak Adizes survived, so we can benefit from his contributions to help us be a more civil society, for having the strength and courage to share, so honestly and openly, his strength and weaknesses, his hopes, loves, traumas, demons, dreams, angels, incredible achievements, and frustrations.

Thank you, Ichak Adizes, for being such an inspiration to all of us.

Abraham Foxman
Former National Director of the Anti-Defamation League

ABOUT THE AUTHOR

Dr. Ichak Kalderon Adizes is the founder and CEO of the Adizes Institute, which delivers the Adizes Program for Organizational Therapy to clients in the public and private sector around the world.

Leadership Excellence magazine named him one of the Top Thirty Thought Leaders, and *The Holmes Report* named him as one of the Best Communicators Among World Leaders for 2017, alongside Pope Francis and the Dalai Lama. In recognition of his contributions to management theory and practice, in 2019, Dr. Adizes received the Lifetime Achievement Award from the International Academy of Management and twenty-one honorary doctorates from universities in eleven countries. He has been made an honorary citizen of two countries for his contribution to their governments.

Dr. Adizes lectures in four languages and has appeared before well over two hundred and fifty thousand senior-level executives in more than fifty-two countries. He has published twenty-six books, which have been translated into a combined total of thirty-six languages.

He lives in Santa Barbara, California, and loves to play the accordion, meditate using the Heartfulness method, and practice yoga.

ACKNOWLEDGEMENTS

I want to thank my editors, Gene Lichtenstein and Claire Nuttall, and most of all, Nina Wiener. They were more than editors. They were my advisors and supporters, and without their contributions, this book I have been working on for over ten years would never have seen the light of day. Thank you, all.

Many people read an early version of this manuscript. Among them, three stand out: Carlos Valdesuso from Brazil, Dragoslav Grinvald from Belgrade, and Costas Petropoulous from Greece. To all, my gratitude for taking the time and commenting, making this book more readable.

To Boris Vukic and Zvezdan Horvat, leaders of the Adizes Institute Southeast Europe, my special thanks for taking the initiative and leading me to write this book.

I thank Maya Korling, Louis Torres, and Yura Lysenko for the dedicated work in putting all the footnotes in order and assisting me in finalizing this book.

I thank my half-century friends, Monroe Price and Abe Foxman for their foreword and afterword. In the Serbian language, the saying is "a good friend is more than a brother."

I am in debt to Larry Schiller, my literary advisor, whose advice should be measured in gold and I thank his assistant, Collin McCarthy.

Thank you with all my heart.

Ichak K. Adizes
Santa Barbara County, California, and Tel Aviv, Israel

PRAISE FOR THE ADIZES METHODOLOGY

"The [Adizes] Institute's methodology has enhanced internal communication by encouraging habits of participatory management and by helping us accept change as normal and as a continuous opportunity for the bank."
—Samuel H. Armacost, former CEO, Bank of America

"The Adizes methodology for managing sustainable, accelerated growth has been a major contributor to our success. In the ten years that we have worked with and retained the services of Adizes LLC, we have grown our capitalization from two hundred and sixty-one million dollars in 1992, to three and a half billion dollars in 2002, making us one of the largest corporations of the continent."
—Ricardo B. Salinas, CEO, Grupo Salinas, Mexico

"I have read a lot of books by Dr. Adizes, and in each of them he writes about difficult situations that every manager deals with sooner or later in a structured and crystal-clear way. However, Dr. Adizes's methodology of management can be implemented not only in a business point of view.

It is a unifying theory, which covers all of life and is essential for every human being."
—Herman Gref, CEO, Chairman, Sberbank, Russia

"Adizes is the Darwin of corporate evolution."
—Monroe E. Price, former Dean, Benjamin N. Cardozo School of Law, Yeshiva University, New York

"At times the recommendations of Dr. Adizes . . . are some of the most quoted in the business world."
—Dmitry Medvedev, Prime Minister of Russia

"I've been using the Adizes method for over forty years. It has been instrumental in our being able to grow our business during that time from about $50 million per year to over $4 billion. The lessons of balanced management recognizing all the disciplines necessary in every organization, regardless of size, have been a driving force in our success."
—Stewart Resnick, President and CEO, The Wonderful Company

"The US foreign policy world—as well as the international community as a whole—would benefit greatly from a deeper understanding of Ichak Adizes's insights and theories."
—Ambassador Kenneth L. Adelman, former Director of the US Arms Control and Disarmament Agency and former US Representative to the United Nations

"Adizes is one of the truly great innovators of our times. He cuts through pretentious management principles to get to the core of what it takes to bring about effective change in organizations."
—Kirby Warren, Dean Emeritus, Columbia University School of Business, New York

"Dr. Adizes's theory of management can be applied beyond business uses; as a political manager, I have found it to be particularly useful in my day-to-day work. Kazakhstan has been working closely with the Adizes Institute for a number of years, and its methodology has proved to be very useful in our decision-making process."
—Karim Massimov, former Prime Minister of the Republic of Kazakhstan

"Ichak Adizes is one of the few management consultants who has converted a whole array of theory-based concepts into unusually practical guidelines for managers. And even more impressive, he has integrated these guidelines into a comprehensive system of management . . ."
—Monroe Price, former Dean, Benjamin N. Cardozo School of Law of Yeshiva University

"When we began hearing about Ichak Adizes from various companies' presidents we knew and respected . . . they simply said that he was a new breed of management consultant, one who really understood how businesses work and what could be done to make them better. Adizes is, in fact, more than a consultant. He is a pioneer in the field of management; a serious, insightful, and astute observer of organizational behavior, which he has been studying for 25 years."
– The Editors of *Inc.* magazine

THE ADIZES INSTITUTE

Since its founding in 1970, the Adizes Institute has guided companies to achieve exceptional results by managing change rapidly and without disruptive conflict.

The Institute uses the Symbergetic™ proprietary methodology, developed by Prof. Ichak Adizes. This approach is timeless, unique, and adaptable to every company, no matter the industry, size, or maturity. It represents a paradigm shift from traditional consulting or coaching.

Our programs enable companies to achieve four *simultaneous* goals: solving chronic problems, building teams, leadership training and development, and producing exceptional results. Our clients have included Applied Materials, SanDisk, Bank of America, Royal Dutch Shell, Sberbank, and various governments around the world (see testimonials at Adizes.com).

From offices in various countries, a variety of Change Management services are delivered by Certified Adizes Associates—professionals who are exclusively qualified to deliver the Symbergetic methodology. These services foster and nurture a culture of mutual trust and respect and empower organizations to diagnose their own problems and agree on effective solutions. Those solutions, as our mission states, can be rapidly implemented without destructive conflict.

The Adizes Institute Training and Certification Academy provides training and certification in the methodology to qualified applicants who, by and large, already possess advanced degrees in business or other disciplines and have multiple years of executive experience.

We have documented the theoretical framework of the methodology in twenty-eight books, some translated into as many as thirty-six languages (see Publications.Adizes.com).

We are passionate about and committed to enabling organizations to reach their full potential. We are governed by a code of ethics that pledges us to deliver the best to our clients. Profits are our constraint, not our goal.

For inquiries on the Institute's services, please visit www.adizes.com.

PUBLISHED WORKS

1. Adizes, I. *The Power of Collaborative Leadership.* Forthcoming, 2023.
2. Adizes, I. *Systemic Coaching*. Forthcoming, 2023.
3. Adizes, I. *The Accordion Player: My Journey from Fear to Love.* Newtown, PA: WS Press, 2023.
4. Adizes, I. *What Matters in Life*. Newtown, PA: WS Press, 2023.
5. Adizes, I. *Insights On Socio-Political Issues: Volume III.* Santa Barbara, CA: Adizes Institute Publications, 2019.
6. Adizes, I. *Insights on Personal Growth: Volume III.* Santa Barbara, CA: Adizes Institute Publications, 2019.
7. Adizes, I. *Insights on Management: Volume III.* Santa Barbara, CA: Adizes Institute Publications, 2018.
8. Adizes, I., with Yechezkel and Ruth Madanes. *The Power of Opposites*. Santa Barbara, CA: Adizes Institute Publications, 2015.
9. Adizes, I. *Mastering Change*. Santa Barbara, CA: Adizes Institute Publications, 1992. Revised edition, Adizes Institute Publications, 2015.
10. Adizes, I. *Insights on Management: Volume II.* Santa Barbara, CA: Adizes Institute Publications, 2014.

11. Adizes, I. *Insights on Personal Growth: Volume II.* Santa Barbara, CA: Adizes Institute Publications, 2014.
12. Adizes, I. *Insights on Policy Issues: Volume II.* Santa Barbara, CA: Adizes Institute Publications, 2014.
13. Adizes, I. *Food for Thought: On What Counts in Life.* Santa Barbara, CA: Adizes Institute Publications, 2012.
14. Adizes, I. *Food for Thought: On Change and Leadership.* Santa Barbara, CA: Adizes Institute Publications, 2012.
15. Adizes, I. *Food for Thought: On Management.* Santa Barbara, CA: Adizes Institute Publications, 2012.
16. Adizes, I. *Insights on Management: Volume I.* Santa Barbara, CA: Adizes Institute Publications, 2011.
17. Adizes, I. *Insights on Personal Growth: Volume I.* Santa Barbara, CA: Adizes Institute Publications, 2011.
18. Adizes, I. *Insights on Policy: Volume I.* Santa Barbara, CA: Adizes Institute Publications, 2011.
19. Adizes, I. *How to Manage in Times of Crisis (And How to Avoid a Crisis in the First Place).* Santa Barbara, CA: Adizes Institute Publications, 2009.
20. Adizes, I. *Leading the Leaders: How to Enrich Your Style of Management and Handle People Whose Style Is Different from Yours.* Santa Barbara, CA: Adizes Institute Publications, 2004.
21. Adizes, I. *Management/Mismanagement Styles: How to Identify a Style and What to Do About It.* Santa Barbara, CA: Adizes Institute Publications, 2004.
22. Adizes I. *Corporate Lifecycles: How Organizations Grow, Age, and Die.* Initial publication by Prentice Hall, 1990. Reprint, Santa Barbara, CA: Adizes Institute Publications. New revised edition: *Managing Corporate Lifecycles: Complete Volume* or *Volume 1 and Volume 2*, Santa Barbara, CA: Adizes Institute Publications, 2004.
23. Adizes, I. *The Ideal Executive: Why You Cannot Be One and What to Do About It.* Santa Barbara, CA: Adizes Institute Publications, 2004.

24. Adizes, I. *Conversations with CEOs*. Santa Barbara, CA: Adizes Institute Publications, 2004.
25. Adizes, I. *The Pursuit of Prime*. Santa Monica, CA: Knowledge Exchange, 1996. Reprint, Santa Barbara, CA: Adizes Institute Publications.
26. Adizes, I. *How to Solve the Mismanagement Crisis*. Homewood, IL: Dow Jones/ Irwin, 1985. Reprint, Santa Barbara, CA: Adizes Institute Publications.
27. Adizes, I., and E. Mann Borgese, eds., *Self-Management: New Dimensions to Democracy*. Santa Barbara, CA: ABC-CLIO, 1975. Reprint, Santa Barbara, CA: Adizes Institute Publications.
28. Adizes, I. *Industrial Democracy: Yugoslav Style*. New York Free Press, 1971. Reprint, Santa Barbara, CA: Adizes Institute Publications.

Some of these titles have been translated into other languages. All are available from Adizes Institute Publications, Santa Barbara, California, www.adizesbooks.com.

Link to Author on YouTube:
https://www.youtube.com/c/DrIchakAdizes-channel
Link to Ichak Adizes website: https://ichakadizes.com/
Link to Adizes Institute Worldwide: https://adizes.com/